The Beer and Bacc

Joly Harpic's Househusband's Slightly Ca
Fulfilling Post-Care

By

Damian P.O'Connor

Disclaimer

Diets don't work (except this one obviously). If you are foolish enough to follow them then nothing I can say will stop you doing your thing and you have no-one else to blame if things go tits up and you die of something horrible or you get a yeast infection or bloat up like a Zeppelin. Just to emphasise this, you should know that I have no medical qualifications beyond a few First Aid badges picked up in the Boy Scouts, the army and at several dismal work-related training sessions and so you shouldn't think that I'm some mumbo-jumbo miracle worker who can magic you down to a size zero just by telling you to eat pumpkin seeds. I could probably stick a plaster on you and I once put some stitches in a chap's bum but you shouldn't infer from this that I know what I'm talking about regarding dietary programmes, allergies, wheat intolerance, food-related disorders, homeopathy or any sort of medical, psychological or biological science whatsoever. Go see a Doctor or someone who knows what they're talking about if you're going to be slavish about this.

This is a work of fiction and any resemblance to persons living or dead is purely coincidental. The author of this book is Damian P. O'Connor and is Copyright© 2014. The author retains all rights.

Contents

Monday: The Odyssey Begins

'Bacon has no Calories'

Tuesday: Picking up the Pace.

'There is no such thing as a Free Lunch'

Wednesday: Hump Day.

'A New Take on the 5:2 Diet'

Thursday: A Difficult Sort of Day.

'You are what you Eat'

The Eagle Flies on Friday.

'No need to be Abstemious on a Friday'

Saturday: I go out to Play.

'Even Watching Rugby is a little Tough for Yankees'

Saturday Night and Sunday Morning.

'Alpacas, Harpic'

Stormy Monday.

'The Earth Groans'

Famine Tuesday.

'The Spawn of Satan'

Humpday Revisited.

'Sometimes you just have to eat the Bear'

Black Thursday.

'Always shoot Early or Late'

Just Desserts.

'The Secret of Happiness'

Introduction

When my career came to an unexpected halt – 'spectacularly crashed and ostentatiously burned' as my wife Louise rather overstated it - I, Joley Harpic, the longest serving Lieutenant in the British Army and Consultant to Large Corporations vowed I would never subject myself to the ritual humiliations of the daily grind, the thankless task, the busted gut, the up-hill struggle, Captain Kirk or Cathy Burke, ant-ification, up-sizing, down-sizing, prairie-dogging, paper shuffling or indeed any form of *work* and all that awful word entailed ever, *ever* again. No longer would I festoon myself in the chains of wage slavery and trudge, bowed and defeated, towards the daily exhaustion of my productive capacities, my intellect or my very soul. I would seek new fulfilment, recognise and embrace my WAD (Work Aversion Disorder) and make it work for me. I would become a Househusband and I would send my wife out to work.

At first my friends were sceptical. What would I do for money? How would I pay the mortgage? Would this not emasculate me? Scornfully, I batted away their cowardly fears. My wife would take care of the money from now on. Feminism had liberated me, as those far-seeing daughters of Pankhurst had predicted, just as it had liberated my wife from the drudgery of housework, the kitchen sink and the carpet-beater. Of course, there would be sacrifices to make. We had been Double Income No Kids all our lives but I felt that there was something especially serendipitous about making the transition from Dink to Oink.

When, on that rainy September morning, my dear spouse Louise, scion of the House of Horthy Worthy, stepped out bravely into our Brave New World, I was confident. Indeed, more than confident: I knew in my heart that she was more than capable of bringing home the bacon and fulfilling my dreams. She headed out, never looking back, with a chin as strong and determined as the prow of a trireme, her proud Eastern European stock ready to do battle with the future, to push back the frontiers of gender liberation and to give her all for the cause, for education, for our mutual happiness. Never had she looked so beautiful. Her dark, storm-tossed hair, raven and defiant, her alabaster skin almost translucent in the grey light of dawn, her eyes flashing pure fire at the crackling thunder and the iron sleet. I waved, but so absorbed was she in the challenge of the voyage ahead that she could not bring herself to acknowledge the fluttered handkerchief that I held high in her wake.

As the car turned the corner at the end of our lovely cul-de-sac, I resisted the impulse to phone and tell her that she had forgotten to indicate and that as the car only had Third Party insurance, she should not take unnecessary risks at busy junctions. Given that it was her first day at St.Wiccas Preparatory School, I thought it might be a little insensitive. Instead, my thoughts turned inwards and to breakfast.

Monday. Day One: The Odyssey Begins.

'Bacon has no calories.'

George Bernard Shaw.

Breakfast is the most important meal of the day. This is because it is the first and after it you can eat lots of others. However, if you are on a diet there are certain restrictions on the number of meals you can with a clear conscience eat. There are no hard and fast rules about this but, generally speaking, the more you eat, the fatter you get. This is something that is worth bearing in mind. Louise has something to say on this issue from time to time and her valued input is one of the reasons for my embarking on this journey. If she is to go out to work and act as the family bread winner then it only seems fair that I should maintain my svelte figure so that she has something visual to uplift her after a hard day. So I'm doing all this for her. It is important to be unselfish in one's motivations.

'Breakfast is the best meal of the day,' said Eve handing over the apple, possibly. Actually, I have just Googled for some appropriate breakfast related witticisms and wisdom but I couldn't find any so from this point on, please assume that any quote that is not properly attributed is made up by me or is something I heard in the Pub. Still, it *is* a good quote and brings me nicely to the subject of bacon.

'Bacon is the food of the Gods,' said Winston Churchill. Not *all* Gods, obviously, but enough to be going on with. I cannot think of anything that tastes as good as bacon and no-one else can either. There isn't a sentient being on this planet who does not smell bacon frying and wish to eat it. It is irresistible to all Homo Sapiens without exception. I have known devout Jews and Muslims weep at the distant whiff of a bacon bap even when it has been cooked up in engine oil by a hairy knuckled unwashed ungulate outside a leaking sewage works in Scunthorpe. I have known vegetarians lapse faster than a Catholic nun after her first orgasm on the first taste of this forbidden fruit. In 1597, Prince Septicus of Anhalt-Serbst declared war on the Archbishop of Pomerania over possession of a flock of prize porkers known to provide the most succulent sizzle, while Salzburg was conquered specifically by the Holy Roman Emperor to provide salt for the curing of the royal bacon. Philosophers have debated its merits; the 1st Viscount St.Alban preferred to be known as Francis Bacon and even had his parents similarly renamed, so convinced was he of its essential truth. Mozart's Second Clarinet Concerto is known as the 'Bacon Overture'. Christian Bernard had bacon for breakfast before performing the first ever heart transplant and this in itself should indicate the wealth and extent of its medicinal benefits. Who would trust the trembling scalpel in the surgeon's hand without it first having been steadied by a good slice of streaky? It would not be too much to assert that Hitler lost the Second World War because he didn't like bacon, although of course some Historians may disagree and assert the relative importance of other factors, like D-Day or the battle of Stalingrad. This is neither here nor there though; what we can all agree on is that bacon and breakfast are synonymous.

Of course, you can have other things alongside bacon for breakfast – sausages come naturally to mind – and we'll be dealing with all the marvellous multi-cultural diversity of breakfast as we continue on our journey. The fact remains though: you simply can't have breakfast without bacon and there is no simpler way to eat it than in a bacon butty.

Today's Recipe: The Basic Bacon Butty/Sandwich

There has been a long debate over whether bacon is best eaten in a butty or in a sandwich and over the years this has been exacerbated by the North/South divide. Those who argue for the butty tend to come from above the Watford Gap and are sometimes stigmatised by the supporters of the sandwich as dirty finger-nailed proletarians mumbling unintelligibly from under flat caps. Those who prefer sandwiches are equally often unfairly characterised as 'Southern Jessies' who wouldn't know a Black Pudding from a dildo, but in fact, there is no need for class divide, homoerotic fantasies or any other such unpleasantries. Both the sandwich and the butty can be comfortably eaten without recourse to sectarian rivalry or aggression. The difference is that a butty is folded, whereas a sandwich is cut. Nothing much to really fight over now is there? Perhaps the Arabs and Israelis might learn a lesson from this?

The real advantage of bacon for the slimmer is, of course, that it has no calories. So follow this simple guide and tuck in without guilt, remorse or worry.

Step 1. Take some bacon out of the fridge and put it under the grill. We'll leave the issue of whether to fry or grill until later. Many people ask me 'How much bacon should I grill?' There is a specific formula for this when dealing with sausages but right now the answer is, simply, five. Don't skimp. It is important to get your Five-a-day.

Step 2. Turn the grill on and grill the bacon until it is done on one side. Then turn it over and repeat. You will know when it is done because everyone knows this.

Step 3. While it is doing, get some bread and put some butter on it. Spread the butter. Don't get side-tracked by debates over different kinds of spreads or margarines just yet. We'll cover this when you are *au fait* with the basics.

Step 4. Take the bacon from the grill and put it on the bread. If you are using a single piece of bread, remember to fold so that you will have the perfect butty. If you are using two pieces of bread, go ahead and enjoy your sandwich by cutting it in half. You might begin with a straight cut. I prefer a diagonal stroke myself.

More adventurous or experienced cooks may wish to skip ahead a few pages for variations on this theme but, as this is a holistic approach to weight loss, I can't recommend it. Beginners should walk before they can run.

This brings us neatly along to the next part of our day but before heading there it's probably worthwhile reminding Northerners to wash their hands before cooking, especially if they have been down a coal mine, as fingerprints on the bread are a bit of a turn-off if you have guests.

Today's Exercise Regime: A Lovely Walk.

Joining a gym is a common error for those seeking to lose weight or effect a general lifestyle change. They appear to offer a steady, scientific and disciplined approach to the burning of calories accompanied by a novel and pleasing change of wardrobe. The seeker of the svelte often makes the mistake that buying expensive sports equipment such as branded shoes, designer tee-shirts and expandable lycra cycling shorts will somehow provide a boost to the recently diminished willpower that is at the root of the overall weight gain experience. Nothing could be further from the truth. You are fat (and probably poor) because you spend too much time shopping.

Similarly, the attractions of the Yummy Mummies of St.Wicca's Preparatory School leaping out of powerful mechanical machines fresh and flushed from the excitement of a school run accomplished at speed and over rough terrain are to be distrusted, especially for those Househusbands who live in a small community. Superficially, the panting exertions and athletic gyrations of the 9.30 Zumba class may be of passing inspiration and, of course, the Zen like calm of 10.15 Pilates might appear to offer possibilities of striking up stimulating training partnerships that reach across the gender divide. These are rarely consummated. I knew a chap who tried hanging out by the water-cooler and engaging young mothers in conversation of a more or less louche kind. He ended up going into the wrong sauna and that did him no good at all. Also, gentlemanly attentions, however innocent or well-meant, are apt to be misunderstood; highly-charged female executives with careers paused by child care issues can sometimes be testier than a Feminist in a monastery.

The mere mention of lycra clad Yummy Mummies is also fraught with difficulties for those lucky to have working partners. I have noticed that this is a characteristic found particularly in female Prep school teachers, especially among those who have the daily charge of the offspring of those same ladies with time to go to the gym.

Gyms also cost money to join. When Louise expressed an interest in joining a gym, I made a point of telling her that we really could not afford such luxuries now that we were down to one income and that she was not really fat enough to justify the expenditure. Perhaps next year? She did not take this entirely in the spirit in which it was offered and responded a little acidly at first. She did come round to my point of view after I pointed out that she would hardly have the time now that she was working and that it was her sacrifice that allowed all those Yummy Mummies to go to the gym in the first place. She should be proud of that, I said.

'I shall be in the garden, Harpic,' she replied.

'In February?'

'It will be healthier for both of us,' she said.

A further reason for avoiding gyms is that unless you are already in possession of perfectly crafted abs, sculpted pecs and a six-pack you can bounce coins off – as I had until relatively recently – then you are likely to become an object of derision for all those who have already got them and this is not good for the self-esteem necessary to a happy life and effective weight loss.

All in all, therefore, beginning your fitness regime by joining a gym can be safely marked down as 'inadvisable' alongside those lycra shorts that you recently bought but keep hidden, for good reasons.

No: it cannot be stated too often or too firmly that gyms are for fit people not fatties. Better to start with a lovely walk.

To get the best out of walking, you should try to live in the countryside. The best place would be a small village close enough to interesting places to visit like London, Cambridge or Aldeburgh but far enough away from Birmingham, Burnley or Blackpool to deter the people who live there from coming to visit you. Here in Slimstead, we are fortunate to possess all the necessary attributes for a holistic exercise regime. There are two pubs, a church, a village hall, a stately home cum wedding venue, St.Wicca's prep and some homosexuals from London to give the place an agreeably modern Metropolitan hipster feel.

We take a straightforward approach to directions in Slimstead so the church of St.Moses the Black is situated on Perdition Drive, the two pubs are to be found on Hope Street and the stately home cum wedding venue is at the end of Cane Lane opposite St.Wicca's. Just past the far end of Cane Lane is the Slimstead Golf and Country Club, which is a mixed blessing for those who prefer to watch paint dry but tolerance is our middle name in Slimstead. All around are fields and farms and woods to walk in and so there are endless options for the determined lifestyle freestyler when it comes to a lovely walk.

Walk Number One: The St.Wicca Circuit.

I always like to give my walks names so that I can refer to them easily whenever I tell Louise about my daily activities. The St.Wicca Circuit is so named because it takes me past the Prep where she works and affords me the opportunity to give her a cheery wave whenever I see her. So now, our breakfast being over, it is time for our lovely walk.

Walking is very efficient for burning calories, especially if one pays attention to selecting the correct the type of footwear. Many people choose branded training shoes for their daily constitutional but it should be borne in mind that in the countryside things can sometimes get a little muddy. Also animals can sometimes be less than considerate when they do Number Twos and this shows up conspicuously on white training shoes. Wellington boots are a better option – but remember that you will need to wear two pairs of socks (one thin cotton, the other a heavier wool variety) if you are to avoid an unpleasant balling at the toe of the boot. It is important not to buy those Wellington boots that have little laces at the tops or be tempted to wear anything other than a green shade; black Wellingtons are for workers or for African mine dancers, while laces are inescapably louche in the mind of the Countryman. In the summer, a stout pair of Oxfords or some good sturdy brogues are ideal. Sandals are to be avoided as they provided no protection whatsoever and a stubbed toe is really no laughing matter.

Walking technique is also important. There are alternative schools of thought on this issue and it is as well to be informed of them before starting out. All are agreed, however, that slouching about with one's hands in one's pockets like a spotty teenager deprived of crack cocaine or mooching along, feet splayed, kicking at stones like a Shop Steward looking for a strike is to be avoided. My own view is that a determined, purposeful stride is best, where heel and toe are pointing in the exact direction of travel, and progress is assured. There is no need to pump ones arms as though doing Zumba nor to swing them in a military fashion. Just a natural, easy motion is all that is required. A chap I know from the pub, Denning, an ex-barrister, follows the theory that one should always keep one's hands folded behind one's back while walking as it is conducive to a more dignified bearing and deters policeman from making unfounded accusations of loitering. Wall-eyed and cursed by a habit of unconscious gurning, he has the high domed forehead and unsightly ear hair characteristic of the legal profession, which has combined to make him generally unattractive as a potential sexual partner and rather blighted his life; he does not revel in the status of Slimstead's most highly educated Lone Wolf. Nevertheless, his opinions are worthy of respect. He always adopts the hands-behind-back stance when going into the spinney behind the graveyard although I have noticed that he abandons it when leaving, usually about fifteen minutes later. Then he moves in a fashion closer to my own theoretical approach.

Walking attire suitable for a lovely country walk may safely be left up to the individual. I am aware that specialist gear such as an extra pair of socks and a windjammer may be required for Snowdon or the Cairngorms but here in the civilised parts of the Kingdom such extremes are not required. If it rains severely, a Barbour jacket is all that is necessary but beyond that pretty much anything goes. In summer, it is delightful to see ladies abandon layers of outer clothing the better to enjoy all the health giving properties of the glorious English sunshine and in winter there are few more pleasant delights than rosy cheeks warming by the fire after a good jog through the country. My own tastes extend to plus fours, which though out of fashion these days, make the perfect walking attire but being hard to come by in Primark, I usually make do with khaki shorts. In winter, long trousers are important. For the upper body, a loose fitting Norfolk jacket is ideal because it has lots of pockets to keep useful things in but again, Primark may not be so big on this traditional line of outdoor wear. If in doubt, stick with the Barbour as it is both practical and ensures that you will not be mistaken for some dreadful proletarian townie.

On this lovely sunny day, the Wicca Circuit is an easy, level walk which takes about an hour depending on how long you might be distracted by watching the young PE teachers do sporty things on the playing fields. I leave the house after carefully checking to see that I have locked all doors and windows behind me and proceed at a good pace down the cul-de-sac, making sure to look in to all those of my neighbour's windows that are not covered by net curtains. This is part of my regular contribution to the Neighbourhood Watch and I sometimes supplement it by a closer inspection if I feel that there is something suspicious. I *do* not, as has been alleged, pay any more attention to Mrs Johnson's windows than to any other of the other recent divorcees in the village for that would be intrusive and likely to generate ire in some quarters closer to home.

Turning right onto Berkstead Road and neatly avoiding the Gazpacom truck thundering down the road at high speed and doubtful braking capacity, I head towards Hope Street which is shaded by dappled elm trees artfully sculpted into a shady tunnel by the said passing Gazpacom juggernauts. Turning left would take me to Berkstead where I sometimes do my shopping but as this is a Monday I will probably not go to the shops. Instead, I will go a little way down Hope Street and then head up Cane Lane towards the stately home cum wedding venue. This business is a boon for the village as it provides part-time employment for some of the younger, less skilled members of our lovely community and welcome extra trade for the two pubs. I have often noticed that at many wedding celebrations some guests prefer to investigate the local hostelry as an alternative to the free beverages provided during the speeches. This is not a phenomena restricted to young men in ill-fitting morning suits with short attention spans but also to a number of young women, who sometimes are by turns bitter or weepy. Under no circumstances should a gentleman notice these women and absolutely no attempt be made to offer consolation until much later, when they are feeling more agreeably approachable. By that time, the risk of a young man in an ill-fitting morning suit returning with a hang dog expression and a bad attitude towards sympathetic gentlemen will be much reduced.

The stately home cum wedding venue was once home to the Earls de Slimstead, a much respected family of French origins who made their fortune in the slave trade and then devoted the next few generations to rack-renting tenants, enclosing common land and putting out man-traps for honest poachers. They returned to France for a long holiday and to the surprise of the village were bought out in 1789 at a surprisingly modest price by the Bluntnose family, who also inherited the Slimstead title shortly after it became unexpectedly vacant. The Bluntnoses extensively remodelled the 17th Century Palladian construction and extended it to accommodate a pig farm and a water-mill which provided welcome employment to the distressed peasantry. Sometime in the 19th Century, the Bluntnoses fell upon hard times and the stately home passed into the hands of Sir Thomas Higginbottom, a wealthy northern mill owner eager to escape his humble origins and assume gentlemanly status. The pig farm went at this time, followed by the mill, which improved the aesthetics but depressed the local economy to the point that the Slimstead peasants had to live off mangel-worzels or go up north to go down a pit. Sir Thomas Higginbottom was not popular and made himself even less so by introducing the practice of Total Abstinence to the village. This abhorrent and alien concept took physical form in the shape of a Coffee House that abjured anything stronger than tea, coffee, two sugars and unpasteurised milk. It was burned down twice. The heirs of Sir Thomas did not prosper particularly; many of them were killed in the First World War and Death Duties after the Second World War finished off those who were left. The stately home 'went on fire' as the saying among insurance assessors goes, whence the estate was broken up and sold off to provide the buildings and grounds for St.Wiccas Prep (the pig farm) and of course the (re-built 1977) stately home cum wedding venue. Its style is now described as Wimpey eclectic.

I usually arrive outside St.Wicca's just as morning break is about to begin, buoyed up by the notion that my Dearest Louise is about to enjoy a well-earned cup of coffee in the staff room. It is only rarely that I see her outside on break duty, partly because I have a copy of the rota, and partly because her turn does not seem to coincide with Miss Peters' jogging, which is a very pleasant sight and reminds me of my own school days when I spent many fulfilling hours in the woods competing at cross country with the girls from St.Hilda's Grammar. Back then I was not as fit as I later became, but observing those superb female forms leaping like gazelles through the forest from a position at the rear of the pack is not something that I would willingly forget. It was educational. The building is quite nice and painted a cheerful blue.

Moving on, I take a left turn towards the church which will take me down through the fields of barley. For any city dwellers reading this, barley is a crop which to the untrained eye is indistinguishable from wheat. Flour is derived from wheat and you can easily purchase it at retail outlets in the city and use it to make bread. Barley is a little more complex and is not the first thing that one puts one's hands on in the Tesco Metro by the Council Estate. However, it is important because beer is derived from it which is, of course, the first thing that Council Estate dwellers do put their hands on in Tesco Metro and often at the public expense. There is also a thing called Pearl Barley which used to be quite popular for use in soups and stews in Boarding Schools. I last ate it in the mid-1980s when I was in the army and cannot really recommend it. It is perhaps something that vegetarians might find a use for, poor things.

Unexpectedly appearing (as he is wont to do) beside me as I enter upon the path that flows through the golden field is Old Father Timeon, a village regular of druidical appearance and philosophy. He is dressed in his usual dusty denims, desert wellies and CND T-shirt and carries his scythe held high above his magisterial mane of wild grey waist length hair. I have always eschewed those who hold that his appearance reminds them of a cross between Karl Marx and Charles Manson and prefer to regard him as a figure of biblical proportions, though given his religious proclivities, he probably wouldn't thank me for this. He is a keen ecologist and conservationist, lives in a tepee and earns his living by charcoal burning, hedging and ditching and supplements his income by tending the Wicker Man which the village constructs annually just a little way on from the Nature Reserve. He and fellow village worthy Carruthers are said to get on like a house on fire, sharing as they do similar views on the sustainability of mankind in the face of serious and mounting threats from the environment, although Carruthers' are rather more concerned with the issues of rhino poaching and the possibility of untreatable epidemics crossing the species boundary than the awakening of vengeful Gods through excessive open cast mining and the related activities of extractive industries.

'The Earth groans, Harpic,' he says, with a wild eyed visionary stare.

Accompanying him is his raven haired daughter, Chickadee Southern Comfort, who though conceived in a Californian commune and spending her formative years following a *Grateful Dead* tribute band has turned out remarkably well. Well, fairly well: like her father, there is a hint of woad amid the patchouli, but it is the crescent moon tattoo on her forehead and the Bronze Age torque on her arm that marks her out as a full citizen of Loonyville. On the positive side, she has gone into business for herself as a tree surgeon and although being self-employed necessarily involves some small concessions to the capitalist system maintains her alternative society credentials by being a staunch Feminist – principles which she underlines at this moment with a chain saw. She is a regular help to her father in his timeless struggle with nature and can be seen with him on moonlit nights at certain times of the year cutting Mistletoe or dancing naked around sacred trees (I had this from Denning, who refuses to reveal the exact whereabouts of the said sacred oak for fear of violating her privacy; the photos he took are good though; very atmospheric).

'The Earth groans, Harpic,' repeats Old Timeon, portentiously. 'There is unrest within her bowels.'

Old Timeon is a bit of a prophet of doom and most villagers take his warnings with a pinch of salt – although one should note that he predicted last year's snowfall to the very hour and made a killing by selling short at the top of the Dotcom boom. (Much good it did him too: his wife had the proceeds and buggered off to live an alternative lifestyle on a yacht in St.Tropez). He does seem rather agitated today though.

'Is he alright?' I ask Chickadee. 'Taken all his medication as directed?'

'The Moon is orbiting, Harpic,' she replies, a faraway look in her eyes. 'The Mistletoe is singing.'

'Have *you* been at his medication, Chickadee?' I enquire. 'You know that isn't strictly allowed.'

'The corn fears, Harpic,' says Old Timeon. 'It *fears*.'

'Well, I suppose it would do if harvest is due along in a couple of weeks – if it was a sentient being, that is,' I reply.

'Listen to the Earth, Harpic,' he replies. 'It groans.'

'Yes and I shall certainly listen out for singing Mistletoe, too.'

I give them a cheery wave and walk on with an extra spring in my step.

By the church, I give a similarly cheery wave to my ex-barrister friend Denning, who today has his hands behind his back. It is a wave similar to the one I was intending to bestow on my Dearest Louise, indeed identical, and I'm sure she would not want it to be wasted. Strangely enough, he does not seem to see it even though I had the distinct impression he was looking in my direction a moment ago. Never mind; perhaps he has weighty matters of legal import on his mind. From here I turn sharp left again and walk briskly up Perdition Drive so as not to intrude on his thoughts. This brings me to the Old Queens Head, the first of our two village Pubs and affectionately known as the Freddy Mercury Arms. It is a half-timbered beauty of age and staid steadfastness and we will certainly visit it before our dietary adventure is over but as it is not open yet, it will remain for now as a delight for the future.

Up Hope Street and back into my own dear cul-de-sac takes no more than ten minutes and completes our first lovely walk. Slimstead is a lovely, lovely place as yet untroubled by development, fracking, environmentalists or any of that nonsense associated with pressure groups and the modern world. Here, we are Nimby and Proud Of It, though it has to be said that the Parish Magazine, the *Slimstead Insinuator* has indicated that the frackers and developers are indeed prowling.

(Wildlife sighted: 2 rabbits, one muntjac, several swallows).

Lunch is for Wimps.

'Lunch is for wimps' declared Gordon Gecko and he was as right in this assertion as in all things. It is pleasing that our great captains of finance know how to set a standard so that our pensions and investments might grow at an inflation beating rate and thus we can do no better than to emulate them in our own, less stressful, lives. We should also bear in mind that both Mussolini and Stalin ate lunch and that some very strange people sit on benches eating sandwiches at lunchtime in London. It is also a well-known fact that lunch has got more calories in it than any other meal, so in order to be beautiful, it is necessary to suffer a little. And it is only a little. Missing lunch is not like being crucified. Put that out of your mind right away.

Housework.

Having elected to embrace the role of Househusband there is really no escape from housework however much a chap might want to. Of course, having a job and earning a wage outside the home in a busy and demanding career has naturally exempted men from taking the lead on the domestic front and women have, in turn, naturally plugged this gap - often excellently. It is both fortunate that the modern liberated woman has acquired the necessary multi-tasking skills to hold down a real job and do housework and indeed admirable that she has shaken off any suggestion that being a Jack-of-all-trades means that she is Master of None. No, she has done well on the whole, even if she might be guilty of going a little out of the way from time to time in pointing out her own achievements. I know Louise has fallen into this trap on occasion, but I have always found it better to forgive this small lapse than to respond in a tone of matching shrillness.

Puzzling though it undoubtedly is, the truth is that there is no great mystery to housework and much of the claims about its complexity and difficulty are, to my mind, exaggerated. A chap who can command the IT system, the BMW and the TV remote will hardly find it beyond his powers to master a twin tub and a mangle and one has to consider the possibility that the whole issue has been blown out of proportion to serve a Feminist agenda. This is not entirely a bad thing because housework is now actually counted as 'work' thanks to England's very own Abel Magwitch, Germaine Greer. It is a Feminist advance that Househusbands should own and celebrate.

At the root of the housework issue is the mistaken notion that Cleanliness is next to Godliness. You may have noticed over the years a female obsession with cleanliness that to a rational mind borders on OCD. This is not to belittle that mental disorder - which is treatable now and carries little stigma - but the female insistence on heightened levels of hygiene is readily observable both by working Husbands and Househusbands. It is something to do with their vaginas. This is probably a well-known fact. From this we can probably infer that cleanliness is emphatically *not* next to godliness because there is nothing in the Bible about Lesbians and they do very well at housework.

No, the key to being a successful Househusband is to quickly master the housework and the essential concept to internalise here is what I call 'Bloke Clean'. This means keeping the house in a state easily habitable without expending excessive effort sure in the knowledge that anything requiring higher standards will be achieved when she is home at the weekend. A quick example; the bathroom. It does not need to be steam cleaned every five minutes. A quick run round with a damp cloth to remove pubes will suffice for all practical purposes. Nor does the toilet need to be flushed every time you go for a pee – and in middle age that can be more often than expected – because it wastes so much water and water bills are never going to get cheaper are they? The maxim is 'if it's brown, flush it down; if it's yellow, let it mellow' because no-one likes looking at a toilet trout but you hardly notice a bit of stale piss in the urinals in the Pub. And here's a killer tip; instead of flushing when you pee, stick some bleach down the bog. When she comes in from work the smell will make her think you've cleaned the bathroom properly. Louise falls for it every time.

Sundowners.

It is important to know that alcohol is a chemical element and the body cannot metabolise it. This was made known to me by a chap I know who has a First Class Degree in Zoology and is thus as reliable a fact as any. It is vital for our purposes because it means that alcohol has no calories and can therefore play a full role in any successful diet. Ignore all unhelpful speculation and claims to the contrary from either the media, the scientific community and especially the government. They are all interested parties who stand to gain from peddling the horrible untruth that booze is in some way bad for you. To believe that alcohol is bad for you is to deny the wisdom of centuries and become a wizened creature of spiteful misery, a bloodless prig, a bore, unpatriotic and undeserving of consideration. Johnny Rotten said that one should never trust a hippy. I would say that you should never trust a Teetotaller.

People do not get fat because they drink alcohol either. Putting weight on is due to all sorts of other reasons. I knew a fat woman of Italian extraction who swore blind that she had piled on the pounds simply because she had inherited a slow metabolism from a distant Mediterranean forebear. I believed her; she only ever drank diet coke with her vodka and only ate chocolate to speed up her metabolism so that she could lose weight faster and more efficiently. Drinking is not only a perfectly reasonable and sociable activity – indeed, there is none better – but it is also almost guaranteed to help you lose weight. As Someone Once Said: if you're drinking, you're not eating.

Which brings us to the subject of Sundowners, the well-deserved reward for a day of honest labour. To the sentimental Englishman it conjures up marvellous visions of sandy lands and other days when the Union Jack fluttered high above palm and pine, mountain, desert and veldt and drinks were served by grateful natives in white jackets and turbans. To the uncouth Australian, it is the six o'clock slurp. To the Chicago gangster, suave in his double-breasted pinstripe and Thomson sub-machine gun, it means cocktails, molls and speakeasies. To the decadent lounge-lizard Frenchman it is a *pastis* and a filthy cigarette trailing smelly smoke into his over-oiled receding hairline. I don't know what they do in China, Africa or South America but I dare say they enjoy a good piss up like the rest of us. It is a multicultural celebration of the end of the working day and so not to be taken lightly.

The hour at which Sundowners may be embarked upon naturally varies. It would be absurd to wait for the sun to go down in the middle of a long English summer because that would mean waiting until ten in the evening and that would never do. Similarly, mid-winter in England means that the sun is rarely seen after three in the afternoon and drinks at that time would come under the Afternoon Session appellation rather than Sundowners. For those disordered enough to choose a life inside the Arctic Circle, the tradition would be redundant for most of the year, as indeed the inhabitants themselves are, and may go some way to account for the legendary high levels of suicide in Scandinavia (but not in Canada or Alaska: death in that part of the Arctic is almost always due to being eaten by Polar bears). Things may also be complicated by geography. Those Americans who live on the Eastern seabord may have difficulty because the sun goes down behind them un-noticed while Californians desport themselves with abandon on golden beaches lit by spectacular Pacific sunsets – although it is an interesting perversity that the famous West coast easy listening rockers *The Eagles* should name their most famous cocktail song *Tequila Sunrise*, after something they might never see because the sun comes up behind them when they are gazing out at the Pacific Ocean. (Mind you, they are hardly reliable *rapporteurs* on anything important; in their barnstorming anthem *Hotel California*, they refer to 'the warm smell of colitis rising up through the air' when everyone knows that colitis smells of things bowel-related and is the last thing you want running through your hair on any highway, dark desert or not). All things considered, therefore, it seems wise to rely fully on the tried and tested wisdom of the English seadogs who established six o'clock as the time when the sun went below the yard arm of the ship as the time to break out the grog. So six o'clock is the proper time for Sundowners.

Except for teachers. Many teachers I know begin to think about a cool one round about eleven in the morning and by two they are sweating with enthusiasm for the comforting sharpness of white wine or lager. This is a throwback to the days when they were in Teacher Training College and were not expected to do much outside those hours, or in the holidays or at weekends beyond learning how to blow smoke rings and teach children to be beastly little Communists. Nowadays their workload has increased to the point that they are rarely able to access alcohol before 3.30pm unless they work in the private sector where a glass of port is often served at tiffin or perhaps a little earlier if they are Housemasters. My own Dearest Louise is apt to show enthusiasm for a glass of white wine from the moment she enters the door and as the *Major Domo* I take great pleasure in providing for her needs. Her enthusiasm can sometimes get a little ahead of her so, in the interests of marital harmony I have perfected the perfect His 'n' Hers cocktail, ideal for late afternoon or early evening on a Monday. And just to reiterate – being full of alcohol, cocktails are completely free of calories.

The Monday Cocktail.

Step 1: Empty the contents of a good bottle of chilled white wine into a large bucket-sized glass and add ice. Soave, Pinot Grigot, Sauvignon blanc or perhaps something from *Entre deux Meres* are ideal but try to avoid Chardonnay as chavs drink it and it tastes of aluminium pans. Add crushed ice.

Step 2: Add sparkling water to taste (not too much). Soda water may be substituted.

Step 3: Add a twist of lime and serve in a fluted glass.

Now, while she is getting on with her drink, you can make your own. Just follow **Step 1**, but don't bother adding any of the other stuff and serve in one of those glasses that look civilised but actually hold a whole bottle.

Dinner.

Dinner is very important because you haven't had lunch today. The evening repast should be quick and easy to prepare without any of that horrid old slaving over a hot stove that used to oppress women. A few slices of cold meat – ham obviously – and a light salad are all that is really required because your wife or partner will probably have eaten lunch and will not want a heavy evening meal however skilfully prepared. Louise is fortunate that school meals are provided free of charge at St.Wicca's. She is doubly fortunate in that she gets to bond with her little charges over that same shared lunch. We might also say, triply favoured because school meals just keep on getting better and better – there were no Turkey Twizzlers, Pizzas or Burgers in my day, I can tell you. No - such delicacies were not for us. *We* had to make do with whatever the school farm could provide and whatever Monsieur Blanc deigned to produce that day. I remember everyone got so tired of *foie gras* and the over-wrought fripperies of *Cordon Bleu* that we would have given a testicle for a pizza.

However, just because dinner may be quick and light, it is still worthy of serious consideration. Just to get the gastric juices flowing therefore, I'll introduce you to my special salad.

The Monday Salad.

Step 1: Open a bag of spinach leaves and arrange on a plate. Add fresh basil from one of those little pots that you buy from the supermarket and watch wilt after a couple of days despite following the twee and patently made-up care instructions. Serve.

Step 2: While your wife or partner is inspecting the green salad for wildlife, take some ham from the packet in the fridge and put it on a plate. Ditto some cheese – a good cheddar is always acceptable.

Step 3: Put jars of pickled beetroot and gherkins on the table. These are much underrated as vegetables and their use should be encouraged, especially in conjunction with Branston Pickle.

Step 4: Serve and enjoy. Note how low calories, low carbs and a high protein content are cleverly combined in this dish. No doubt you are beginning to guess my secret to successful weight loss by now? Keep the white wine handy.

'Harpic,' says my Dearest Louise, on eyeing up the cocktail and the salad. 'If you are going to commit serial enormities while I am slaving away at the chalk face to keep our bodies and souls together, at least have the decency to spread them out across the week.'

'Enormities spread throughout during the week, it is,' I reply, with a winning smile. 'Have another cocktail.'

After-Dinner Drinks.

Everyone has their own view on this. There are those who swear by cognac or port, while others prefer a soothing liquor like Amaretto to finish off the perfect repast. On a Monday, however, and bearing in mind it is only the beginning of the working week, it is probably advisable to stick to the white wine or perhaps a couple of tinnies. Louise prefers to stick to her 'special' and sometimes I make up a second batch for her if she has marking to do, which will see her through to the early hours. Meanwhile so as not to disturb her and if it is summer, I will repair to the back lawn with a grassy Sauvignon to listen to the trilling of birdsong. In winter, I might put on earphones and listen to Heavy Metal with a warming pint of ale until it is time to snuggle in beside her under the duvet. There I will drift off knowing that a good day has ended well and that Louise is so happily absorbed in her work that she will not lightly lay down her red pen before 2 am. I was the longest serving Lieutenant in the British Army, so I can easily sleep with the light on.

Tuesday. Day Two: The Odyssey Continues and Picks up the Pace.

'A man would rather come home to an unmade bed and a happy woman than to a neatly made bed and an angry woman.'

Marlene Dietich.

'And vice versa, probably. You never can tell with women though.'

J.Harpic.

The Weigh–in.

The most important thing to remember for those who are so fortunate in their lifestyle choices to have a working spouse is never, *never*, get up before her. Gone are the days when couples sat down to breakfast together and swapped interesting snippets of information from the pages of the freshly ironed, urchin delivered newspaper. Gone are the days of the second pot or the replenished toast rack. Nowadays, mornings are a rather frenetic time of crammed in pieces of toast, curses at empty shower gel containers, lost hair dryers and the constant tyranny of an over-paid, over-enthusiastic idiot of a DJ shouting the bloody time and the state of the M25 at you every five minutes, all conducted to a staccato drumbeat of very short, very pronounced stiletto stamps. Put away any generous or chivalrous thoughts, chaps: you may think that making her a light breakfast of bacon, egg, sausage, fried bread, beans, tomatoes, mushrooms and hash browns might be a well appreciated gesture but – and I must insist upon this point – the noise generated will not assuage her wrath at being awoken before her allotted and finely calculated time. A chap being anywhere near the bathroom or even threatening to cross the direct line between her and the coffee pot is guaranteed to produce imperious demands and sharp rejoinders. Suggesting that she get up ten minutes earlier and take a more leisurely approach to the morning routine is tantamount to suicide. No: experience has shown that it is essential to stay in bed until she has left the building.

Making use of this time can be a challenge for a chap with an active mind but I have developed a real interest in the patterns formed on the inside of my eyelids when subjected to the different angle and intensity of the light. I particularly like the ones that look like parquet flooring or other geometric shapes. I am not sure why these patterns form but I believe they are due to the different types of light receptors known as rods and cones that exist somewhere inside the old *camera obscura*, and they are often jolly pretty especially when they come in those curious shades of green and orange. For variety, I sometimes press gently down on my eyelids with my fingers to observe the changing effects and at other times stretch out my eyelids by pinching them between thumb and forefinger to enjoy even more shapes and patterns. Be careful not to get your eyelashes caught if you intend to try this.

Sometimes I ponder on curious etymological facts; did you know that the words for *mother, father* and *baby* are almost identical in the English language, Mandarin and Zulu? Or that the Finnish for *coffee* is *kahvi*? The word for *book* in Xhosa is *incwadi* – an ink wad! – while *bint* is Egyptian for *girl*, which is a bit un-PC. I wonder how this came about. Does it mean that we are all descended from a common tribe located so far back in geological time that no trace of it is now left? Or is it just a coincidence? I have no idea. Just as I have no idea whose idea it was to invent paper hats to wear at Xmas lunch. Still, it is a comfort to know that there is so much that we don't know and can't know even if we wanted to. Imponderables are important, I find, even though they are by their very nature, imponderable.

At other times I wonder about subjects related to names. Would, for example, Giuseppe Verdi have made such a success in the world of opera if he had been called plain old Joe Green? If the Duke of Wellington had been called Earl Snodgrass, would we be wearing Snodgrass boots? Why are so many people called Smith? I understand that many people are named after professions; Thatcher, Farmer, Cooper spring naturally to mind and Christopher Plummer who (coincidentally, considering we have mention his eponymous boots) played the Duke of Wellington in the 1970 film *Waterloo*, is probably descended from someone who picked plums for a living. I can only conclude that the village Smith must have been putting it about a bit more than he ought to have done; perhaps his profession forged him a muscular stature that horsewomen found all too irresistible and he ended up doing more than just shoeing their horses? It is a theory. Puzzling too is why there are no people called Robber or Thieving-Bastard when there are plenty of them about, especially in the North Country. Similarly, I have met people called Butler, Baker, Nurse and Patel (which is Urdu for Farmer) but never anyone called Electrician. This goes for people named after places too; I have known people called Chester, Holland, Lancashire, French, Middleton and Churchill but never anyone called Archipelago. Curious isn't it?

Other pastimes include trying to remember the names of all my old girlfriends in the correct order and giving them marks based on a variety of criteria that I vary from time to time, or pretending to have seagulls in my head – it is very soothing to think of them flying high and free in a blue sky atop a blustery cliff; if only we could all be so free. A really hard one is getting all the Swedish monarchs in the right order; start with the House of Vasa before attempting anything in the Kalmar Union or Bjalbo periods, would be my advice.

Some people swear by a bit of Buddhist PTin the morning but I find all that deep breathing and contortion of limbs a bit of a trial in the mornings and the sight of you coming over all relaxed, yoga'd-up and spiritual while she's trying to find the bloody car keys can test her patience too far. Similarly, don't roll over and go back to sleep as a habit; once or twice a week, if it is one of those horrid cold, sleety mornings, is fine but otherwise it is a waste of the time that has been given unto you. *Carpe Diem* is what I say.

Anyway, to the Weigh-in. The first thing you will notice when you step on the bathroom scales this morning is that you will have lost weight. It will probably be a pound - not much more - but the secret to successful dieting is to get the right mix of bacon, booze, exercise and lifestyle for you and so this might take a little while. Everyone is different. If you have lost a kilo then you are in danger of losing weight too rapidly and need to slow down. Nothing good ever came from rushing. If you have gained weight then you are guilty of snacking or slacking and you will need to pull your socks up if you intend to achieve your goals and enjoy a general feeling of well-being. Whatever your situation, take heart and do not be disappointed; look forward to breakfast. The very worst thing you can do is skip it. Remember Rome fell because the people demanded Bread and Circuses. If they had stuck to toast and bacon all would have been well, I feel.

Bacon for Breakfast.

Bacon comes in many forms and all are worthy of consideration. The first choice faced by the questing breakfaster is whether to go for smoked or un-smoked. This is quite important because they have different flavours. Smokey bacon tastes a bit smokey, but in a pleasant way, not like it has been in a fire in a carpet warehouse or held over French cigarettes and is very good with baked beans. Some people wait for it to go cold and add it to salads and one can only marvel at such patience but it's safer on the whole, I feel, to eat it hot. You can easily recognise it because it looks a bit orangey around the edges or, if you are unsure, you can look at the label on the packet for identification information. Unsmoked bacon is not smoked or rather, it is bacon that has not undergone the smoking process and is still in its natural form. In some places, it is known as 'green' bacon and this is not because it is off, but because it is more natural. Some people think it looks a bit pasty but don't let it put you off. It's not like its lard or anything like that. Really, it's more like the colour of a Scottish girls thighs but without the goose pimples.

Bacon can be thick cut or thin cut and somewhere in between. This is entirely a matter of individual preference but there are some things that the savvy breakfaster should be aware of. If you get your bacon from a butcher like the one in the Barkingham just up the road, you may be asked to state the number of 'rashers' or slices that you require. He will then cut that number of rashers to your order. When you come to pay your bill, however, you may be surprised to find that it is more then you expected. This is because he cuts the rashers extra thick so that you must pay more. This is because bacon is sold by *weight* rather than by number of slices. It is a good marketing strategy and obviously good for his cash flow but for those of limited means, it can be a challenge. I have brought this to his attention on several occasions despite his sometimes surly responses but he still persists in his sharp practice.

It is the same with supermarkets. They too sell packets of bacon which advertise the number of rashers contained, only in this case the rashers are sliced very thinly so that you may be fooled into thinking that you are getting *more* rather than *less*. It stands to reason that eight rashers of bacon from Tesco does not automatically equate to eight rashers of bacon from the Butcher of Barkingham, doesn't it? So 'always go by weight', as a chap once told me and I have taken this sage counsel as my motto.

The next choice to be made is between Streaky and Back, both of which come in smoked an unsmoked varieties. Back bacon comes from the back of a pig and Streaky comes from the part next to it (but not the bottom). Both have their supporters. Back is meatier and is particularly suited to sandwiches, being toothsome. Streaky is favoured by those who like their bacon crunchier and who can blame them? There used to be an extra choice to be made of 'rind on' or 'rind off' but this seems to have fallen into disuse. Almost all bacon comes 'rind off' now, which is a shame, for one does not like to see consumer choice needlessly diminished in this way. The Butcher of Barkingham disagrees with me on this point too, even though I have made it several times.

In recent times, Middle Bacon has been making a come-back. Middle bacon comes from the middle of the pig, as you would expect, and neatly marries up both Streaky and Back in a harmonious horse-shoe shaped union. It was very common up North where I lived for a while as a child while my father was engaged in Missionary work and usually came 'rind on'. Cooking it presented its own particular challenges because the centre point of the junction between the Streaky and Back sections would often shrink and rise up under the grill presenting a very real possibility of a burned section flanked by under-done extremities. My father overcame this challenge by using a pair of scissors to snip through the rind, which was quite hard to do because the rind could be tough. Fortunately, being the determined sort of man he was, he persevered and discovered the solution in the form of my mother's dressmaking sheers, which she used to make shawls for the poor. They were as equal to the task of snipping through bacon rind as they were for snipping through the poverty of the undeserving proletariat. Happy days!

A word of warning: Collar bacon. Collar bacon has been gradually sneaking back onto supermarket shelves under the guise of 'cooking bacon' (what else would you do with it, for heaven's sake?). In itself it is no more harmful to the conscientious dieter than any other kind of bacon but still, I cannot think of it without experiencing a momentary shudder. This is because it is popular with Northerners who do not grill or fry it, but *deep fry* it in old, square tins. Hard though this is to believe, it is indeed true. They use a fork to fish the stuff out when it is cooked and although this in itself is no real bar to enjoyment the medium they use for frying is called 'dripping' and is laden with calories. For those unaccustomed to Northern customs, 'dripping' is like lard but worse and comes from cows which have been rendered down to make the tinned corn beef so favoured by them as a Sunday treat. It is not for human consumption, whatever it says on the packet. It is the bacon lovers' equivalent of the abominable deep fried mars bar, which is what Northerners often have for dessert (or 'pudding' as it is known up there).

So now, turning away from such unpleasantness and thanking our lucky stars that we are on the right side of the North-South Divide we may proceed to enjoy our bacon in whatever guise we choose to enjoy it. Remember: there is no such thing as bad bacon. Have an extra rasher.

Today's Exercise Regime: Pottering in the Garden.

When I was younger I failed to appreciate the attraction of gardening for the middle-aged man and tended to delegate it to menials whenever I decently could. All that tugging at dandelions under a hot sun, sweeping up leaves in autumn and sweating behind a lawnmower all year round when one could be sitting quietly on a patio chair enjoying a cold drink or playing cribbage in the snug with a pint served at room temperature! I was unmoved by gardening programmes (except for that detective series with Felicity Kendal in it, though the producers could have done without the fat one; Miss Kendal needs no foil to highlight her charms). When I saw a film about prisoners winning the Chelsea flower show, possibly with the late Pete Postlethwaite starring, I hooted with derision. Who would give a convict a shovel? They might use it to dig a tunnel under the walls or excavate a shallow grave for a rival prison gang warlord in the exercise yard. If they were capable of the honest effort required for gardening then they would have found jobs on the land, perhaps even hedging and ditching, and become respectable members of society and not end up in prison for being the violent, lower class recidivists they, in almost all cases, are. (The exceptions are Labour MPs banged up for expenses frauds; they are usually champagne-swilling upper class recidivists). On a more literary note, when I saw that ill-favoured, unpleasant little gold-digger who married the smarmy vicar in the BBC production of *Pride and Prejudice* pushing that unfortunate churchman out into the garden while she drank tea in the back parlour – which was off limits to him! The rightful property owner! – I suspected that gardening was a Feminist plot to deny frustrated husbands their conjugal rights. Now, having moved into a post-employment phase after a satisfyingly varied series of career experiences, I can see things differently and in a clearer light. The attraction of gardening is simple: *no one bothers you there*. Never are you hounded by bosses waving pieces of meaningless paper; never are you importuned by members of the general public seeking redress for some pootling mistake that you are alleged to have committed with dangerous chemicals or to return a product which was fit for the purposes it was sold *at the time of sale*; no-one minds if you fart and as long as you are discrete and make full use of the shrubbery, you may pick your nose to your heart's content and wipe the bogies on the leaves where caterpillars will eat them and so prevent your own small children (if you have them) learning dirty habits; and I have never once been shot at in my garden, even though we are used to guns here in the countryside.

Pottering in the garden is good exercise and can be done at a moderate pace. One need never break into a sweat while gardening if one adheres to Don's Dictum. Don is my next door neighbour and a gardener of no small ability. He knows the value of moderation, unlike some of the more competitive types in the Slimstead Horticultural Society, many of whom take things to ridiculous lengths. I wrote to the Chairman of the Parish Council (it is always a man, so *Chairman* is the correct usage here), a miserable little Communist by the name of Ostrakov, about this but I have yet to receive a reply. He is a busy man, obviously. Anyway, Don is a man who knows his onions and his dictum is 'Half an hour at a time'. He sticks to this rule, interspersing bouts of gardening of thirty minutes duration – no more and no less (unless it is raining, obviously) – with reading the paper and walking the dog (a pleasantly yappy Yorkshire terrier named Billy). His garden is perfect by any reasonable man's assessment, whatever that pedant Norman at the end of the cul-de-sac says. I have therefore adopted this dictum as my motto. Norman, by the way, is obsessive in the matter of his front lawn which he insists must be Wimbledon standard and will not tolerate a single daisy appearing in it. I have gained much pleasure over the years from seeing him repeatedly dig up, re-seed and re-lay the so afflicted turf in his war on the humble *Bellus Perennis*. He now has Astroturf – and I plant plastic daisies in it on my way back from the Pub.

Half an hour is enough to mow part of the lawn and water some of the hanging baskets and this is really enough to be going on with. Anything that requires more strenuous or sustained effort can wait until the weekend when Louise has more time. She enjoys weeding, I know it. She sees some parallels with teaching in it, I think. Tending to the education of children is obviously a lot like gardening when you think about it; planting the seeds of intellectual growth in a young mind so that they might grow into bulbs, then bloom into beautiful flowers displayed for decorative purposes or deadheaded as the case may be.

After half an hour, have a rest or read the paper. There is no need to feel guilty about this if like me, your spouse is busy at work. She will probably be enjoying a nice cup of tea and a chocolate biscuit in the Staffroom about now. After a decent interval, resume your activity and in no time at all, you will have a lovely garden and your pottering will have been worth all the effort expended. You can spend all day like this in the summer. Also – a good tip - remember that if you time this right and ensure that you are carrying a spade or shovel about around the time she gets home from work, you can claim that you have been too busy to complete all the housework tasks you set yourself.

Of course, not everyone is so lucky to live in the countryside and have a garden. Many people live in cities or in the North of England. In the first case, it might be possible to alleviate such a depressing condition by the purchase of a Gro-bag which you could keep in the corridor outside your Council flat. Consult a gardening manual on those varieties best suited to thrive on fluorescent light and urine. Better still, fix a window box on the security bars and grow something that doesn't need much care and attention – a cactus perhaps, for added protection against ram-raiders. Indoors, urban gardeners will find endless opportunities for Bonsai in a specially purchased glass cabinet or for growing orchids in the wet room. At the end of the day, it really doesn't matter how you overcome your unfortunate choice of dwelling as long as you try your best. The aim is to lose weight not to win all the prizes at the Slimstead Horticultural Society like that bloody Norman at the end of the cul-de-sac. Northern gardeners may wish to wait for the glacier to recede from the slag heap before planting some hardy and useful edible crop, like turnips, which will be both a comfort and a welcome change to eating each other.

Lunch.

You may only eat lunch if it is free.

Afternoon Beers.

Afternoon beers can sometimes be a problem area and open to criticism on a number of levels. The first is, of course, the possible and wholly understandable danger of objection from working spouses. That those in a post-career phase should spend time in the Pub while the breadwinner is slaving over a hot computer, attending Health and Safety training sessions of monumental ennui or guiding eager young minds to a greater knowledge of algebra can sometimes be seen to be a little unfair, is true. I know from my own experience what Louise's strongly held views on the subject are and I have come to respect them. She has made them completely plain on occasions too numerous to count and we have agreed to differ on the subject in the interests of marital harmony. I fully appreciate her point of view and so to avoid unnecessarily upsetting her and in consideration for her admittedly high stress levels, I just don't tell her if I've been in the Pub at lunchtime. This solves the dilemma. And any evidence that might lead to renewed suspicion on her part may be dispelled by plying her with alcohol the moment she gets in from work, which she is grateful for. Do not be tempted to disguise beer breath with Listerine or any other forms of spearmint based mouthwash. It stands out like a whore in church: who the hell brushes their teeth in the middle of the afternoon?

The other difficulty with afternoon beers is that they may cloud one's judgement on matters of import for the rest of the day. (Do not, for example, attempt housework: and never hoover naked – those things on the internet are *not* real). This difficulty may be resolved by not doing very much – having a nap is an excellent way to fill in any spare time and the restorative powers of the siesta are not to be underestimated. It is also very Zen. What *is* to be avoided is staying in the Pub all afternoon and then attempting to grapple with the evening session. Don't do this; you are not as young as you once were and parking a tiger at your age is not the fun it used to be. Nor is your spouse likely to display the tender understanding that she showed for your boyish japes before you were married, especially as it is only Tuesday. You might stand a better chance at the weekend but I wouldn't swear to it.

It's all about choosing the right beer for an afternoon session. I prefer to go with a mid-range lager of between 3-4% strength or perhaps one of the blonde beers that are gaining in popularity these days. The big 5% knicker-dropper lagers are best avoided at lunchtime if one wants to retain one's dignity when the kids from St.Gollum's Comprehensive pile off the bus in their customarily rowdy fashion outside the Old Queens Head at some improbably early hour of the afternoon. Pale Ale is not ranged among my favourites at the moment, but I am working on this and so I would not rule it out completely at this stage. A good craft Bitter is chosen by many and I have never found it necessary to object when someone has generously provided me with a great foaming pint of ale to quaff. White or Wheat beer, which is made from flour as opposed to barley, is not to be recommended because flour is also used in the making of bread and so has calories in it. Never forget that you are on a diet. Spirits are completely forbidden, although wine is acceptable and in summer, if you are in the company of yokels or beefy peasants, cider might have to do, especially if you are holidaying in the West Country.

In winter, the motto is 'Low cloud? High Stool' and I have always felt that this ancient wisdom from Ireland has served me well, although Guinness is filthy stuff. I once drank some Guinness in Nigeria when I was Consultant to a Large Corporation there and regretted it. Not to be deterred or fall at the first fence, I tried a rival brand called McWilliam's Stout but it tasted like the stuff they seal roads with. My cook tried unsuccessfully to make a beef and stout pie with it. It was inedible but it did fill in a pothole in the driveway quite nicely. 'Mild', I am pleased to say, seems to have disappeared with the rising prosperity conferred on the southern part of our great nation by Margaret Thatcher and since almost squandered by the dreadful Gordon Brown, who comes from a place so far north that it may well be closer to the Ultima Thule than even a rudimentary form of civilisation. 'Mild' was made from stale beer to which was added all the leftovers and spillage from the other beers being pumped; a very unsavoury proposition, but popular with proletarians of the lower sort who had little choice but to appreciate its charms. We developed folk in the South do not find it necessary to drink anything from out of a slops bucket and now that it has been removed from civilised bar tops can rest easier knowing that grim Northern proletarians will not be attracted by its scent. I believe it is still available in certain Northern mining towns where they make it out of coal dust, tripe and black puddings, but can't guarantee it. In Scotland they drink 'Heavy' which we all know may result in liver damage and freckles.

Pre-dinner Drinks.

Always be home for when your spouse gets in from work, even if you are having an affair. As she is working hard to bring home the bacon it is only right that the dutiful Househusband should be on hand for her as a welcome helpmeet at the end of a tough, perhaps even harrowing day, drink in hand and dinner preparing. And what better drink can there be for the harassed female mid-ranking executive than a good, solid, elegantly crafted Gin and Tonic? 'None' is the answer. It is the quintessential English drink and I include a recipe here which I downloaded from the internet. It's not copyright or anything. Nothing on the internet is copyright: everyone knows that.

The Perfect Gin and Tonic.

Step 1. Choose a good English brand of quality gin like Bombay Sapphire, Holland's or Hendrick's.

Step 2. Slice up a lemon or a lime.

Step 3. Put some ice cubes in a nice, big clean glass. Sometimes I polish the glasses for that extra shine, especially if there is lipstick residue present of a shade that Louise does not use.

Step 4. Pour some gin into the glass and add tonic. The exact proportions are up to you but in general a ratio of one slug of gin to five of tonic is probably right. In Istanbul they do things differently and reverse these proportions, which does have a certain logic to it and I can understand the attraction, but is not for beginners. Swimming the Bosphorus is fraught with unexpected difficulties and a lot harder than it looks. It can also land you in trouble and the policemen in Turkey are not at all as polite as the ones at home, I can tell you.

Step 5. Combine the other ingredient and drink responsibly.

Dinner.

Dinner is essential for mopping up all that gin and tonic but it doesn't have to be anything particularly complex because, of course, your spouse will have taken advantage of the discounted company catering or the heavily tax-payer subsidised generosity of the productive part of the population if they are Public Sector 'workers'. Louise has her school dinners which, being regulated by statute for nutritional value, guarantee a healthy and varied repast. Simplicity does not mean skimping though and so here we can turn to a lively low calorie snack, easily prepared, tasty and ideal for both the diet conscious Househusband and the working spouse.

Welsh Rabbit.

In some recipes this is called 'Rarebit' but it is obviously a spelling mistake as there is no such animal as a Rarebit, especially in Wales. When I was growing up my mother often provided me with this wonderful delicacy but strangely she never referred to it as being Welsh in any way. She was from Hertfordshire and this might account for it. Instead, she always referred to it as 'Cheese on Toast' which was elegant but I am going to stick to its original name out of respect for the Welsh who have not been so stupid yet as to demand their independence. Can you imagine an independent Wales? No, it is too absurd. Who would pay their dole money?

Step 1. Take some bread and grill it – but only on one side.

Step 2. Slice some cheese up. Any sort of cheese will do except for those nasty, runny French things or those horrid plastic squares that come in individually wrapped portions. Cottage Cheese is probably a no-no too. Best stick with cheddar or, if you are feeling particularly Swansea, why not crumble a Caerphilly? The more adventurous might try Stilton or Gruyere for a Continental feel, though not Edam obviously or your toast will look like it's been hit by one of Saddam's Blister Agents.

Step 3. Take the bread from under the grill when it is nicely toasted and reserve.

Step 4. Un-reserve the bread, which is now technically known as 'Toast' and on the side that is un-toasted, carefully place the cheese. Some people like to add tomato ketchup at this point in the hope that it will turn into a pizza, but it won't. Others experiment with Worcestershire sauce with more success. I prefer to keep Worcestershire sauce for my American friends. It is often amusing to hear them try to pronounce it.

Step 5. Pour another Gin and Tonic for your spouse as her serotonin levels might be dangerously depleted.

Step 6. Put the combined ingredients back under the grill and toast until the cheese is nicely melted and going brown on top. Try not to let it slide off into the grill pan as this is a waste and food prices are never going to come down as long as we have all these Greens demanding that we stop chopping down the rainforest. How else are we to provide GM soya for a growing population? Serve on a plate.

After Dinner Activities.

Tuesday can be tricky for evening amusements, especially if you have had afternoon drinks and got away with it. There is little chance of going down the pub because your absence will be noted, especially if you live in a small house. They may be greater if you live in a crack den but then it's probably not worth the bother. Parish Council meetings are an obvious answer but they usually only happen once a month and rarely on a Tuesday. I have raised this with the Chairman of the Slimstead Parish Council several times by e-mail with a view to having meetings conducted more frequently on Tuesdays but I have only received one answer and that was to the effect that the Parish Council can no longer accept communications by e-mail due to the low speeds of rural broadband.

Stay away from on-line dating sites. Your interest in recent divorcees might be misconstrued by a vengeful partner, although I should say that my own Dear Louise is almost free of jealousy in this regard, being descended from East European nobility. Let's be clear: when spouses say 'Help yourself, you ridiculous old man,' they *do not really mean it*. It is just part of the natural contrariness of the average female. Worse still, I knew a chap who met a woman on a dating website, had a few dates and then ended up marrying her. What was the point of that?

Sometimes the computer option is not available because your spouse needs it to fill in some reports or arrange a business plan or review a serious miscarriage of justice, which are all too frequent these days. Louise often needs to do a bit of lesson planning or upgrade her Child Protection training which often can be so absorbing that she stays up until one in the morning. On these occasions I open a couple of tinnies and enjoy the birdsong in the back garden until it is time for bed, making sure that I do not disturb her when she has put her head down on the desk for a moment. She looks so peaceful in her sleep, and although I'm not sure it's good for her posture, on balance I prefer not to disturb her. I usually tip toe past the study door then and being careful to remove my shoes head silently up the stairs to bed. I was in the army, so I know how to move silently.

For a lot of people, the preferred after dinner activity is blanking out with a good wodge of mental chewing gum in front of the idiot box. Louise avails of this option from time to time is presently engrossed in *Grisly Murder Series 8* since she finished off the *Myra Hindley and Rosemary West Directors Cut Special Extended Edition* Box Set which I bought her for Xmas. She is never so relaxed as when she has a good meal inside her and a corpse or two to hand. I have pointed out to her that there are other genres to be explored but she is resolute in her particular tastes.

'This is therapy, not viewing, Harpic,' she intones, over the sound of someone rapping at the door which, this being after 7pm, I ignore. 'And it is considerably cheaper than psychotherapy.'

'As you wish,' I reply, edging down the sofa a little. 'What's on after this then?'

'*The Burke and Hare Hogmanay Special*,' she replies. 'Followed by *Midwinter Slayings*. Any objections?'

I am about to come up with something witty but that blasted rapping repeats itself in a rather insistent manner and I decide that I must just go and see who the devil it is.

'I am not At Home to callers,' says Louise, regally. 'And your friends I will have legally debarred should they attempt to put one foot inside the door. Do you understand, Harpic?'

'No callers and legal penalties for Denning and Carruthers it is, Ma'am,' I say, heading for the front door.

I open the door and before me is a small wizened pendant of a man who is clearly unemployable in any other capacity than that of a rat-faced little runt of a sneaking tell-tale who should have been more thoroughly bullied during his wastrel years at a fetid Dame School in Doncaster.

'Are you the legal owner of this property?' he says, in a high pitched Nazi Gauleiter voice.

'Who wants to know?' I reply, a freeborn Englishman standing on a Freehold piece of the finest part of God's own country.

'Are you watching TV at the moment?' he squeaks, ingratiatingly.

'What's that to you?' I reply.

'I'm from the BBC Licencing Enforcement Unit and I am here to suspect that you are illegally viewing content in respect of you not possessing a TV Licence which, according to our records you have failed to purchase, despite being sent numerous reminders,' he squeals, menacingly, his rat-faced little nose sniffing greedily at the prospect of a slice off someone else's hard-earned cheese.

'Well,' I reply. 'I do not pay the Licence fee because I believe the BBC to be run as an exclusive club for Communists, Traitors, Journalists, their various offspring and Fatty Pang. Plus it's all repeats and un-talent shows. And rubbish soap operas.'

The yellow faced little weasel is stunned.

'Fatty Pang?' he niggles.

'So you don't deny my charges?' I put on my best approximation of Denning's legal tones. 'Then you stand convicted.'

'Fatty Pang?' He repeats, floundering like a loathsome toad speared on the beak of a noble heron.

'I shall never pay the Licence Fee after what Fatty Pang did to me in the Gun Hill Barracks in Hong Kong,' I declare. 'So now, get off my Freehold, Servant of Reptiles.'

'Who's at the door, Harpic?' calls Louise, pausing the TV.

'Ah! So you are watching TV,' cries the vile Enforcer of the Metrosexual Champagne-swilling, Socialist Liberal Elite. 'You're bang to rights!'

'You'll have to do better than that,' I say. 'How do you know it's not the DVD? Or the Internet? Or the radio? Or BBC iPlayer? None of which you need to have a Licence for?'

'It's my word against yours,' he says, with a filthy guttersnipe rubbing of his hands. 'And the BBC Dirty Tricks Department will smear any judge who dares rule against us in a Court of Law.'

'Not if I can prove that the BBC knew about the 9/11 World Trade Center terrorist atrocities in advance,' I powerfully counter. 'Because then I would be in contravention of Section 15 of the Terrorism Act for providing funding to a Terrorist organisation. See Rooke vs BBC, Horsham Magistrates Court 2013.'

'He lost that case,' replies the snivelling shit.

'Oh no, he didn't,' I reply, with all the benefits of an expensive public school education behind me.

'Oh yes, he did,' says the stupid little parasite on the intellectual health of the nation.

'Harpic!' cries Louise. 'Who is at the door?'

'It's the BBC Nazi come to violate our Human Rights and collect the Licence Fee,' I say.

There is a rumble of discontent.

'You brought this on yourself, remember,' I say to the grovelling slave-imp of the Self-Righteous British Bolshevik Corporation and step back from the door.

There is a grumble of movement, not a thousand miles away from the sound of a Cape Buffalo going from 0-60 in under five seconds. She blots out the light from the lounge as she appears in the hallway, catches sight of the cowering lackey of the Broadcasting Bullshit Cartel and loses it.

'Disturb my viewing would you?' she hisses. 'After the day I've had?'

She has the scrivening little gnome of the Bestial Beeb by the collar and shakes him like a terrier with a rat. His feet are off the ground doing a hanged man's tap dance and he is emitting a mewling sound decidedly pleasant to my ear. She flings him bodily down the length of the lawn.

'Your implied rights of access are rescinded,' she declares, placing a sharpened stiletto heel on the grovelling goblin's chicken-necked throat. 'And if you ever darken this door again I will send you to my cousins in Bosnia who will broadcast your guts over a wide area after first having introduced you not so much to Logie Baird - or even Yogi Bear – but to several real bears. Do you understand, lackey?'

The minion of the British answer to Pravda is still mewling but is now showing that multi-platform multi-tasking capability for effective news gathering, editorial and comment for which it is famed and is now moving through the rolling dynamic of the news-cycle towards an accurate understanding of the crisis. He is nodding vigorously. He also appears to have shat himself.

'Right then, off you go,' she says, hauling him to his feet and giving him a hefty crack round the ear.

'You'll pay for this,' the fleeing coward seethes. 'I'll put the news hounds on to you, I will! I'll have you door-stepped, hacked, exposed, tried by media and vilified the length and breadth of the land, so help me I will!'

'One word from you, *faszfej*,' she replies, partly in Hungarian. 'And believe you me, I will make you *very* famous in a way that you will not like.'

'I should pay heed, old chap,' I say, between holding my sides and wheezing with laughter. 'The Bosnian authorities are still looking for the last person who doubted her. They claim they've found most of the bits but I think they're making it up.'

With that the snivelling Lord Haw-Haw of Islington and Primrose Hill scuttles back to his Licence Fee payer funded car like a kicked cockroach and hurtles off down the cul-de-sac chastened, but no doubt ready to apply his strong arm intimidation to single mothers too poor to afford the Licence Fee subsidy to socialism in an attempt to rebuild his shattered pride. Still, one may hope that he will remember this salutary lesson meted out to him by Louise, scion of the Countess Theresa Horthy-Worthy of Borsova and Chop in Sub-Carpathian Ruthenia and Prince Selim Seljuk of the Sanjak of Novi Bazaar, c/o Bosnia.

'Well done, old gel!' I say, heartily. 'Exit pursued by a bear! Most impressive on several levels. Now, back to your Murder Therapy, where I shall bring you a nice glass of warming wine.'

'Harpic,' she says, darkly. 'I gave you money to buy a TV Licence.'

'I have invested it more wisely,' I reply, stepping backwards into the shadow of the hedge. 'I have used it to re-float important sectors of the local economy.'

'I bet I can name both of them,' she says. 'God give me strength.'

Harpic exits, pursued by a bear.

Day Three: Wednesday – Hump Day.

'Sausages are not the only fruit.'

J. Winterson.

The Weigh-in.

Wednesday is known as 'hump day' because it marks the point when our 'warriors for the working day' reach the mid-point in the working week and can begin to look forward to the weekend. Completing three full days of arduous labour is a great accomplishment and though we Househusbands are grateful for their efforts we may take pride in the fact that our own working week is significantly longer. Our hump day does not come around until Thursday because we have to work weekends too. There are some fairness issues involved in this division of labour but we need not be distracted by them here. Our business is with the bathroom scales.

You will have lost another pound or 485 metric grammes overnight, guaranteed.

Sausages for Breakfast: The 5:2 Diet.

The ideal accompaniment to bacon is a good sausage and the relationship between them is regulated by a ratio of five rashers of bacon to two sausages. This provides a satisfying balance on the plate while maintaining interest in the bacon which less committed dieters might feel is waning after the third day. Put that yoghurt down, o ye of faintheart! Stick to your guns, as we used to say in the army.

Sausages come in all sorts of shapes and sizes with a dizzying choice of ingredients guaranteed to provide a lifetime of culinary pleasure but, unlike bacon, there *are* bad sausages out there. When I was growing up in the sixties and seventies, sausages had acquired a reputation for being dumping grounds for all sorts of nasty bits of pig. My suspicions as to the purity of the then humble sausage were first alerted at the time my father was doing missionary work in the North. It was whispered that the local butcher was engaged in a practice known as 'blowing the sausage', which involved artificially enlarging the product by placing it in the mouth and engorging it with air. This did indeed result in a bigger sausage but once it went into a warm oven for Toad in the Hole or into the frying pan for a more controlled handling, the air expanded and either escaped with a bang or deflated in a very disappointing manner. I brought this reminiscence to the attention of the Butcher of Barkingham recently and asked if he had ever 'blown a sausage'. He did not deign to reply but pointed to his new Point of Sale advertising leaflet which stated 'Look Good: Feel Good: Eat My Meat'. So I took my pound of pork and leek and left it at that.

Nor was I much impressed with the 'snorker' a sausage-like object which was issued to the loyal troops of the British Army for exercises during the Cold War. This was a turd-like object of the colour and consistency of plasticene, was possessed of marked constipatory properties and came in a tin of lard. It was popularly believed to be part of the deterrent holding back the Communist Hordes and the thinking was that after three days of eating these, when the constipatory properties had worn off, the invading Russians would be faced with the whole of the British Army going for a Tom-Tit at once and producing ordure in the order of megatons. They would naturally recoil in horror at this monstrous biological weapon and flee screaming all the way back to the Urals, which are in Russia. Fortunately for them, the theory was never tested. I once offered a snorker to a Belgian comrade in arms but he declined to eat it.

Right up until the early 1980s, sausages were things to be avoided or only eaten when drunk, much like the modern kebab. Then there was a Risorgimento in the sausage industry driven by independent souls keen to roll back the tide of skinless wonders and restore the sausage to its rightful place in the nation's culinary arsenal. I well remember the first specialist Sausage Shop opening in London and have happy memories of standing awed under its awning reading through its list of offerings as though it were the menu in a Michelin starred restaurant, my tongue salivating so much that I had to use my tie to wipe the drool off the window pane. Alongside the traditional pork, there was pork and leek, pork and sage, pork and cider, pork and apple, pork and garlic – known in France as 'Toulouse' after the famous artist. The ground-breaking chef within had added port wine, madeira, ales of every wondrous variety to his offerings and then had pushed on into the unexplored hinterlands of the mighty South African *Boerwors*, the Beef and Guinness (not my particular favourite, admittedly), the spicy Morroccan lamb *Merguez,* laced with fiery harrissa paste. One might choose Red Wine and Forest Mushrooms (actually these looked a bit like bruised penises and took some getting used to: Louise still won't touch them), Wild Boar varieties, Lincolnshire with its unique blend of Parsley, Sage and Thyme fully deserving of its protected status; the peppery Cumberland Ring, distinguished in both its white and black pepper forms; the magnificent Gloucester Old Spot; the gingery Marylebone and perhaps the Queen of them all, the Newmarket whose recipe is so secret I would have to kill you if I told you. The chicken sausages were a bit ropey though and I wouldn't recommend them.

Sausages have come a long way since the heady days of that breakthrough and even supermarkets stock passable varieties in their 'Minimum Acceptable Quality' ranges, which they choose to market as *Select* or *Finest* or some other such marketing speak. Beware though: the true sausage is made by stuffing pig's intestines with good tasty stuff. Supermarkets spray collagen on old mattress frames to make 'casings' and then stick whatever they feel they can get away with inside. Collagen is what models inflate their lips with and is pumped out of people by liposuction. It has got nothing to do with pigs at all. This is a Well Known Fact and germane to your breakfasting pleasure.

If you are not blessed with a conveniently situated specialist sausage-meister, the safest way of sourcing your sausages is to strike up a mutually beneficial commercial relationship with a traditional local family butcher of good reputation and respected standing in the community. That way you won't get anything but the permitted antioxidants and preservatives and if you don't like what he gives you, you can complain to the other people in the queue and ruin his reputation. This won't work at Tesco because they are Too Big To Fail but it works with the Butcher of Barkingham sometimes.

So now, bacon and sausages in a 5:2 ratio for breakfast. On, On, you noble hound! Gird your loins, stock up your frame, fill up your tank and get ready for the day.

Today's Exercise Regime: A Lovely Walk.

Walk Number Two: The Aerodrome Circuit.

We are very fortunate in the countryside to have quite a lot of open space and can thus take every opportunity for a spot of bracing exercise which is free of charge and healthy. It is important to have a spot of bracing exercise. I understand that if you live in a town or city this might be difficult to achieve and that a stroll past the noxious canal or the grim Council Estate might be anything but pleasant but one must just do one's best in the circumstances. Perhaps combining it with a bit of voluntary litter-picking will give you an uplift, if the Trades Unions allow it.

So now, we sally out down the cul-de-sac going straight over Hope Street, through the snicket on the Barkingham road and into the hay field which is always a delight. Heading straight on and being careful to stick to the bridleway we approach the Slimstead Community Woodland and Nature Reserve for which the Parish Council has applied for status as a Site of Special Scientific Interest to deter development, fracking or the construction of modestly priced homes. Bill Gon, Chairman of the Parish Council Planning Sub-committee has bred some great crested newts in his pond for deployment if and when the developers ever attempt to get their hands on Slimstead. We don't want affordable housing and all that comes with it here, do we?

Just past the delightful buttercups and daisies one can discern an amount of concrete which would be unpleasant and unwelcome in normal circumstances, but looking closer we can see that it is actually a symbol of our freedom, for here is the Slimstead Aerodrome. It was constructed during the Second World War to throw the Hun back into the sea but after only a brief but exciting period under RAF direction, the USAF arrived and it played host to the Air Legions of the Arsenal of Democracy right up until the end of the war. The Luftwaffe raided it twice in 1944 and although several Americans were killed, no real harm was done. When the Cold War began it was decided to maintain this important facility as the runway was still pointing in the right direction and in 1955 it was upgraded to take more powerful jet aircraft, more large, wealthy pilots and a bigger PX store, bar and disco. This development was met with mixed feelings and for a while there was a pronounced gender divide in the village, the females being generally in favour of this development, and the males generally against. During the 1980s the gender divide seemed to reverse when a Feminist protest group set up a peace camp and chained themselves to the railings in a very smelly fashion. The ladies of the village tended to regard this development as deleterious to their chances of landing a pilot while the gentlemen, among whom Bill Gon counted himself, saw the prospects of peace and nuclear disarmament as outweighing the opportunities for Stateside travel provided for the village lasses. With the collapse of the Soviet Union in 1989 the peace camp packed up and left, rather glumly I'm told, shortly followed by the US Air Force itself and things got back to normal within reason. The Ministry of Defence resumed responsibility for the aerodrome but don't use it very much. From time to time groups of burly young men in ill-fitting suits fly in and out of it, often coinciding with a crisis somewhere in the world speedily and decisively averted, but apart from that it is mainly deserted. There has been dark and loose talk of an extraordinary rendition facility being located there, but nothing has gone through the Parish Council on this. Certainly, the night flights and helicopters can be distressing to the elderly from time to time but we have been more fortunate than Stanstead, whose reward for hosting the Lancaster Bombers that wrought such righteous retribution on Dresden was Ryannair and hordes of chavs dressed in sombreros rowdily heading off for stag parties in Bratislava.

Bill Gon is very knowledgeable about the aerodrome and has been very useful in filling in some of the gaps in my own knowledge. He has a house on a slight rise which overlooks the the runway and I give him a cheery wave as I go by and congratulate him on the new Range Rover sitting on his driveway. He is a big man, slightly stooped, of vaguely Turkish appearance, with a yard brush moustache over a strong dimpled chin, playful eyes under beetling brows, and a broad forehead. Actually, he reminds me of someone that I can't quite put my finger on.

'How are things going with the developers?' I ask in a tone of neighbourly enquiry.

'Pretty well,' he replies, with a tight grin. 'But there is some way for them to go yet.'

I notice that he has an Eight metre radio antennae of the type used by my regiment during the Cold War attached to his drainpipe and enquire if he still keeps up his radio ham hobby from back then. He answers 'Foxtrot Oscar' in the affirmative.

'I would have thought that e-mail would have made communication by radio rather redundant these days,' I venture.

He gives another one of his tight grins. 'Not with GCHQ, MI5 and the CIA monitoring the web,' he replies. 'Some times the old ways are the best.'

I cannot agree more. Although the Internet and social media are on balance a good thing in that it keeps teenagers in their bedrooms and out of the way, it can also be terribly irritating when cats are constantly rammed down one's throat. I note that he also has a large diameter telescope pointed out through one of the upper windows. He informs me that he has always been interested in star-gazing and, bringing our intercourse to an end, climbs into his Range Rover with a tight grin. From what I hear Bill used to be in both the CND and the Communist party, but these rumours I dismiss as smears from his political opponents on the Parish Council. Communists *do not* drive Range Rovers. I move off the driveway smartly to avoid being sprayed by loose chippings.

Just past Bill's well-appointed dwelling the road turns left and then meanders pleasantly towards the hamlet of Sticky End. Here we see red-jacketed, red-faced Chubble the Postie, a man with a wide bottom and a hopeful mien, in his recently privatised red van arriving to 'deliver a heavy load to a recent divorcee', as he often describes his labours. This is a *double entendre*, I believe, although I may be mistaken as I know for sure that Chubble did not have much formal schooling up at St.Gollum's Comprehensive. The reason I think it may be a *double entendre* is that he sometimes varies his traditional response to my cheery wave and neighbourly enquiry as to the progress of his daily tasks with 'emptying my sack in a bored housewife's letter box'. This is a coarse expression, I believe, with some very louche connotations. Besides, it is all boasting as Louise has made clear.

The journey from Sticky End to Slimstead proper can sometimes be a little arduous as the road is of a gentle but steady uphill gradient for about a mile or so. It is also perilous for those who prefer to take their constitutional after imbibing at The Sticky Wicket public house located there. Bill Gon's grandfather fell off his bicycle into a ditch several times on this stretch of road, even though he had survived being torpedoed twice during the First World War. Eventually, he was forced to change his routine and acquired a motability scooter from the NHS, which although providing him with a steadier platform, proved harder to get out of the ditch. This tale of woe only came to an end when The Sticky Wicket closed down after being taxed out of existence by Gordon Brown. That's socialism for you. I give a cheery wave and step smartly onto the verge as Chubble the Postie speeds past in his recently privatised red van scattering loose chippings to ping against my shins and akles.

Once back in Slimstead, it is but a hop, skip and a jump back to the cul-de-sac where I check on my neighbours' welfare with a quick peek in the windows to make sure they are all safe. I note that the recently divorced Mrs. Johnson is still in her negligee and going through her post, which is rather late for her.

(Wildlife spotted: 2 rabbits in Miranda McNulty's vegetable patch. No bears).

Lunch.

My contemptuous disregard for the midday meal is well known and has its origins in what Fatty Pang did to me in the Gun Hill Barracks in Hong Kong during the 1990s. I was having Dim Sum for lunch when the call from Governor Patten came and so I leaped out of bed and dressed hastily. Dim Sum was understandably upset at being left in the lurch so suddenly – a lovely girl, but with higher expectations than I had been led to believe – but when you are in the army, duty is duty. I donned my service cap and Sam Browne and headed to the Officer's Mess where the Governor was waiting.

For those of you who do not possess an encyclopaedic knowledge of politics, 'Fatty Pang' was the name awarded by the Chinese to Governor Christopher Francis Patten, now Baron Patten of Barnes, then the pallid, pasty-faced sloven who Tony Blair had appointed to give Hong Kong back to the Chinese and then put in charge of the BBC. I had been posted out to the Intelligence Branch to give what help I could to the service of the Empire but, it has to be said, I was fairly surprised to learn soon after arrival that the role involved participation in handing over the most successful and prosperous city state in the world to a bunch of grasping Communists who had already reduced their own country to a state of penury. Where was the sense in that? I asked myself. There was no sense and I made my disquiet at such proceedings known as soon as I decently could. In the first instance, I raised my objections with Major Dunwoody-Tring, the Officer Commanding Intelligence Branch, to which I had been attached. His response was to show me a painstakingly constructed chart detailing the number of divisions of the People's Liberation Army currently massed along the border complete with tanks, guns, aircraft, Agit-Prop detachments and Saboteurs. He then turned to the window and pointed to Private Scroggins of the Highland Light Infantry then engaged in whitewashing a line of stones with a clapped out paintbrush and making a damn bad job of it.

'He'll be fine with the right weapon and a liberal supply of ammunition,' I gamely ventured.

'Since the latest round of defence cuts, those *are* his weapons and ammunition,' he replied, bringing the meeting to a close.

Undeterred by such negativity, I took a few minutes and came up with a brilliant plan which would save Hong Kong, boost the British economy, please Dim Sum and put one in the eye for the grasping and avaricious Chinese Communist hordes. Jotting the main points down on an opened out pack of fake Marlboro Lites, I commended it to the Governor's attention which within a day or so, resulted in the surprise visit of Fatty Pang to our humble regimental abode and *coitus interruptus* with my lunchtime Dim Sum.

'Is this a joke, Lieutenant Harpic?' were his first pallid and insipid words.

'Certainly not, Sir,' I replied, dignified in bearing and clear of speech. 'I see no reason why the people of Hong Kong should be consigned to the Communist jackboot when they might all be shipped to Liverpool in a straight swap for the Scousers, whereupon they will recreate their success and boost our GDP in no time at all. '

'And you don't feel that the people of Liverpool might have any objection to being relocated to Kowloon and the New Territories?'

'Why not?' I replied. 'Have you seen Liverpool recently? I'm sure that Liverpudlians would view Victoria Island as an improvement on Toxteth.'

'What about the Triads or the Chinese?' said Fatty Pang, with a sneer unworthy of a Baronet.

'The Triads will surely welcome such an addition to their skills base,' I replied. 'And who cares what the Chinese think? The important ones will all have moved to Liverpool and the rest will be too busy dealing with a Scouse crime wave to be bothered with anything else.'

'I suppose you'll be relocating Anfield too? And John Lennon International Airport.'

'Sir,' I replied, defiant but respectful. 'The loss of eleven *prima donna* football players and four tawdry minstrels would be a small price to pay for the retention of this jewel of Empire.'

Well to cut a long story short, my posting to the Intelligence Branch was terminated and I was posted to the rocket range at Benbecula in the Outer Hebrides, which is almost Ultima Thule. Fatty Pang lost the Empire and Dim Sum lost any chance of a British passport. I never saw her again, she being the only person in eleven years of Labour immigration policy to be refused a visa. It was a traumatic time and I can no longer think of lunch without thinking of Dim Sum.

Afternoon Pottering.

Assuming that one has decided not to go down the Pub for afternoon drinks, the thorny question arises as to how to fruitfully spend the period between lunch and pre-dinner drinks. There may be a temptation to browse the TV stations but this should be avoided not just because the schedules are woefully inadequate and full up with orange people with unfeasibly good dentistry enjoying lifestyles that us non-media mortals can only dream of. The pornography on offer is dreadful too and not a patch on what you can get on the internet. The real reason for avoiding afternoon TV is that it has lots of calories in it and makes you fat. Proof of this assertion may easily be obtained by standing at the checkouts in Tesco and carefully observing which customers are possessed of a larger stature and carrying one of those dismal glossy magazines full of more orange people with equally unobtainable lifestyles funded by those of us forced to pay the Licence Fee. How do you think those people got so fat? By watching too much TV and turning into couch potatoes, that's how. No - Afternoon TV: Best Avoided. It rots your mind too.

A bit of pottering in the garden is ideal, especially in early spring after the April showers have loosened the earth enough to allow for easy weeding. There is no need to get involved with anything contentious like brambles but the savvy dieter will be pleased to be on the lookout for the marvellous gifts that a bounteous nature provides. These can be found in any hedgerow or country garden plot, but if you live in a town the practice is not to be recommended until the Council cleans up all the dog shit. Edible plants that are readily available include nettles, which make a tasty soup if you can be bothered, and marigolds (not the French variety) which are an attractive garnish for any salad. The humble dandelion leaf makes for very good eating and is preferable to rocket, which was introduced into British cuisine by that odious man Blair and his equally odious 'Cool Britannia' campaign. For the record, I am not 'cool', have never been 'cool' and have no desire to acquire its dubious distinctions. This I will hold to until the Union Jack is hauled down from the flag pole atop Edinburgh Castle at which point I will be English and remain scornful of the whole concept. Rocket is too Nu-Labour to be countenanced on an honest man's plate. Stick to dandelions or Boston lettuce if your neighbour's vegetable plot is within easy reach.

Sticky Willy, or *Galium Aparine,* is often known as Goose Grass and grows plentifully in areas where geese are common visitors. They are known to devour it in large quantities whenever they get the chance which is a blessing because if you don't keep on top of it, it's all over the village in no time at all. But what's sauce for the goose is sauce for the gander; countrymen know that the plant is also edible and provides a good source of green stuff for no financial outlay whatever. It tastes like spinach when blanched in hot water, but it can taste bitter and give you a rash if eaten raw. It also has mildly sedative properties so in the spring afternoons I make a point of gathering a good several handfuls of the stuff ready for Louise later. It comes up easy so there's no danger of a crick in the back either. Sticky Willy patrol is rewarding therefore on so many several levels. Not only am I engaging in a healthy and absorbing pastime, I am also foraging for the next meal and keeping the garden looking tidy.

Pre-Dinner Drinks.

As already noted, in recent years the Health Lobby, led by that deplorable band of charlatans at the BMA, have put it about that drinking is bad for you and have come up with a totally arbitrary measure of alcohol consumption known as the 'unit'. Men are supposed to limit themselves to a ludicrously low number of these units spread interminably across a whole week while for women it is even less and possibly longer. I stress; this is a made-up figure and has no scientific basis whatsoever, so ignore it. Louise can easily get through her week's allowance in a day when she's on form so what on earth is she going to do for the rest of the time?

The reason for this nefarious attempt to interfere with the well-being of the nation is so that Doctors can guarantee themselves cushy jobs with generous allowances and gold-plated pensions at the public expense. It is part of a long trend of inventing two diseases for every one they cure and thus justify ever more amounts to be lavished on them from the public purse. When I was growing up my father contributed through his missionary work to the reduction in many diseases prevalent in the dismal industrial squalor of the North. Working voluntarily alongside the NHS, he played a minor but nonetheless valuable part in reducing rickets, ringworm, smallpox, measles, whooping cough and host of other virulent impositions. They were checked, bought to book and vanquished. This should have resulted in the closure of the NHS as no-one needed it any more but the doctors intervened and invented a whole host of new conditions to blight the landscape and pillage the Treasury. ME, ADDH, Anorexia, Bulimia, HIV/AIDS, Dyslexia, Dyspraxia were all invented with no other purpose than to boost the wages of indolent GPs and provide lavender scented consultation rooms for Napoleonic consultants.

To illustrate my point. Once, during my second career as a Consultant to a Large Corporation, I worked in the Middle East where I had the misfortune to have a fat Feminist fresh out from Frodsham foisted on me. Within two days she phoned in sick with 'ME' and could not envisage returning to her well paid duty before the end of the month. I rang her back and told her that there was no Statutory Sick Pay in the Middle East and so she was fired. She was back at her desk the next day.

Which Proves It.

I brought this theory up with Doctor Shipman at my regular MOT at the Emily Pankhurst Memorial Clinic in Berkstead. He made no comment but found grounds to examine my prostrate anyway. Bastard. Give me a drink someone.

Anyway, the sound of gentle laughter drifts up the driveway as Louise returns home from St.Wiccas, although normally it is not so high pitched. I am ready with her helpmeet.

The Hump Day Helpmeet.

To complement the foraging theme earlier encountered, the Hump Day Helpmeet draws on that greatest of garden crops, the apple. What could be more English than an apple and more readily available than a pear? I am fortunate in my choice of neighbours because Barney the Builder is a real countryman with the beefy face, strong arms, thick wrists and knowing grin of the true yokel and a man who knows the value of hard work, a creative approach to the Taxman and how to benefit from the good things that nature provides free, *gratis* and for nothing. He produces very good cider from windfall apples which he chops up with a spade and sticks in an oil drum to ferment. The results are remarkable, the batch is large and the results astounding; don't talk to me about synthetic highs. Like many of the best things in life, however, it is soon gone leaving only a memory and sometimes not even that. Fortunately, I understand that cider is available in towns and is particularly popular among the lower socio-economic groups that exist there, so this cocktail is democratically for everyone.

Step 1. Take a bottle of Calvados and measure two stiff measures into a pint glass.

Step 2. Fill the glass up with cider. Dead easy, piece of piss and does the job in no time.

When Louise enters the house on a Hump Day I am often ready for her with a little joke to lighten the load, which she appreciates.

'Where was the Magna Carta signed?' I say brightly and hand her the Hump Day Helpmeet.

Sometimes she returns a blank stare.

'At the bottom,' I quip as she takes the cocktail.

'Thanks, Harpic' she replies. 'Thanks. I really needed that.'

As a reward for her appreciation, I hand her the second one and leave her to gather her thoughts while I prepare a light supper.

Dinner.

The reference to the founding document of our freedom was not without purpose because of course it is written in Magna Carta that just as it is the right of every freeborn Englishwoman to own property, it is the right of every freeborn Englishman to go to the Pub on a Wednesday night. This interpretation is apt to be disputed but you may rely on the fact that very few spouses have a working knowledge of Medieval Latin so you have a pretty fair chance of pulling it off if you argue with conviction, at least in the early years of marriage. Later on, you may need more subtle arguments so, bearing in mind the sedative qualities of *Galium Aparine*, you may wish to try this recipe.

A Healthy Humpday Supper in Two Courses: Nettle Soup and a Warm Summer Salad.

Step 1. Collect some nettles and put them in a pot of water to boil. Add some other vegetables like leeks or onions and pop in a couple of chicken stock cubes. Season with salt and pepper and cook it for a bit.

Step 2. Pour it into a bowl, add a couple of shots of Calvados and serve hot or cold, depending on whether it is winter or summer.

Step 3. While she is enjoying the fresh flavours of the soup, take the Sticky Willy and blanch it in hot salted water. You can use the soup pot as long as she doesn't notice. It'll save on the washing up.

Step 4. Drain the Sticky Willy and combine with the dandelion leaves that you gathered earlier and placed discretely in an area of the fridge she is unlikely to visit with too much curiosity. Add some basil from the pot over the sink if it is still alive.

Step 5. Add some garlic mayonnaise and arrange some marigold petals around the plate nicely. Garnish with a tomato (in season) and serve with another Humpday Helpmeet cocktail. That should do the trick.

'Harpic,' says my own Dear Sweet Louise. 'You are feeding me weeds.'

'Nonsense my dear,' I reply. 'It is a vegetarian treat.'

After Dinner Activities.

After such a hearty meal, I usually help Louise through to the lounge where she can put her feet up on the sofa and drift off to the sounds of some easy listening music along the Celine Dionne lines. She does work hard and it is important for the conscientious Househusband to go the extra mile to ensure that his spouse gets all the rest she needs. On this day, however, just while I am looking for some change in her purse I spy a note on lavender notepaper from the Headmistress, Miss Hatcher. It is badly crumpled but I smooth it out and discover that it is a missive informing her of the addition of a new pupil to her class tomorrow. Clearly, the Head was overcome at the joy of this news as there are the unmistakeable tracks of gentle tears upon it. I also note that the new pupil is Bill Gon's daughter, Madeleine. I know the child slightly and I am sure that Louise will be gratified at the addition of such a spirited child to her already charming collection of little dears. Sometimes I wish that I had become a teacher.

Shouldering on my blue double-breasted blazer with gold buttons and perfectly matched taupe chinos, I tip toe out and leave her to her reverie. The Pub calls.

The Old Queen's Head.

The Pub. What a small word for such a place of wonder. I have always loved Pubs and always will love them. All life's troubles are here relieved and all life's mysteries are revealed. It is a place where more wisdom resides than in all the libraries of the world and in a more accessible form to boot. It is a place where a man might think quietly, nestled in the snug away from the hurly-burly of a stressful job or an over-enthusiastic, over-demanding wife. Here he may talk rubbish and not be held to account for talking rubbish; indeed, he may be honoured for it. Here he may float the most outrageous of theories before a sympathetic crowd of worthies experienced in the weighing of complex matters and should his audience be not convinced, he will not be thought the less of for airing them. He may rant, protest, rage, rage against the dying of the light, be witty, talk of many things, of cabbages and of kings and always be assured of an attentive and respectful audience, whether elevated in intellect or Northern-level dim. And it matters not what outrage of wit, what sheer, dizzying leaps of imagination, what daring journeys of investigation into the nature of man and his place in the cosmos are essayed upon but found wanting on grounds, metaphysical, scientific, geographic or historic and so rejected. No one will remember in the morning and you can start all over again. Here, above all, is a place where many men meet the one, true love of their lives be she a lovely pale blonde as light as dew on a spring morn, a spicy, chocolate brunette smouldering like the embers of a Yule-tide log dipped in cinnamon, a dark-haired Killeen from Dublin, a hoppy red-head full of autumn gold and summer lightning, the continental Stella or my own particular favourite, JCB. It is a romance not to be sneered at for the passion will burn long and ardently and as long as a man has a liver, he will always have a lover.

The humble Pub is a temple to life, liberty and the pursuit of the clarity of thought only to be found after a couple of pints. Once, when having drunk deep of the glass of clarity, I penned a little poem in praise of the Pub and I humbly offer it here.

> This royal home of beers, this optic'd isle,
>
> This glass of lager, this seat of ease,

> This other Eden, demi-john of paradise,
>
> This fortress built by boozers for themselves,
>
> Against teetotallers and the ravages of time,
>
> This happy breed of men, this little world,
>
> This precious plonk set in a vinous butt,
>
> Which serves it in the office of a wall.
>
> Or a moat defensive to a house,
>
> Against the envy of more sober types.
>
> This local, this refuge, this bastion, this Pub!

Shakespeare himself couldn't have put it better.

The Old Queen's Head is an agreeably rustic setting with an agreeably predictable crowd. Prominent among the characters to be found there are three very venerable gentlemen known as Shocking, Outrageous and Shouldn't-Be-Allowed. One might have been a teacher, the second something in agricultural machinery, the third involved in grommet-related industries but nothing much is known definitively. Sartorially, they belong to the string-for-a-belt school of couture but at least they dress better than Jean-Paul Gaultier. No-one now remembers their real names, nor even whence they originated from. Rumour has it they were unearthed in a geophysical survey by a team of archaeologists hunting for the bones of Richard III on a horribly mistaken premise. Since then they have been a permanent fixture of the corner trestle, aside a small Heinz 57 of a dog called Bark, and are treated with great respect as indeed such venerable gentlemen should be, given their contribution to cash flow. They acquired their appellation as a direct result of their expressed considered opinions when consulted on a variety of issues. In an attempt to discern which end of the political spectrum they abided at, I once asked them what they thought of gay marriage. The response was swift, decisive and to the point.

'Shocking,' said the first, slamming a pewter tankard down.

'Outrageous,' responded the second, banging down his personal glass jug.

'Shouldn't be allowed,' answered the third, bringing down his pot with all the authority of an auctioneer's gavel.

'Bark,' said Bark.

Satisfied that I had located them at the less tolerant end of the liberal attitude, I was then amazed to hear a colleague offer them a similar proposition.

'What do you think of the plans of the Ugandan government to feed homosexuals to the crocodiles for even dreaming of buggery,' said Barney the Builder.

'Shocking,' replied the first, deep from his tankard.

'Outrageous,' said the second, through a froth of best bitter.

'Shouldn't be allowed,' called the third, holding up his pot for more.

'Bark,' said Bark.

'There you go,' said Barney, conclusively. 'That should answer your question.'

It was an argument to which I had no answer and which still has the power to stun me with its existential brilliance.

Tonight, Carruthers is in his normal place under the dart board polishing his elephant gun. Stark and spare, his thin legs testimony to a lifetime in the outdoors, his worn, tanned face, supporting evidence for a career spent in unspeakable malaria-ravaged places, and his cold, sharp, unblinking eyes focused always on a point a thousand yards on the horizon, where the elephants or guerrillas are usually to be found. He is a perfect choice as the leader of the Slimstead Neighbourhood Watch and I have given him my personal assurance that he can count on me to join any lynch-mob that he cares to raise. Next to him, Chubble the Postie deals with his blisters, bunions, flaking, dishevelled, dried and desiccated disgusting, odiferous pedal members in a dish of warm water and suspicious unguent thoughtfully provided by the management, who are used to it. The dog likes to lick it too. Along the bar are ranged the usual Wednesday night volcanoes; Barney the aforesaid builder, Higgins the Trucker who is of Peruvian extraction, like his regular but unofficial cargo, and 'Ark' Slymstead, who claims to have come over with Noah and settled in Slimstead in plenty of time to bare his arse at the Romans. All are fine, upstanding members of the community mainly.

There is football on the telly and the usual argument over which team is likely to win is raging. The stakes are high and the weekly prize for the most accurate forecasting of the Premier League results can sometimes be as high as £15. Experts abound but Barney's missus usually wins it. Her method is the subject of much speculation, but I know for a fact that she just guesses – much like the rest of them, although they choose to dignify their efforts by appeal to arcane statistics and occult knowledge. Tonight's match is between a team in red shirts and a team in blue shirts and I add my three-pennies worth to the analysis whenever I feel the assembled might benefit from it. I am fond of saying 'control it from the middle' whenever the teams are running around at one end or the other and 'they need to be more clinical in the box' whenever a shot goes wide. I also like to shout 'big Jessie' whenever one of the players goes down like he's been shot by a sniper but most of all I like to shout 'side' when they toss a coin before kick off.

International matches featuring England never cease to amaze me because, of course, England always lose and always disappoint in doing so. The experts debate this at length, usually with furrowed brows and much shaking of heads and yet I have told them on many occasions the reason for the national team's repeatedly dismal performance. It is because football is a game played mainly by Northern proletarians who decided that kicking a football around was a far better alternative to the education on offer. This in itself is not an unreasonable premise in those places like Manchester where football is much revered and education reviled, but any human activity requires some problem-solving ability and although footballers only just fall into this categorisation, it is as true for them as it is for the conquest of space. They keep losing because the foreign teams play in a different manner to what is customary at home and being devoid of educational attainment, the low brows of English football fail to understand this and are thus unable to respond to changed conditions. The employment of expensive foreign imports in the domestic game exacerbates the situation because the job of scoring goals and thinking is left to them and thus do England fail. The answer is to ensure that only chaps with degrees be allowed to play in the national squad.

'That's bollocks,' opines one of the experts. 'You can't expect a load of bookworms to do better than the Sons of Charlton.'

'They could hardly do any worse,' I witheringly reply.

I am always amazed by the passion that twenty two grown men kicking a bag of wind between two sticks can engender. I stopped watching seriously when the authorities brought the legendary crowd violence of the 1970s under control and ruined what artistry was left in the sport. It is true that the gladiatorial nature of the beautiful game remains, but the violence and bad language on the pitch is no substitute for a good punch up in the stands. The refereeing is woeful too, as everyone seems to agree; I have never ever heard anyone utter the words 'well, the penalty might have been awarded to the opposing team, but I agree that they deserved it.' And don't get me started on Maradonna or Thierry Henri who ought to be the volleyball league rather than the premiership. Here in the Old Queen's Head things can get passionate but Carruthers is always on hand with his elephant gun in the event that witty banter spills over into anything unpleasant, which is a blessing. I'm a rugby man myself.

The best bit about Hump Day football is the pies that are served free of charge at half-time by Perky Pete the landlord. I sit close to the space on the bar where they are normally placed so that I can eat two, despite my contempt for the stupid game. We will be returning to the subject of pies at a later date but, suffice it to say at this point that they are safe for the dieter to eat because they have no calories in them.

I like to be home by midnight on Hump Day so that I can tuck Louise in on the sofa, put her coat over her and arrange the cushions in such a way that she doesn't get a crick in her back. Then it's off to bed ready for the challenges posed by that most difficult of days, Thursday, which is neither one thing nor the other.

Day Four: Thursday – A Difficult Sort of Day.

'I can't decide whether I'm between a rock and a hard place or faced with Hobson's choice. It's a bit of a dilemma.'

J.Harpic.

Thursday is a difficult sort of day because although it is better than Wednesday, it is not quite Friday. The soldiers so movingly portrayed in Stanley Kubrik's *Full Metal Jacket* were fully aware of the Disney Corporation's view that Wednesday was 'Anything Can Happen Day' and the scene in which they sing Mickey Mouse's© favourite anthem, M-I-C-K-E-Y M-O-U-S-E© amid the ruins of Vietnam is a lesson for us all. Sir Bob Geldof reminded us of the hazards of Mondays and his warnings are worthy of consideration. The famous Alabama rockers Lynyrd Skynyrd held the equally prescient opinion that Tuesdays were apt to be 'Gone with the Wind' and Fridays have never been regarded as particularly lucky on Wall Street since 1929. Even so, I find the baffling possibilities of Thursdays more troubling and nothing good ever comes of being baffled.

The Weigh-in.

After three or four pints of the old JCB last night, you will no doubt be called early to the potty and this brings us conveniently to the subject of 'Doctor' Gillian McKeith, a dietician made famous by the appalling Channel 4 'documentary' *You are What You Eat*. Here, an inhabitant from a place just south of Ultima Thule attempted to deal with weight loss by sniffing at people's poo, recommending quinoa (whatever that is) and administering colonic irrigation, which really is a load of shit. She then wittered on about the unhealthy qualities of pork scratchings which I personally found offensive; how can anything that tastes so good be unhealthy? It is the only snack food with hairs on, for shame. This unscientific smear was only one of a number of wild food-related claims for which she may well have been hauled up before the American Holistic College of Nutrition (but I doubt it), and possibly done over by the British Dietetic Association in an alley behind the offices of *The Guardian*. She might well have deserved it too, considering the possibly litigious nature of her relationship with the Medicines and Healthcare Products Regulatory Agency over her alleged sex aids; neither *Fast Formula Wild Pink Yam Complex* nor *Fast Formula Horny Goat Weed Formula* ever worked for me. There were other recommendations in the programme involving zits, tofu and mung beans plus the ritual humiliation of fat people which achieves nothing beyond improving the ratings; always remember, Winston Churchill was fat and so are you. The wise weight-loss seeker will never be drawn in by this sort of macrobiotic nonsense.

One of her most distressing weight-loss mantras was 'a stool for your stool' in which she argued that placing your feet on a footstool while dumping the lump encouraged every last drop of shit to come out and that subsequently you wouldn't be carrying around more than was absolutely necessary. For the true life-style conscious dieter, this is the equivalent of losing weight by cutting off an arm; accept that your shit is part of you and you will come closer to grasping the truly holistic. Another was that she could tell the state of your liver by examining your tongue; the only proper response by the civilised person to this balderdash is to invite her to do so first thing in the morning after a garlic balti and a vat of Old Hookey. I doubt also if the good 'Doctor' ever considered the dangers faced by a small person forced to elevate their feet while perched on the porcelain. They might easily lose their balance and topple over backwards.

The success of her programme may be partially attributed to shit of this sort though, as there is actually a serious academic debate as to whether one should weigh oneself *before* the daily movement or *after* it. Obviously, weighing *after* the prisoner has been discharged will result in a lower reading on the scales and thus may provide a welcome boost to morale. Those who weigh in before the Dambusters' March claim that the subsequent release of the bombs improves their motivation by fixing in their minds the near certainty that they are already losing weight, even before breakfast. In truth, it doesn't matter when you weigh in, as long as you stick to your routine. You will definitely lose weight whatever. I'm an *after* person, if you are of so prurient a nature that you need to know these things; if I've hand a few pints of JCB the night before, I don't get the choice anyway. It goes down the pan like a flock of starlings.

Breakfast.

Although sausages are native to our shores, we have already noted that they are not unknown in other parts of the world and I have recently had the opportunity to embrace the Polish Kielbasa. This noble pork delight is usually smoked, has a good shelf life and can be eaten cold or hot as required. This versatility makes it as eminently suitable for light suppers as it is for breakfast. I was introduced to it by Stefan and Lucas, the newest East European additions to our shores, who made such a good job of replacing Carruthers' roof tiles after the negligent discharge of his elephant gun. They have a younger sister called Karolina who also made a good job of replacing Big Mandy behind the bar of the second of our village hostelries, The Hanged Man. There could be no denying that Big Mandy had become slovenly when she forsook her bra and embraced the inverted double arches punctuated, so it was only a matter of time really. Admittedly, her father, a native roofing specialist of windswept and brooding temperament, did not care for this turn of events, but his objections were mainly related to Carruthers' decision not to accede to his inflated quote for the necessary repairs.

'Bloody foreigners,' he muttered darkly, from beneath beetling brows.

'Cut your prices and compete, Heathcliff,' advised I, sternly. 'This is the free market. And you should address the neglect of the roofing deficiencies of your own house before you criticise hard-working New Britons.'

'It's all right for you,' he responded, before leaving, like the miserable git he is. Apparently he got jilted in his youth by a bit of Yorkshire fluff and he's never got over it. Why he doesn't join an internet dating site is beyond me.

This intervention in Karolina's defence earned me a pleasant smile from the said barmaid. As a young man, I was sometimes guilty of a deplorable censoriousness towards gerontophilia in young females when I saw them getting into the fine cars of sprightly elder gents, but my feelings on this have mellowed over the years. I now find that the spectacle of females cradle-snatching young men and inviting them to ride alongside them in their powerful, sporty machines is much worse. The young men in question have no conversation and nowhere near my wit, charm and charisma.

I considered embracing the clear-skinned, milky blonde Karolina, just as I have embraced the kielbasa, to demonstrate that there are plenty of native born Britons who still have manners enough to welcome visitors to our shores, but thought better of it. Louise would have got to hear of it, Stefan and Lucas are big blokes and Tredegar, sitting in the corner with his UKIP leaflets and pint of Spitfire, would not approve. I stepped back in the interests of village harmony.

The Keilbasa does pose certain challenges to the traditional breakfaster, especially on a Thursday when one can't quite make up one's mind as quickly as one would like. The nub of the decision revolves around the critical question of *tracklements*, those traditional accompaniments to the greater enjoyment of sausages and bacon and which we may for the purposes of analysis divide into the handy categories of Ketchup, Brown Sauce and Mustard. We'll take ketchup first.

No one knows where the term 'ketchup' comes from although theories abound as to its supposed origins in French, Arabic, Malay or American English. The Chinese have attempted to claim it as their own *gwai zap* but we may dismiss this as no more than a Communist plot; all Chinese words have four or more meanings so they can claim anything. Similarly, the claim of its American English origin in the corruption of the spelling from *catsup* to *ketchup* may also be dismissed; it might just as easily have originated from *Fetch-up*, given the American propensity to miss-spell everything. The idea of a snooty French *cordon bleu* chef inventing it is also ridiculous; it's hard enough to get a *Big Mac* in France without negotiating a subsidy or avoiding a line of tractors dumping the whole of the principal raw ingredient of ketchup on the pavement outside in protest at American imperialism or some such rot. As to an Arabic origin this is palpable rubbish; all the much vaunted learning of the Arab world never produced much more than Zero, which is hardly fundamental to the foundation of Western civilisation. Besides, Arabs are often Muslims and so don't often eat bacon; there would be no incentive to invent ketchup. In reality, the word is just a made-up word and we should just leave it at that if we are not to be embroiled forever in unlikely etymologies and unintelligible languages.

Similarly, various food writers have identified recipes for the sauce dating back to the fall of the Roman Empire but these recipes lack credibility because ketchup is made from tomatoes and tomatoes weren't invented then. The truth is that ketchup was invented by Heinz in 1876 and although the market has since been flooded with all sorts of imitations, we need not engage with them. Ketchup is Heinz Tomato Ketchup and anyone who says they prefer another brand is quite obviously a liar. And while we're at it, Mushroom ketchup is a completely different product and you don't put it on bacon.

Tomato Ketchup is perfectly acceptable on bacon, especially on sandwiches bought at Transport cafes. It has a pleasing colour and adds a sweet, tangy flavour of tomatoes. Children, I am told, love it and I am reliably informed by Randy, the cook at St.Wicca's, that they will eat dog shit as long as it's got ketchup on it.

'Does the brand matter?' I ask.

'Not at all, Harpic' he replies, with a shake of his head. 'Children have no standards at all.'

Ketchup on sausages is another matter and I cannot really recommend it. I should admit a bias here; ketchup is not my favourite breakfast condiment at all. It has too many proletarian connotations and sometimes, when I do spread it on a good piece of well grilled smoked back, I have unsettling flashbacks to when my father was doing Missionary work in the North. There is something of the Dark Satanic Mill about ketchup so I tend to prefer Brown.

Brown sauce is a much more complex subject but is full of commensurate reward for those prepared to put in the effort to study it. The basic recipe for Brown sauce is ketchup plus Worcestershire sauce but as the ingredients for Worcestershire sauce are something of a mystery, the leeway for experimentation has always been pleasingly wide and has thus produced the resultant variety of offering. Let us start with the tamarind-infused Houses of Parliament Sauce which, with its Royal Charter and iconic label, remains a refreshing symbol of Britishness in a changing world despite being made in Holland. This rich and tangy melange of good malt vinegar (from barley, which is used to make beer, remember), molasses (a posh name for treacle), dates and possibly anchovies has been a breakfast favourite since 1899 and is certainly a regular feature of my daily routine. It is worth its weight in gold on bacon and equally welcome on virtually any native variety of sausage, whether grilled or fried. It goes magnificently with Baked Beans and may be added to soups and stews without fear. A generous brown smear down the side of a Cottage pie is a delight to behold and it is a peerless addition to cheese on toast. When a man is tired of HP, he is tired of life.

The addition of oranges, mangos and chillies to the base recipe produces the feisty HP Fruity, a veritable fiesta on the tongue. Deployed in exactly the same way as HP and with equal and undiminished confidence, it rarely disappoints. In the North country it is added to *Hash*, a traditional dish made of minced beef, the noble onion and the humble carrot, which is popular there and brings cheer to many a shivering hearth. Aboard that bleak Scottish ship of state popularly known as the *Tartanic*, HP sauce is diluted by Act of Scottish Parliament, then distributed free from chip shops to the huddled masses reeling from their pints of Heavy and casual violence. Taken together, HP and HP Fruity make a formidable partnership whose rivals at Branston and the more specialist Wilkins find difficult to outwit.

From the West Indies comes Jerk Sauce. This tastes better than it sounds. Once, when I was Consultant to a Large Corporation in Nigeria, I was asked to visit a school to give a Careers talk on what made a successful executive. Indeed, my boss had sent me out to Nigeria for this express purpose as part of his commitment to a Third World Outreach project; the Large Corporation felt that I was exactly the man for the job – indeed the only man for the job - and put so much store by the project that they told me I was to take as much time as was necessary to spread the message and that I should not feel constrained by any arbitrary time frame in determining when I should return. I was even allowed to take Louise with me, for which she has been eternally grateful. However, I digress: on arriving at the JaZee Sixpac Muthafucka Academy, I was alarmed to be invited to witness a Jerk-off in a school dining hall, which had been cleared for the purpose. Unable and unwilling to disappoint the Headmaster, who was very keen to show off the school's Jerking, I followed and was thus present when a very lithe young man by the name of Chukwubeke lifted the trophy for the best Jerk. He was cheered to the rafters and unselfishly congratulated by his fellow Jerkers. As you have guessed, *Jerking* is the local word for *dancing* and not for playing the fool.

During the 19th Century many Africans were exported to the West Indies from Nigeria until William Wilberforce put a stop to it and the Jerking went with them. Once established in that tropical paradise, the Africans, or West Indians as they quickly became, were exposed to some very cosmopolitan South American influences, especially in the matter of samba and salsa. Not satisfied that these cultural forms fully reflected their own proclivities they therefore invented their own music – which we know as reggae – and their own salsa, which we know as Jerk Sauce. The sauce may be described as a more robust variant on the milder HP Sauces. The addition of strong chillies, garlic, spring onions and pepper delivers a kick as satisfying as one could wish for in the absence of Gordon Brown's bare arse while the mix of ginger, nutmeg and other exotic spices guarantees its place as a viable barbecue marinade option.

A final word on Jerk Sauce. If by some oversight you find you have a craving for Jerk Sauce at the disappointing moment that you discover the bottle contains no more than the unreachable sludge at the bottom, you need not despair. Simply take your standard HP – it does not matter greatly whether Fruity or not – and add a dash of quality tabasco to taste and your breakfast will be rescued. Don't employ tabasco on its own though; it really isn't acceptable with either bacon or sausages.

The subject of Mustard is equally complex and equally rewarding of extensive study but there can be no debate that does not acknowledge Colman's English as the King of all mustards. Its fiery characteristics are legendary and when spread carefully on a good pork and leek sausage, it is peerless. Carruthers swears by Colman's English prepared directly and personally from the powder and will countenance no other. He has had some improbable adventures in Africa and has thus known the hardship that leads to the acquisition of such admirable qualities of self-reliance, but I am of the considered and settled opinion that it is not necessary to go to these extreme lengths. Ready mixed Colman's is perfectly acceptable and equally good on bacon as it is on sausages. It can also be spread to excellent effect on ham sandwiches but its power can be diminished if tomatoes are added; safer to stick with the simpler pleasures here. In America, almost all mustard shares the same colour as Colman's English but lacks almost all of the strength, being sweeter and developed for use alongside ketchup on hot-dogs. This means that you can play an amusing trick on any American friends that come to visit by encouraging them to ladle on the Colman's as if it were a familiar American variety. This will make their dogs hot indeed and bring tears of mirth to everyone's eyes. We Brits like a little jape at the expense of our American cousins from time to time, but no hard feelings or lasting damage is sought. Sometimes I give it to children of the beastlier sort too.

Denning, the ex-Barrister, is more of a Dijon sort of chap but is difficult to draw on whether he prefers the smooth varieties over the more coarse grained products. For myself, I would go for the smoother, more unctuous Dijon but I have no objection to either, as long as the quality is acceptable and the brand respectable. Denning refuses to give up his secrets though. I have probed him on this issue many times over the years but he has always defended himself with disputational skills learned at the hard school of the Bar.

'The answer that you require is covered under non-disclosure and goes to both poison fruit and the strictures against self-incrimination,' he declares portentiously, through an alarmingly pendulous lower lip. 'I am innocent until pleaded guilty. Next question, M'Lud.'

If I ever need a defence lawyer, I would certainly choose Denning. His gurning alone would be enough to dispirit the prosecuting Counsel.

German mustard is not to be overlooked either. I first came across it when I was in the army deterring the Communist Hordes in Germany during the Cold War. It was a frosty morning shortly after one of the Company commander's tedious Orders Groups, whose contents never varied very much from the four decades old formula of 'Sit in trench; point gun in enemy direction; stay alert,' and which I had not thought it absolutely necessary to accord my full attention.

'War, war, war,' I said testily, upon being nudged awake. 'Is that all anyone can talk about around here?'

'Harpic,' replied Sergeant Makin. 'Nip down the *Schnell Imbiss* and use your military skills to bring back a bratty breakfast for the lads. No mustard for me.'

'Certainly, Sir,' I said, leaping to attention and cracking off a whiplash salute. 'How shall I pay?'

'We'll have a whip round and reimburse you out of Company funds when you get back,' said Sergeant Makin.

'Absolutely, Sir,' I eagerly responded.

Dashing out into the bright morning and mounting my trusty short-wheel-base Landrover, I ordered Robbins, my six foot six driver, to speed ahead and not spare the horses. 'To the *Schnell Imbiss* and don't spare the horses,' I said.

We arrived at the fast food outlet forthwith and I entered, alone, and placed the order with the grizzled veteran of the Eastern Front whose proud symbol of German economic reconstruction and revival this was.

'Kann Ich haben ein hundred and twenty six Bratwurst sausages,' I asked in my flawless German. 'Ein mit no mustard, danke.'

'Yes, certainly,' he replied, in his heavily accented German. 'Take a seat and I'll be with you in a minute.'

The production of this tonic for the troops took a little longer than the proffered minute but my confidence in the legendary Teutonic efficiency of our near-distant cousins was not unduly dented. Indeed, when he marked the mustard-less roll with a swiftly penned 'ohne Senf', I confess that I was rather impressed. I paid up and left, having first had Robbins carry the bounty to vehicle.

'Auf weidersehn, pet,' I said, with a linguistic flourish. 'Deutschland uber alles.'

'Sieg Heil,' he replied, with a traditional Eastern Front gesture. 'Uberprufen Sie Ihre kleingeld, Dumbkopf.'

This was a little above my O Level Grade D, so I simply responded with a cheery wave and ordered Robbins, who was looking a little cramped behind the wheel at that point, to return to our castramentation.

'Be a shame not to have ours while they're hot,' he remarked.

The wisdom of Tommy Atkins is not to be sniffed at and so I readily agreed to his suggestion and I am glad I did. A bratwurst with German mustard on a sunny morning on the North German Plain, even in plain sight of the Communist Hordes, is a magical thing and I still remember the pop of that fine sausage as my teeth went in and the dribble of the mustard as it slobbered down my chin. Later on that morning, we had the opportunity to enjoy the comparative delights of hot, lukewarm and cold bratwurst several times over because, the exigencies of Cold War being what they were, the Company had moved to a new castramentation in our absence and it took some little time to find them again. The sour look on the face of the Company Commander when we finally rejoined the regiment was presumably due to having missed his breakfast and was something to see but fortunately its deleterious effects were expunged by Sergeant Makin's happy welcome.

'You found us then,' he said, as I handed him his bratwurst *ohne senf*.

'Oh, no,' I replied. 'It was Robbins.'

'I must congratulate him,' he replied. 'Now where did I put my fatigues roster?'

More recently, there have been many worthy attempts to revive interest in the field of domestic mustard and now it is relatively simple to get hold of the good seed fortified with both ale and cider, in addition to the traditional vinegar, in a range of strengths and combinations. Honey and mustard has also acquired a pleasing popularity as a barbecue marinade or salad dressing – it works well with dandelion and Boston lettuce. Perhaps the most uplifting development for the patriotic food critic is the resurgence of Tewkesbury Mustard, which is characterised by its *melange* with horseradish. Traditionally, horseradish is eaten with the Roast Beef of Olde England and is not usually found on the breakfast table but in its Tewkesbury form it provides an excellent tracklement. It must be good because Henry VIII liked it and look what a fine, strapping, healthy fellow he was. I particularly enjoy it with kielbasa, which does not seem to lend itself to brown sauce or ketchup in any of their main forms. I raised this delicate dilemma with Karolina and she suggested I try Polish mustard which, serendipitously, also contains horseradish! It can be obtained from any East European delicatessen but as the Polish language has no vowels in its written form you will need to look out for jars labelled 'Mzstyrdsky' to avoid disappointment.

Today's Exercise Regime: Gardening Desolation; the Key to liberation.

Women love flowers and when providing them for your loved one, do not skimp. It is always a mistake to skimp. Flowers should mark every significant anniversary and are also a perfect decoration around the house on dull days and in the deep, dismal winters experienced anywhere north of a line drawn between the Severn and the Wash. Always prepare for the purchase of flowers well in advance because your chances of recovering from a missed anniversary by stealing from a churchyard or picking up a few forlorn stems from a petrol station are slim. This is because if you live in an urban environment then the decline in church attendance will have reduced the number of churchyards to hand and thus increased the competition from the blighted denizens of the Council Estate. Petrol station flowers are instantly recognisable by spouses; they just *know*.

I get my cut flowers from Jim the Brum in Berkstead who appears every weekend outside the Co-op without fail. As an independent retailer, his products are often cheaper, always of a higher quality and served up with more cheer than you'll ever get out of Big Mary, who's working on a checkout at the self-same Co-op since the wonderful Karolina supplanted her at *The Hanged Man*. He is also happy to share tips on how to extend the vase-life of the stems he sells and I have found two of them to be most applicable; add a bit of aspirin or a spoonful of sugar to the water, and always trim off the leaves. Louise appreciates this very much, as indeed I do. It has got me out of many a tight situation.

Jim the Brum cannot be the whole answer to the question of florality when a single packet of seeds can be purchased for a sum so paltry I need not even write it down as an item worthy of note in the family account book and thus provide a wondrous summer display for only minimal effort. There is some capital outlay involved in the form of soil, seed trays, small pots and a watering can and the like, but the rewards far outweigh the costs and one need never violate Don's labour-saving Dictum ('Half an hour'). The beauty of this pastime is that it requires little input, largely because flowers grow on their own even outside. This is, of course, a contributory factor to its popularity with those chaps in a post-career phase. Even in the concrete jungle, plants may be nurtured with minimal effort on balconies, window sills, the roof-top gardens of exclusive penthouses for successful executives and beneath the 'garden flat' gratings of the grim hovels of the poor. Indeed, this is a hobby that even the most humble may enjoy. Many of them may improve their moral condition if they save up hard for the opportunity to rub shoulders with their economic and social betters at the Chelsea Flower Show or its rival, the Slimstead Horticultural Society.

Choosing the right plant for you is a matter of individual choice and purchasing power but in the end it does not really matter because the truth is *desolation* is the key to gardening success. My preference is for *Cosmos*. This is originally a South American variety of feathery foliaged flower transplanted from the Argentine to South Africa during the Boer War when it came in the horse feed. There it quickly established itself along the roads to Pretoria where it remains as a lasting reminder to the fair inhabitants of that far country of the folly of challenging the might of the British Empire – something that Fatty Pang might have borne in mind before doing what he did to me in the Gun Hill Barracks in Hong Kong. It is a hardy plant and prolific, known in the local Afrikaans language as 'that bladdy roinek weed' and thus admirably suited to the British clime.

Sow indoors early in February in good compost and water accordingly. Transplant into individual pots and grow on, being careful to ensure that your spouse's attention is regularly drawn to the efforts you are making to make her life rosy. Harden off by leaving them outside from time to time and visibly worrying about them as though they were children off on their first overnight school trip to Broadmoor. Bring them in and out during March and April regularly until you feel confident that they can be planted out in a flowering position. Then, ensuring that the danger of frost is not yet passed, plant out in a prominent position where she can't miss them. When the Met Office warns of the inevitable sharp, hard and late frost, dismiss it as the alarmist rambling of a discredited institution run by Communist environmentalists bent on destroying all planetary human life to make way for pandas and polar bears. Go snugly to your bed.

When the sparkle of the rime glitters through the flowerbeds in the early morn immediately adopt a distraught mien. This is guaranteed to illicit a 'told you so, you bloody man, Harpic' from Louise and no doubt your own spouse will say something similar at first. However, your drooping shoulders and haggard face will soon soften her; women love flowers and hate to see them go down to the last gasp of Jack Frost. 'Plant some more and you never know,' is soon to follow, a sympathetic encouragement which you will be sure to embrace if you value her love. Sow your seed once more, but this time directly outside in May, and your labours *doubly wrought* will inevitably build you up in her estimation. No-one loves a quitter. And she will get flowers because they are *Cosmos*. Weeds have no problem producing flowers. Look at the bloody dandelions.

Lunch.

Missing lunch can be a challenge for some people and in the early days the seeker of the svelte may be tempted to fall at the mid-day fence. For the benefit of all, therefore, I recommend the perusal of this, the greatest *nouvelle cuisine* lunch menu ever invented. It was the brainchild of Cindy Mokonuwi, an antipodean chef with a taste for absinthe who persuaded a now rarely mentioned, long bankrupted landlord of The Hanged Man, to give her *carte blanche* in the creation of a new menu.

The Hanged Man Tasting Menu

New Commonwealth Asian Traditional with a Twist

*

To Start

Borlotti Beans and Pigeon Sausage with Breadfruit Sauce

*

Curried Haggis with a Lime and Kiwi Compote

*

Egg Chutney with Minted Garden Peas

*

Gwent Camembert toasted on Maize Meal Sadsa

(Suggested accompaniment: A fresh, full fruited Canadian Ice-wine)

*

Soups

Cowheel Consomme with Tripe Croutons

*

Lamb bouillabaisse

(Suggested accompaniment: Moroccan Pinotage)

*

Bon Bouche

Venison Falafel

*

Goat's Cheese Hummus

(Suggested accompaniment: a sparkling Odessa frizzante)

*

Entrees

Tahitian Fried Cassowary served with Seaweed Mayonnaise and Durian Chips

*

Grenouille Australienne

*

Bombay Duck Sushi in a Scotch Bonnet Reduction

*

Bush Meat Steak Tartar served with a Thousand Year Old Egg and Locally Sourced Leeks

*

Zimbabwean Elephant Game Pie with Tequila Gravy and Turnips

*

Grande Escargot Africaine avec Moules

(Suggested accompaniment: Cremant de Cote d'Ivoire)

*

Sweets

Melon Boat drizzled with a Raspberry and Garlic Coulis

*

Peaches with Wasabi

*

Liver and Pineapple Sorbet

(Suggested accompaniment: JCB)

Still hungry? Thought not.

Housework: Managing the Family Finances.

Let us get one thing clear from the outset, conjuring money out of the ether *is* work. Do not listen to the rabid Communist or the anarchist banker basher slurping his *Starbucks* Lemon Frappe through a Brazilian made 'V' mask and complaining about globalisation. They are both motivated by low envy and have no understanding of the beneficial effects of greed in enhancing the wealth creation process, as Gordon Gecko reminded us before being jailed. It is emphatically not the same as bunging a monkey on *Last Hope* in the 4.30 at Newmarket; the principles are entirely different, as the good lady bursar at St.Wicca's will tell you on any Wednesday you happen to be going by the bookies in Berkstead. Investment is a legitimate occupation which oils the wheels of global growth and returns due reward to those with the courage and foresight to engage in it. Like any other business, it has rules and principles to which everyone sticks; pariah status awaits those who break these rules and get caught as I, once a Consultant to a Large Corporation, can readily attest.

The first principle is called 'risk'.

If she can't afford to lose it, she shouldn't have let you invest it. Stocks and shares can go down as well as up. It's how money is made. Live with it. It's a tough world out there.

The second principle is called 'spread'.

Make sure you spread your dealings around a baffling number of accounts, brokers and offshore holdings to keep the Tax man at bay and her curiosity limited. This last point is important and may be achieved by regaling her with the ins and outs of the new thinking on annuities and draw-down income schemes. When she says 'Harpic, you tedious little bore, one more word and I will garrotte you,' you may count her curiosity so limited as to allow the full spreading of the wings of your financial creativity.

The third principle is 'getting good advice'.

This is essential; do not choose a financial advisor too young, for they are likely to be brash, flash and loose with your cash. Stay away from the old and bold who are too close to retirement, too well-versed in the thickets of financial law (and probably in possession of bolt-holes in the Philippines) to be trusted. Always choose a financial adviser whose shoulders are narrower than his hips because that means he has what my father called 'bottom'. My father was fond of men with 'bottom' and never failed to point them out whenever he saw such a man. He was also firmly of the opinion that although 'bottom' was to be found mainly in the professional middle classes, it was not unknown among the lower orders.

'There, is a man with *bottom*, Harpic Junior,' he would say as the police escorted the lone blackleg through the picket line. 'Talk about the nobility of labour? Well, that's it. *Bottom*, lad, *bottom*.'

Watching the spittle flecked man force his way through the howling mob of miners fighting for the Right Not To Work was an inspiration for the young Harpic and the lesson my father taught me has stuck. I always choose my financial advisers on their ability to ride roughshod through the flying picket lines of the regulatory authorities whose contempt for the straightforward working of the free market is at the root of our recent financial crises.

The fourth principle is 'caution'.

These are the family finances you are dealing with and the change in status from Dink to Oink means a greater degree of due diligence is essential. Remember, in the absence of a pre-nup, what's hers is yours and it's got to go a long way if you want to keep yourself in beer money.

After-work Drinks in the Pub.

As a Househusband it is important not to be so ground down by everyday chores that you neglect the intellectual life. So this afternoon, it's off to the half-timbered fastness of the Old Queen's Head to help me ponder on the solution to all life's problems. Many great philosophers have attempted to solve this little mystery and few of them to any good effect. Most of 'em never wrote a word you could understand while even more of them were completely hopeless idle bastards; expensively educated Karl Marx claimed to understand the whole economic system of the world, yet never managed to get a paying job and died without a pot to piss in; Diogenes claimed that living in poverty was the only way to go but was banged up for debasing the currency. The rest of them came up with such bollocks it's a wonder they were ever taken seriously at all. Take for example Xeno's Paradox; Achilles, the greatest athlete in the world, was set to run against a tortoise and because Achilles was the greatest athlete in the world the tortoise was granted a head start. Fair enough, you might say. So off went the starting pistol but each time Achilles halved the distance between them the tortoise took a couple of juddering steps forward and so stayed ahead long enough to put his nose over the finishing line ahead of the thoroughly humiliated Achilles. This is supposed to be some clever mathematical thing but it really is just a con and you wouldn't venture a fiver on it down the bookies. Emmanuel Kant was even worse; he said that you should never tell a lie or you would deny your humanity. Obviously, he had never been asked the question 'Does my bum look big in this' or his humanity would have been roundly battered. No, you shouldn't get hung up on philosophers; for true wisdom, the Pub is always the place to start if you want to know the answer to all life's problems.

Stark and spare Carruthers is quick to proffer a theory. When I ask him what the solution to all life's problems is he quickly replies, 'a shotgun, a shovel and a shallow grave in the Transkei,' which though potentially worrying makes more sense than Xeno, Aristotle, Bertrand Russell or the rest of them.

'Shoot them in the back first then turn them over and shoot them in the front,' he adds sagely. 'It will confuse the prosecution endlessly. And be liberal with the quicklime.'

My admiration of the legal mind is increased still further when Denning answers.

'What is the answer to all life's problems, Denning?'

'Doesn't that rather depend?' he replies, sagely, his face contorted into a fair approximation of a gargoyle's bum.

I agree, it does.

Barney the Builder is less sphinx like. 'Money,' he states confidently. 'Money is the answer to everything. There is no problem that money cannot solve.'

'But it cannot make you happy,' I challenge. 'Look at how miserable rich people so often are.'

'That's because they don't think they've got enough,' he ripostes, rapier-like. 'They're always happy when they get more,' he adds, doubling my intellectual discomfiture.

'Could money make Gordon Brown happy?' I demand. 'Could lucre ever lift those heavy brows to bestow happiness on his mien?'

'That *is* his happy face,' answers Barney. 'You should see the bastard when he's miserable.'

The Pub being a very democratic institution, it is natural to find Ark Slymstead at the bar. He is the very epitome of the bullet-headed, sometimes belligerent, mainly honest working man that used to be the backbone of this country until Labour invented the Trades Unions and taught them to be idle bastards; Ark is among the last of a dying breed; a man who needs no cocaine to get through his allotted productivity targets; who is capable of joined up writing; who nicks no more of the left over copper than is strictly traditional. He scratches his blunt nose, furrows his wide brow, licks his normal sized lips and summoning up all his long experience of a life serving the local community in a variety of skilled and semi-skilled ways, joins the debate with vigour.

'The answer to all life's problems is a job well done,' he argues. *'That's* why Gordon Brown is such a miserable bastard.'

'A couple of beers will do for me,' says Higgins the Trucker. 'Served up in my beach-side mansion by a rotating selection of ethnically diverse experienced hookers at regular intervals.'

I direct my enquiry to the corner trestle.

'Shocking,' says one, slamming his pewter tankard down.

'Outrageous,' says two, banging his personal glass jug down.

'Shouldn't be allowed,' says three, hammering his pot on the table.

'Bark,' says Bark.

'Not much use, was it?' says Barney. 'You should stick to JCB, mate.'

I have to agree and noting the clock, time my several pints so as to ensure that I am home in time to prepare drinks and dinner for Louise.

'Have you been at the soup already, Harpic?' she enquires, as I hand her a large glass of simply prepared red wine.

'Only a little snifter, while cooking supper for you,' I lie. 'It will be ready presently.'

Dinner. Stew.

A chap I knew once was such a creature of habit that he would entertain no change in his evening routine for any reason at all. He came home from work expecting to find his appropriately unadventurous stew at the appropriate time of 6.05pm and in the appropriate place set at the appropriate end of the table, just as he had done for twenty years straight. On this occasion he came home to find, to his surprise, that the house was empty though showing signs of a struggle having taken place and on enquiring next door he was informed that though it was difficult to be absolutely certain of the sequence of events, the said neighbour had heard a significant level of banshee wailing. Going back into his own house, he found a post-it note stuck on the microwave which fully and comprehensively explained the mystery of his missing wife and stew-less state. 'Have gone to the loony bin,' it read. 'Your dinner is all over my tits.'

I relate this cautionary tale to reassure the nervous reader that variety is the spice of life and that the humble stew need not be dull, repetitive, unappealing or lacking in interest. Indeed, it is to be found present in all the great cuisines of the world under a variety of guises and served up with a variety of accompaniments. The famous spaghetti bolognaise is actually beef stew with an elongated form of pasta; *coq au vin* no more than chicken stew in red wine. In Spain they cook rice and fish together and call it *paella* but, let's face it, Spain doesn't really have a cuisine in the classic sense. I include it here because a lot of people go on holiday there and may have experienced it. In India, which *does* have a cuisine, even the mighty curry is no more than lamb stew with chillies while in the Andes, *chilli con carne* is beef stew served with guinea pig.

I first learned how to make stew at the knee of my driver, Robbins, during the Cold War. His recipe was called 'All-in' and consisted of opening up all the tins and packets in my ration pack, emptying the contents into my mess tin and then warming it over a hexamine stove. It was capable of refinement, as I saw from the outset, but he only modified it once I had lost another filling to a lurking Rolo. He also agreed to leave out the tea bags after a while.

So taking this as my inspiration, I give to you my recipe for stew.

Step 1. Open some wine or beer.

Step 2. Get some meat and vegetables, chop them up and put them in a casserole dish. You can add spuds too if you want to save on the washing up.

Step 3. Add wine or beer. Put some in the casserole too.

Step 4. Add some Oxo cubes, then fill up with water – the casserole, not you, obviously.

Step 5. Put it in the oven for a couple of hours.

Step 6. Add more wine or beer – to you, not the casserole, obviously. Serve when it is done.

There are many variations on this theme, and it is the very indecisive nature of stew that makes it the perfect dish for a Thursday, but this will suffice to get you started. If you decide to risk serving your choice of starch distinct from the stew, whether that be rice, potatoes or spaghetti, bear in mind that the expert chef always contrives to serve them at the same time as the stew goes piping hot to the table.

After Dinner Activities.

'Does this Purgatory have a name, Harpic?' asks Louise.

'Beef Bourguignon,' I reply, emptying another 250 of Chianti into her proffered beaker.

'It is *not*,' she replies. 'I have eaten it. This is *not* Beef Bourguignon.'

I bring up the subject of the Extra-ordinary Special General Meeting of the Parish Council meeting tonight and my possible intention of attending.

'Indeed you will,' she says, taking the bottle from my hand. 'But as you value your manhood you will vote in favour of Tabitha Greenwood's amendment. Do you understand Harpic?'

I nod gravely.

Political Drinks.

It is one of those marvellous conundrums that keep Historians up all night arguing over the port; how is it that Hitler wasn't doomed to failure from the moment he launched his Beer Hall Putsch in 1922 without telling the assembled beered up Bavarians that he himself was a Teetotaller? Keeping *that* dirty little secret from the German masses must have had Goebbels up all night in a muck sweat and when you add in the fact the odious little fellow was vegetarian and so a non-partaker of either sausages or bacon, it is nothing short of a marvel that the nation that gave us *Bierwurst* ever took the wretch seriously.

He was up against some tough opposition too. Once the abstemious Neville Chamberlain had been given the bum's rush in favour of Whisky Winston, the writing was on the wall and duly underlined when Uncle Joe Stalin found out that he had made the Nazi-Soviet Pact with a Teetotaller. (It is an interesting point that most of the Soviet intelligence service was purged for not telling Stalin this earlier, thus clearing the way for the Cambridge spies to be promoted to full traitors because they were all heroic pissheads). As soon as Old Rotgut Roosevelt got in on the act, the game was up; weak lemon tea was never going to stave off the grand alliance of the British Boozpire, the Union of Soviet Socialist Soaks and the United Rakes of America for long.

Of course, booze is at the very heart of our political system. There are four bars in the Houses of Parliament and most of the nitty gritty of political horse trading, influence pedalling, bribery, chicanery, backstabbing, innuendo, fleeing for cover, leaking, lying – in short, all the things vital to ensuring the efficient running of the democratic system –is done during receptions of one sort or another within the Westminster village. The booze is almost always free too. Harold Wilson sought to quell the influence of the Trades Unions during the 1960s with beer and sandwiches in Downing Street itself, which must have been something of a sight; Mick McGahey of the Scottish NUM was always plastered and virtually incoherent by lunchtime. Mind you, Wilson himself didn't make much sense drunk or sober. The Sainted Margaret was fond of a glass of whisky at the end of a hard day's strikebreaking, which is something that 'Mine Fuhrer' Arthur Scargill might have learned from – like Hitler, he was teetotal. During the 1990s, the Liberal Democrats sacked their leader, Charles Kennedy, on the totally unconstitutional grounds that he was a pisshead. If that rule was strictly enforced there would have been no William Pitt, no Wilberforce, no Palmerston, no Gladstone and, as already noted, no Churchill. Tony Blair admitted to enjoying a drink, which is not a bad thing in itself; I just wished he'd hit the Downing Street cellars with as much enthusiasm as his wife trousered the loot from the Human Rights Act he passed, stayed away from Parliament and got totally paralytic for the whole of his time in office. Picking up his bar bill would have been infinitely preferable to picking up the bill that he and Gordon Brown left behind.

The question before us, therefore, is: what is the best sort of drink to enjoy when preparing for a political event?

Cocktail: The Sleaze and Scandal Slush Puppy.

Step1: Always use someone else's booze. You can do this by raiding their stocks or taking money directly from their pay packets to buy the ingredients. Keep a biography of Gordon Brown handy for tips on how to do this efficiently.

Step 2. Always insist that the booze has come out of your own cocktail cabinet or that you have bought the ingredients with your own money and are now generously sharing this expensive and well-crafted cocktail out of the goodness of your heart.

Step 3. For the sleaze, use something oleaginous. The consistency of the drink is important so choose something like Grande Marnier. Put a healthy slug into a cocktail shaker and fill up with crushed ice. For parties or, indeed, party conventions, a slushy maker is a more practical option as it will dispense the quantities that politicians are used to at a suitably reptilian temperature.

Step 4. Add Champagne. The more expensive the champagne, the more scandalous the price; sweeter than a tax payer's wallet indeed.

Step 5. Serve in a trough with Politician Pie (all hot air), Pig's Ear, Tripe, a couple of rent boys and several hookers.

Step 6. Print off bogus receipts and put everything on expenses. If you need help with this consult Denis McShane, Elliot Morley, David Chaytor, Jim Devine, Eric Illsey or Margaret Moran MPs (jailed).

All the way down the cul-de-sac, I ponder the Tabitha Greenwood Amendment. It is a revolutionary motion which will over-turn the founding statutes of the Sir Thomas Higginbottom Total Abstinence Coffee House when it was rebuilt in the Edwardian era. The original building having burned down in somewhat mysterious circumstances, the new erection included a well-stocked bar instead of an expensive and now unnecessary insurance policy. It also changed its name to the Slimstead Men's Club and for many years excluded women from its portals. Since the 1960s, however, this restriction has been honoured more in the breach than in the observance and the women of the village have made free with it as and when they have wished. Recently, however, Tabitha Greenwood has been campaigning for the restrictions to be removed in fact as well as theory and the Club renamed in a more inclusive fashion as a symbolic gesture to the cause of womanhood. This has provoked some controversy and one or more symbolic gestures of their own from the village elders, led by Ark Slymstead.

Neither Slymstead nor Slimstead likes revolutionaries and it is a fool who crosses them. In general though, although I am generally ambivalent about the strident tone of Tabitha Greenwood, I am aware that she will be backed by Ostrakov, the Chairman of the Parish Council, who is a Communist and who I am generally not in favour of. I see him regularly hanging out in the ramshackle bus shelter at the end of the cul-de-sac waiting for a bus to take him to Berkstead to meet his KGB handlers no doubt. He claims not to take his car for ludicrous environmental reasons but I know for a fact that he only takes the bus so that he can rub shoulders with the underclass and so maintain his cover as a champion of the proletariat. He further attempts to maintain this deception by shopping at the Co-op but as an ex-Officer in the Hong Kong Intelligence Branch I know a wrong-un when I see one. Thus my dilemma; do I back Tabitha Greenwood, advance the cause of womanhood, earn the plaudits of the Feminists and the continued forbearance of my dear Spouse or sacrifice it all for the greater good of scuppering the Communist Ostrakov and keeping in with the venerable villager worthies?

My sense of trepidation increases as I draw nearer to this sturdy peasant of a building, each brick redolent of honest sweat and agricultural labour in an age gone by. I admire the simple rigidity of its construction, its four-square no nonsense roof and lowering lintels inspired by the bluff-browed peasants who worship at its shrine. Its perfect proportion and restraint is a rebuke to the wild eyed fanatic Ostrakov who is determined to wreck its ancient stolidity with his new-fangled vision of a female dominated world. Approaching from the opposite direction is Tabitha Greenwood, red-haired, green-eyed, determined of gait and determined of purpose. She is an independently wealthy woman of power and prestige, commander of a property portfolio acquired after four clinically executed divorces and one funeral, which left each of her deluded victims as empty husks both physically, mentally and, more importantly, financially. She is the Preying Mantis's Preying Mantis and those who approach her now do so with extreme caution and a pre-reconnoitred escape route with full back-up. Only Carruthers is known to have survived a recent amorous encounter with her – but even his claims are disputed - and describes the experience in Apocalyptic terms, of being 'sucked in and blown out in pink bubbles'. Those others who remember her in her youth and can recall the sight of her in bathing costume or frilly underwear regard the experience with awe, comparing her to a snow-capped mountain avalanche throwing up clouds of spindrift under a full moon, a tall ship under a full spread of canvass in a roaring topsail breeze, a pale and tumbling orchid of gargantuan and gorgeous proportions. There can be no denying that she is so massively titted that a new definition needs to be sought for the concept of 'Lady Bountiful.' *Tout la monde sur la balcon*, does not even begin to describe the wonder of those orbs, which it may fairly be said are not so much jugs as tuns, medicine balls rather than airbags, Southampton docks rather than Bristols.

From across the road a defiant door is thrown open and the village worthies led by the bullet-headed Ark himself, who have been deep in discussion since the middle of the afternoon, tumble out of the Old Queen's Head like a collection of rude mechanicals and head for what is still the Slimstead *Men's* Club. I sense a confrontation.

'Those are two fine arguments for Women's Lib right there,' says Ark Slymstead in a stage whisper audible in Barkingham. 'How many more do you need?'

'Fine engineering,' agrees Higgins the Trucker. 'A magnificent cantilever indeed.'

'She must have been upholstered by dockyard engineers,' says Barney the Builder. 'Them nipples are like battleship's rivets.'

'Chapel hat pegs,' agrees Ark Slymstead.

'If you're selling those puppies,' crows an unidentified drunk. 'I'll have the one with the pink nose.'

'Gentlemen, gentlemen,' I chide, catching them up. 'Let us not be sexist. We should address the poonts – sorry *points* – on their merits.'

I halt the madding crowd at the gates to the institution to allow Tabitha Greenwood to sashay massively through ahead of us. Tonight she is wearing something low cut in the light brown

Burberry line, tapered from her ankles upwards until it necessarily broadens out somewhere above the waistline and giving her the appearance of an ice cream cone topped with chocolate orange flake. Tottering on stiletto heels so sharp they leave holes punched in the tarmac of the pavement, I step back: woe betide the toe or shin that they land on, but Ark Slymstead holds his ground manfully.

'Pearls before swine,' she says, a bitter sneer playing across her scarlet lips.

'Shit before the paper,' replies Ark, dodging a handbag swung like a chain mace from atop a nostril flared destrier.

'Sexist!' she spits like a spitfire.

'Sevenist,' replies Ark like a Messerschmitt, pouring bullets of invective at her in return.

'Honestly, Slymstead,' she spits back, like the tail gunner of a Lancaster bomber. 'I need you like I need a hole in my head.'

'You've got a hole in your head,' replies Ark, like a Sopwith Camel swooping down on a Zeppelin. 'I just wish you'd keep it shut and save us all the ear bending.'

She is gone with a slam of the Men's Club door moments before I can intervene and silence this ungentlemanly conduct. Ark turns and grins.

'Anyone who votes for her motion gets horsewhipped and put in the Wicker Man,' he says, darkly and then a bit brighter. 'But it shouldn't come to that. Everyone paid their subs?'

There is a mutter of assent. I assure him that Louise paid mine only the other week.

'Good man,' says Ark. 'I knew I could count on you, Harpic.'

Going inside this last bastion of sexist diversity, I breathe in the healthy smell of urinal blocks, admire the trophy cabinet stuffed full of awards for second place at darts and am comforted by the agreeably 1950s jailhouse colour scheme; magnolia and pale green are just so *retro-chic* these days. A trestle table covered with a grey blanket Soviet fashion has been set up by the snooker table, and behind it is arrayed the Parish Commune. Ostrakov in the centre with his pointy beard and cut rate Kaiser moustache, his bald light bulb shaped head, round spectacles and unsavoury trousers, all of which give him a slightly squinting oriental cast, reminding me of someone I can't quite put my finger on, but may possibly be John Lennon in his long haired layabout radical chic phase. There, next to him is Bill Gon, Chairman of the Planning sub-committee counting through the fifties in his wallet while looking thoughtful beneath his yard brush moustache and matching powerful eyebrows. To the left of him is the Right Reverend Richardson, the Vicar of St. Moses the Black, comfortably restrained in his dog collar and looking like a sanctimonious rabbit caught in the headlights of sin.

To the right of Ostrakov is the shadowy but elegantly coiffured Andrea Lloyd, who seems to have weaseled herself on to several sub-committees including the Brownies, the Slimstead Horticultural Society, the Cradle Roll and the Fete Committee. She is an experienced political operator, all peaches and cream complexion, matronly bosom and irritatingly smug expression, and so one to be watched. To her right and completing the steely core of local governance is horsey Patricia Dalrymple, Mistress of Five Chimneys Farm and Queen of All She Surveys. Her fearsome Dobermans, Boden body-warmer, jodhpurs, riding boots, aquiline nose and pinched look of tired forbearance testimony to the last gasp of the aristocracy that runs through her genes like a knackered foxhound. Her historic demeanour, as towering as a ruined castle covered in ivy and Virginia creeper, can be counted on to keep the machinations of Ostrakov in check in the interests of freedom, liberty, the free market and agricultural subsidies. The dogs slaver hungrily.

Around the room, chairs have been set out in rough rows facing the Chair, so that all might have their say in the democratic process. I move through a room buzzing with interested concern, pleased to see that so many of the fairer sex have come to exercise their rights and then take my seat next to Denning near the front. The skin of his domed legal head is stretched tight across his bonce and despite being rather red and cracked like the nose of an experienced boozer, resembles in some ways the head of the creature from *Alien*. He is screwing up one eye while his head twists downwards and to the left, like Quasimodo in a bullfight. I am glad he is on my side.

'Which way do you think it will go?' I whisper.

'That depends if the amendment is voted on according to the rules of the Slimstead Men's Club or those of the Extra-special General Meeting of the Parish Council,' he replies. 'We'll probably find out on Appeal.'

Ostrakov calls the meeting to order by banging his gavel in a sinister fashion. In his silky Communist's voice he prepares to seduce the dim-witted masses with the brilliance of his oratory.

'Today marks a potential milestone in the history of our small but tight-knit community,' he says, addressing his invidious smile to the venerable gentlemen. 'And it really is rather gratifying to see so many of our friends here tonight.'

'Shocking!'

'Outrageous!'

'Shouldn't be allowed!'

'Bark.'

'Order! Point of Order!' cries Ark.

'Over-ruled!' cries Ostrakov, determined to clamp down on free speech. 'I haven't finished the introduction yet.'

Ark scratches his balls ostentatiously and withdraws. Ostrakov polishes his spectacles on his Paisley cravat and continues.

'Now, we have two items on the agenda tonight and I propose that we allow Bill Gon to present his update on the proposed development on the aerodrome first. Any objections?'

There are none.

'Then because this is *not* a matter for the whole Parish Council,' continues Ostrakov, machinatingly. 'The rest of the Council must withdraw to avoid conflicts of interest. The floor is yours, Bill.'

'Thank you,' says Bill, as Ostrakov leads the Rev, the Mistress of Five Chimneys and the Cradle Roll Queen out. Bill Gon then launches into a pretty detailed exposition on the current state of planning regulations at both national and local level and how the negotiations with the developers are going. It seems very complicated and involved, I must say. His diction is not all it should be either and I struggle to hear everything he says, especially as several people are snoring and there is an argument about Sudoko going on behind me. He goes on for so long indeed that even Harpic nods.

'So it's all down to the village envelope,' he says in conclusion, as Denning digs an elbow into my ribs. 'Thank you. All in favour say 'Aye'.'

There are a number of wavering hands tentatively raised and I decide to ask for clarification on the Great Crested Newt situation.

'Excuse me,' I say. 'I just wanted...'

'Thank you,' says Bill Gon, in a clear baritone. 'Motion carried on Harpic's 'Aye'. Over to you, Ostrakov.'

I sit down, determined to put my questions in writing and so get a measured answer in less fevered circumstances. There is a short bar break in honour of drinkers past and then Ostrakov returns at the head of his putative Committee of Public Safety.

'Thank you, Bill' says Ostrakov, sitting down and peering at the room through beady eyes. 'Next up, Tabitha Greenwood.'

'Point of Order!' shouts Ark, springing up like a March hare with a hard on.

'Over-ruled!' replies Ostrakov, waving his gavel menacingly at Ark. 'Tabitha Greenwood, the floor is yours.'

Tabitha Greenwood stands up and presents her case with her usual eloquence and dignity.

'Listen you sexist bastards,' she says. 'This club belongs to the whole village so it's time we women were allowed in.'

Her eyes glitter around the room like an X-ray laser from a lighthouse, shrivelling gonads at the merest sweep of the beam.

'Any objections from the sexist male chauvinist pigs here present?' she says, her tongue flickering in and out like a viper sniffing for egg shaped objects to bite. 'No? Good. *Wise*, even for the stupider sex. Then I rest my case.'

There is a moment's shocked, nay outraged, pause before the storm of principled objection breaks.

'Shocking!'

'Outrageous!'

'Shouldn't be allowed!'

'Bark.'

'Point of Order!' cries Balls of Steel Ark, indignantly. 'Women are allowed in *already*. They were granted *Associate Member* status in 1974.'

'It isn't enough, Ark you dinosaur! I demand equal rights for women!' blasts the fey Feminist foghorn of Slimstead.

'That club was *willed* to the *men* of the village,' replies Ark, with an oratorical flourish. 'You can't overturn a dead man's wishes.'

'Just watch me,' she hisses. 'I'll dig the bastard up and make him see the error of his ways if necessary. The law is on my side. This is a democratic society and we women have our rights. I demand we take a vote.'

'Only according to what the rules of the Club say,' answers Ark, unbowed. 'And the rules say that the only people who can vote are those members who have paid up their subscriptions *in full*.'

'Very true,' interjects Bill Gon. 'You have to pay your subs if you want a say.'

'Seems sensible to me too,' says Richardson the Vicar. 'Render unto Ceasar, eh?'

'Poppycock,' growls Mistress Dalrymple, bristling and pointing her riding crop at Ark. 'Don't even think of tendering for work on any of my farms this harvest time.'

'I will not be intimidated and I demand the vote be taken only in accordance with the rules of the Club,' says Ark, manfully sticking to his guns.

'Who hasn't paid up?' asks Andrea Lloyd, curling a finger in a silver ringlet.

There is a certain amount of shuffling at this but it is cut short by Tabitha Greenwood's contemptuous sneer.

'None of the women have paid up,' she sneers. 'Because payment for Associate Membership is *deferred* until Full Membership is granted by the Club – which for me would add up to several decades of back membership fees. This is a male plot to oppress women, Ark, and you know it.'

'Well, pay up and then we'll talk about voting,' answers Ark, confident in the success of his stratagem.

At this, a hairbrush bounces off the side of his head and the room dissolves into a temporary chaos of vituperation and rather unpleasant insinuation as the anonymous culprit is sought, found, tried, found guilty and sent to cool off in the bar. I cannot but admire the way in which Ostrakov restores order and dispenses this revolutionary justice with no more than a gavel and a fiver borrowed from Bill Gon, which is used to purchase a calming snifter of Port and Lemon for the hysterical offender.

'Order! Order!' cries Ostrakov as the riot subsides. 'Order!'

I note Andrea Lloyd whisper into Ostrakov's conspiratorial ear and then watch his eyebrows shoot up. 'Good idea,' he says.

'There's trouble here,' says Denning, his face as stock still as stone for once. 'I once represented Andrea Lloyd in a legal matter. Shrewd sort. Best be careful.'

'What was the case about?' I enquire.

'Oh, I couldn't possibly say,' he replies. 'Client privilege. Cost the County Council an arm and a leg in compensation though.'

'Would someone on the Committee fetch the membership book, please?' says Ostrakov.

A thrill of horror goes around the room as the book is rummaged for and a large dusty ledger is produced from above the snooker cue rack. Tabitha Greenwood allows a slinky smile of triumph to slide across her seductive features as the book is handed to the taloned hand of Andrea Lloyd. She flips it open and with practiced ease turns the pages. A pregnant silence descends on the Slimstead men's Club as she takes a slim silver propelling pencil and jots down necromancer's marks in a small notebook. She flicks, she notes, she tots and then scribbles and I note the blood drain from Ark's face as she passes the results to Ostrakov. His Communist eyebrows go up again in surprise.

'According to this,' he says, holding up a piece of paper like Neville Chamberlain after the Munich Conference. 'The only people who are up to date with their subscriptions and thus eligible to vote on the Tabitha Greenwood amendment are myself, Ark Slymstead here and-,' he pauses and cranes his head. 'Joly Harpic.'

All eyes are fixed on me. The beery fury of Ark Slymstead's eyes burning feverishly in defence of ancient right and custom bore into me from one side. From the other the tigerish, green eyes of the Feminist fanaticism of the massively titted Tabitha Greenwood claw at me from the other. Arrayed behind each terrible visage, it seems to me, are all the centuries of tradition, wisdom, outrage and oppression that a village can muster and hand on from generation to generation. Cast a vote for progress and Feminism and no bloke will ever drink with me again and I will be scourged by unpleasant appellations forever. Cast a vote for ancient custom and I will earn the enmity of the Sisterhood in perpetuity and be given short measure by the barmaids. Over all floats the shadow of my dear Spouse, complete with a carving knife and an implacable expression: 'As you value your manhood, Harpic....'

Ostrakov eyes me and smiles invidiously through his bookish spectacles, enjoying my discomfiture.

'Denning,' I hiss. 'Apply your fine legal mind and come to my rescue.'

'It has been my experience that a proper adjustment between the weight and the quality of the evidence is what is necessary to come to a correct judgement,' he replies, twitching, his eyebrows fanning up and down like ostrich wings. 'In any given circumstances, that it.'

I make a silent appeal to Higgins the trucker.

'You're on your own, mate,' he mouths in reply. My heart is heavy at such a shallow betrayal, but I am understanding as his wife is sitting behind him with a knitting needle.

Through the window, I see the hitherto absent Carruthers loading his elephant gun by the light of the lamp hanging over the doorway of the Old Queen's Head, like a beacon of heavenly hope. Can he be assembling the Neighbourhood Watch lynch mob in defence of ancient rights? Has he paid his subs?

'Vote!' cries Tabitha Greenwood. 'Vote and be damned!'

Ark is determined and will not abandon his entrenchments, however fierce the storm of the enemy or hopeless of reinforcement.

'Against!' he cries, waving the tattered banner of his defiance on the barricade of his principle. There is an answering roar from the Ancient and Venerable.

'Shocking!'

'Outrageous!'

'Shouldn't be allowed!'

'Bark.'

Ostrakov turns his conspirator's malign gaze towards me and curls a cruel lip.

'Mr Harpic? May I solicit your vote?'

'Wait,' I cry, cleverly playing for time. 'Why don't you go first? You're the Chairman.'

I know he is in favour of the motion and as his vote is worth $1^{1/4}$ votes he can outvote Ark on his own. If he voted 'Aye' then I could abstain and avoid the opprobrium of all while still decently insisting that it was my action that allowed the motion to pass.

'Indeed I am,' he agrees, treating me as his catspaw. 'But I have the casting vote to be used only in the event of you going against Ark's objections and bringing about a tie. I cannot declare before you do.'

Bastard.

'Vote! Damn you,' hisses Tabitha Greenwood. 'And God have mercy on your soul.'

I consider abstaining anyway, but dismiss the thought. Ostrakov might just vote against the Greenwood amendment to spite me and though centuries of village tradition are at stake, it is my testicles that are being wagered. I begin to raise my trembling hand as the word 'Aye' forms on my lips, then think again.

'Is there no way we can compromise,' I gasp. 'In the interests of village harmony, why don't we, say, allow women to be pay to be Full Members but not let them have the vote?'

'That's not a bad idea,' agrees Ark. 'There is some mileage in that.'

'Not likely, Harpic,' says Tabitha Greenwood, wobbling with building rage.

'Why don't we adjourn and just agree to differ?' I posit.

'Vote,' says Tabitha Greenwood, her teeth grinding.

'I really do think that we must vote on the motion before us,' says Ostrakov, the bastard. 'Come now, it really shouldn't be such a big issue and I'm sure the village will respect your decision.'

'Secret ballot?'

'Vote,' says Ostrakov, with a thin smile.

I can't decide whether I'm between a rock and a hard place or faced with Hobson's choice. It's a bit of a dilemma but I have no choice. There are daggers to the right of me, poignards to the left, and a carving knife waiting for me at home. My trembling hand begins to rise once more and the word 'Aye' forms fatefully on my lips.

'Aye,' I say, but before the word leaves my mouth, there is a bang, the window explodes inwards, the lights go out, there is a wild scramble amid terrible screams and baying, howling dogs and I dive for the cover of the table where, in the dark, I am smothered by the massive medicine balls of Tabitha Greenwood.

'What was that?' says the panicky Ostrakov, who has joined us.

'Carruthers,' I say to myself, with a happy sigh. 'Carruthers has saved the day.'

'Well, the motion is carried,' says Ostrakov. 'One way or the other, it's probably unanimous.'

'Harpic,' says Tabitha Greenwood icily. 'Get your snout out of my garden.'

Day Five: The Eagle Flies on Friday

'Like Pepsi, Kool and the Gang were never quite the Real Thing.'

J.Harpic.

As I say, Thursdays are often difficult sort of days, but fortunately they are followed by Fridays, which everyone is grateful for.

The Weigh-in.

At today's weigh-in you will have lost at least another pound. If in any doubt or if you are somehow in fear of disappointment you may be tempted to shift your weight backwards or forwards as required to influence the read-out. This is not recommended as any weight loss will then be only notional. Dieting is governed by the Laws of Science and they are not to be appealed against. What goes in and doesn't come out results in fat. Don't listen to all that 'I never eat anything but I still put on weight' baloney: are they conjuring matter out of nothing? No, they're scoffing Mars bars that they've hidden behind the sofa.

Stand up straight on the scales and only lean forwards if the sight of your toes is a distant memory. Neither should you try to alter the judgement of physics by placing a hand on the towel rail. Your appendages are part of you and a holistic approach is vital if any realistic life-style change is to be achieved. If your body is wholly repulsive to you, you can weigh-in in the dark so as to avoid any embarrassment that the tyranny of mirrors might cause. Use a wind-up torch for extra-safety and try to avoid thinking of the Pier End Fun House. It is a vulgar amusement and not for the refined.

Breakfast.

Who can deny the restorative effect of a fine length of pork sausage inserted in to a cut roll first thing in the morning? Perhaps a good firm pair of melons and a splash of hot Java lava is more to your taste? The squeeze of a fresh bap around the Lincolnshire sausage perhaps? To my mind though, the mouth-watering aroma of a muffin stuffed with a fine Old Spot, or the dribble of creamy butter over a hot crumpet ready for the Newmarket chipolata must be everyone's idea of a perfect breakfast. Ah, crumpet! Everyone likes a bit of innuendo.

However you prefer to take it, there can be no denying that the Staff of Life, white, brown, black or pumpernickel, is a welcome thing. This is a universal truth. The be-clogged Northern waif pushing his bicycle up a cobbled street to deliver the stolen Hovis to his starving family; the unintelligible Geordie tucking into his Stottie ready for a hard day on strike; the meagre Yorkshireman sharing his Teacake with his slattern wife before heading off down a pit; the dull Nottinghamshire oaf clustering around the family cob; even the poor and benighted of this great island nation know what it is to eat bread and are grateful.

One question facing the breakfaster whether rich or poor is: to toast or not to toast? There are two schools of thought on this; we might dismiss any ludicrous ideas of toasting only one side. Those who prefer not to toast are able to enjoy the warm fragrance of the fresh bread in all its natural glory and savour the soft yield of its yeasty flesh. The toasting fraternity swear by the machismo of the crunch and the pure femininity of the melting butter. In reality, we need not take firm sides in this most interesting of culinary debates but feel free to enjoy the benefits of both.

The second question is: how much? This is a more delicate issue because it cannot be denied that while sausages and bacon are entirely calorie free, bread is part of the carbohydrate food group and so needs to be considered by the dieter. Many people say that two slices are plenty but that is a narrow conception and does not take into account the possibility that a baguette might be on the table. In such a situation, which way does one cut? Clearly, two lateral slices of a baguette would constitute far more substance than two vertical slices. In a ready sliced loaf, the question has already been resolved for you and the number of early morning family arguments avoided by the manufacturer's decisive action is the root of the popular saying 'the best thing since sliced bread'. Those who decide that one slice is enough are then faced with difficulties if they choose a bap; what to do with the other slice? Should one freeze it and toast it on the morrow, give it to the birds or send it to a charitable organisation? These are not easy questions to answer.

The question of what to put on the bread whether toasted or not is not so complicated. It must be butter. Since WWII there has been a concerted attempt by the Health Industry to persuade the good yeomen of England that a glop by the name of 'oleomargarine' is actually better for you. I give no credence to this ignorant nonsense but merely note that it is made by emulsifying a blend of vegetable oils and fats, modified by fractionation, interesterification, hydrogenation, chilling, solidifying and working it to improve the texture. Nickel and Palladium are also involved somewhere in the process. No wonder *I Can't Believe It's Butter*. My suspicion is that it was invented to lubricate the engine valves of U-Boats and was then adopted by the Communists after 1945 and then parlayed into a plot to undermine the morale of the Free World in conjugation with Big Pharma and the giant lizards of the Health Industry. I think I read about it on *Wikileaks*. Stick to butter, salted or unsalted, domestic, Normandy, New Zealand or Danish.

Marmalade is another option and here again, opinions differ. Does one combine sausages with marmalade? And if so, does one put butter *and* marmalade on the bread item of your choice before combining it with a sausage? Personally speaking, I prefer to keep the bacon separate from the marmalade, although raise no objection to its proximity to the sausage. What about brown sauce? For the connoisieur, the tart sweetness of the thick cut orange marmalade blending perfectly with the spice of the brown sauce is indeed a thing of wonder, but it is worth pointing out for the beginner that HP Fruity in combination with any marmalade overdoes things on the sweetness side. Similarly, Lime marmalade is only for Advanced Level breakfasters. Thick Cut Oxford is a stout compliment to the intellectual life of that great city while Robertson's golden shred, though embroiled in an embittered dispute over the Golliwog, should not be banished from the breakfast table for reasons of political correctness. Some say that Dundee is the only true marmalade and they may be right; even Ultima Thule has its claim to fame, although how they grow oranges in the bitter wastes of North Britain defeats me. It's hardly Seville in the sunshine stakes, is it? Recently, I have seen Grapefruit marmalade appear on the shelves and this is a welcome addition to our ever expanding breakfast experience.

Taking all this into account, the ideal relationship between bacon, sausages and bread would include the original 5:2 ratio of bacon rashers to sausages but would then add bread or toast in the ratio of $1^{1/2}$. This is achieved by taking an unsliced loaf and slicing it *laterally* because as most reasonable people will agree, one slice is not enough but for the serious seeker of the svelte, two slices are too much. So, here we are on Friday, able to pat ourselves on the back for not only sustaining an agreeable and effective weight loss regime but also establishing it on a scientific and mathematical basis: $5:2:1^{1/2}$ – the new Golden Mean.

Today's Exercise Regime: A Lovely Walk.

Walk Number Three: A Wander Through the Nature Reserve.

Hauling on a stout pair of boots ready for a good tramp in the woods is one of the finer things in life and I have a favourite pair of trusty leather barges whose lifespan I have extended beyond the manufacturer's guarantee by the liberal application of super-glue and, where appropriate, mastic. They have given sterling service over the last year or two and I consider the £15 originally spent on them to be money well spent. New laces are of course a paltry expense and mastic, though not cheap, can be used for other purposes than the repair of shoes; make sure you buy a gun to go with it though as it can be quite hard to squeeze the stuff out of the tube by hand. Re-soling and re-heeling can also be done quite cheaply by a qualified artisan and here I can recommend the Berkstead Cobbler whom I have come to know so well over the years that I qualify for a regular customer discount.

So, on with our boots, and off down the cul-de-sac, ignoring boisterous Chubble the Postie who is calling at Mrs. Johnson's letterbox again. Here *is* there *very* often and I wonder if a short note to his recently privatised employers might not be in order. At the bottom, I head directly for the ramshackle bus shelter mindful of the humiliation heaped upon me at last night's Extra-special General Meeting of the Parish Council by its Communist Chairman. I take Ostrakov's own umbrella, which somehow found itself in my possession in the confusion of Carruthers' negligent discharge, and use it to knock a couple of the tiles out of the roof. I then tuck the umbrella under my arm and, noting that it is coming on to rain, remind myself that revenge is indeed a dish best served cold. I see Ostrakov approaching and climbing over the five-barred gate into the alpaca field, hope that the bus is late.

As the great Rudyard Kipling reminded us, to be a man one must be able to wait and 'not be tired by waiting' even if the brief drizzle that was forecasted is turning into something a little more substantial. Of course, a little rain never hurt anyone and we countrymen are used to it. Living in England requires a certain tolerance of the wet stuff and a little preparation in the Barbour or Gore-Tex line can serve to mitigate whatever ill-effects the descent of a gentle precipitation might bring. The bigger storms flecked with summer lightning and all the drama of roiling cloud and leaden skies may require more precautions and some claim that it is best to be inside on such a day, but I disagree. The drama of the wind, the fury of the sleet, the roar of the thunder are always worth witnessing and an Englishman is not to be deterred by a little tempest or two. I take my stand, partially but not entirely concealed under the broad leaves of a sturdy oak, unfurl Ostrakov's umbrella and prepare to study the effects of a downpour upon his Mao Jacket and on that subversive political manifesto he is currently engrossed in.

When observing the effects of rain on Communists, I like to have a hip flask with something warming in it to hand. Brandy is the favoured cordial of the trusty St.Bernard toiling faithfully through the snows of the Brenner Pass while the heir of the Jameson Whisky fortune chose the family product to inspire his cannibalism in the Congo. My own preference is for *Southern Comfort* which brings grateful notes of warm spice and the scent of cherries from sub-tropical Alabama to our blustery shores and although it is early to start drinking, it is also true that it is, as the great songsmith Jimmy Buffet said, 'Five O'Clock Somewhere'. I pull out the flask and take a warming sip as the heavens open and Ostrakov seeks shelter in the partially roofed structure. His jacket is not up to much and unlikely to resist the storm for long. I take out my mobile communication device and call the bus company to inform them that an accident has closed the Berkstead Road for the next hour or so and that they should seek an alternative route. The controller thanks me and asks if I might pass on the news of the delay to any passengers waiting. I assure them that I will and take another swig. That jacket really is not up to much at all and being collar-less, provides no defence at all against the searching raindrop soaking into Ostrakov's thin shirt nor against the rising wind. He shuffles his feet and jams his hands in his pockets, like Lenin about to give a speech from the podium. The storm approaches. He looks at his watch and peers through the silver grey stair-rods beating down upon the naked tarmac, then tucks his subversive literature into his pocket.

This is England and so everything must be done in moderation. The rain is just enough to give the ploughed furrow a rich chocolate brown hue, to accentuate the verdant lushness of this green and pleasant land, to nourish the bounty of the harvest and to soak through a Mao Jacket. Ostrakov looks up at the sky, consults his watch, wrings out his dripping sleeve and then his horrible proletarian cap. He wipes his glasses and takes out his phone, but there is no signal at the bus shelter when it is raining. I look into the distance and see the silver lining that marks the rear edge of the passing cloud; this is just a cloud burst, but a Communist would never know that. A Communist would not know Kipling either and Ostrakov is the worst sort of Communist, but now a very dispirited and wet one. His enthusiasm for the cause of revolution is washing away with the tears of the weeping sky, his back-bone dissolving at the touch of England's balm; his 'iron will of History' has rusted; anyone would think the rabble was made of salt. As the end of the storm approaches, I step out from the shelter of the oak, furl the umbrella and time my approach at the bus shelter to coincide with the last sprinkle and the first blessing of sunshine after rain.

'Ah, Ostrakov, old boy,' I say, hopping over the five-barred gate of the alpaca field. 'I saw you getting a bit of a soaking and I remembered I had your umbrella. Here it is.'

'Thanks Harpic,' he replies, rather meekly for a firebrand Communist in my opinion. He takes a Conservative Party leaflet out of his pocket and drops the soaking paper in the bin. 'Looks like the dratted bus is late again. I'll have to get the Parish Council together to see if we can improve the service. People depend on it you know. Still, mustn't complain, eh?'

'Indeed so,' I answer, and march smartly on my way, convinced beyond any doubt that revenge is indeed a dish best served cold – but even better if it is served up cold *and* wet. That bloody Communist has no moral fibre at all.

So, a blow for the Free World having been struck, we go on with our walk. The Nature reserve lies across the Barkingham Road and is situated on the edge of the Aerodrome. Originally the site of an attempt by the Bluntnose family to extract silver from what appeared to be an old Roman mine, it was abandoned to its fate until the early 1960s when Billy Butlin proposed to build a holiday camp on it. This proposal was favourably received by the Parish Council at the time in the hope that it might provide employment for the village youth, bring some welcome tourist money to boost the village amenities and stop the young women running off with the Americans at the aerodrome. Unfortunately, Butlins were forced to drop their plans after a concerted effort by a wild assortment of hippies, environmentalists and Greenpeace types to occupy the blasted heath and insisted on Saving the Earth. Thus was the economic development of the village stunted and what was technically a 'brown field' site turned over by some very smelly Soil Association types into what is now known as the 'Nature Reserve'. Bill Gon then buried any hope of putting the ground to future good use by breeding great crested newts, trying to get the area designated a Site of Special Scientific Interest and probably a UN World Heritage Site to boot.

It's a lovely place to walk in all seasons and at different times of the year I take my camera to record the different flora and fauna to be found there. I am particularly fond of the blackthorn in March, the bluebells in April and the jolly Maythorn in May. There is a fair sprinkling of primulas and primroses to be seen, as well as the nettles necessary for the glad butterfly to nest upon. The song of the lark and of the thrush, the tuneful fife of the blackbird and the comforting coo of the wood pigeon are to be heard, along with the hoot of the hunting owl in the fair dusk. There is a small stream to feed the newt ponds, with a small ornamental bridge on which to pause and play pooh sticks and a fine greensward where one might lie in the shade of the weeping willow and tickle the trout. This place is popular with Denning and also with Carruthers, who hunts the fleet deer hereabouts.

Whenever I go for a walk, I like to take a small notebook with me in which to record the sightings of the day. If I see a roe deer, or perhaps the fallow deer as she travels, the shy muntjac or the swift fox, I jot it down in a shorthand of my own devising. Rabbits and squirrels, though common, are not ignored and although my ornithological classification system is not quite as I would like it, I keep a running tally of the different birds as I spy them. Beetles and worms are outside my purview however – I have never met an entomologist who I would give house room to - and apart from the odd encounter, snakes are too rare to be of interest to the amateur naturalist. Carruthers dreams of bagging the Slimstead Beast, a supposed panther said to be a frequent visitor to these parts, but I cannot be brought to believe in its existence and so walk through the woods unfazed by the possibility of a mauling. Over the years I have built up quite a collection of reports, which I commit to a spreadsheet on my computer as soon as convenient, and in this way I hope to construct a unique database of the wildlife of Slimstead and its environs. I have already made provisions in my will for it to be left to the Royal Zoological Society in the event of my death.

Clearly if you live in the urban environment then keeping a wildlife diary will be of limited reward; there is only so much interest to be had in the club-footed pigeon, rats, feral cats and pit bull terriers, but one need not be entirely deprived of the desire to collect and classify. When I was child, my friends and I used to have great fun spotting the 1963 Volkswagen Beetle and its later variants, crying out 'My Herbie!' whenever we were the first to see one. This was very rewarding on long drives and appreciated by the driver for the innocent amusement it afforded children who might become bored and otherwise fractious. Sadly, these vehicles are something of a rarity these days but the principle remains and the urban dweller might venture onto the hobby of *Eddie Stobart* spotting, or for a continental angle *Norbert Dentresangle* with reward. I would not advise embarking on this harmless pastime if you live in an area of social deprivation like Birmingham or near a Council Estate however; you are likely to have your note book stolen. Try counting up items of litter as an alternative.

Walking through the fair meadow towards the Nature Reserve on this morning however there is a disturbance to the peace that does not originate from a non-mechanical source and raising my eyes to the horizon, I see a large yellow earth moving device approach. Within a very short while I discern amid the roar of a powerful engine and the puff of blue diesel smoke the form of Bill Gon, who is driving it. I give him a cheery wave and he pulls over.

'Thanks for last night, Harpic,' he says, cutting the engine and peeling off a £50 note from a roll and dropping it, fluttering, into my hand.

'I didn't know you were in favour of Women's Lib,' I reply.

He looks at me and returns a wide grin.

'They say every man has his price, Harpic,' he says, restarting the engine. 'But you are priceless.'

'What's the digger for?' I ask, pocketing the £50 note.

'I'm making a new pond for the newts in the Nature Reserve,' he answers. 'So I've just got to take a couple of trees out.'

'Surely not? Tear down the mighty oak, the bright beech and the fine maple?' I recoil in horror. 'Surely we have not sunk so low as to destroy our dendrochronogical heritage in so callous a way?'

'That's just the thing though,' he replies. 'They're not native species and so have to be felled in the interests of bio-diversity.'

'How can this be? Surely the oak, the beech and the maple are as English as curry and chips?'

'Sorry mate,' he says with a chuckle and a shake of his head. 'We've been over-run by *Dalmation* oak, *Fagus Japonica* and the *Norway* maple. They've just got to go. They're alien invaders.'

'*Alien* invaders?' I recoil in horror again. 'Hack them down, Gon good man. Chop away. Fell them, I say.'

'Cheers, mate,' he says, happy to be about his work. 'Glad to be of service to the community.'

I give him a cheery wave and stand aside as the bucket of the mighty beast charges towards the Nature Reserve like the tusks of an angry bull elephant.

Our walk thus truncated, we return to the cul-de-sac, being careful to note down three rabbits, two squirrels and two crows cackling in a most unpleasant manner.

Lunch.

William S. Burroughs once wrote a book called *The Naked Lunch* but I don't recommend it. For a start, I couldn't make head nor tail of it and the copy I had seemed to be missing the end, which was a blessing, but it seemed to revolve around a lot of hard drugs rather than food. *Naked Lunch*: really, it's a disgusting and dangerous idea. Try it and I guarantee you'll never look at turkey in the same way again and I will also guarantee that you will lose your appetite for Tabasco very quickly and Scotch Bonnets forever.

Housework: Washing.

Doing the washing has always caused the bitterest of complaint from women. I well remember my mother watching the Northern women breaking the ice at the horse trough preparatory to lathering up and beating their husbands' malodorous rags clean on the bare cobbles. Back then, the weekly wash was hard work, women's work, time-consuming, labour intensive and of uncertain results as evidenced by the very grubby appearance of many of the working classes. Being closely supportive of my father's missionary work, she always felt a pang of sympathy for those poor drabs to whom the task fell and from time to time allowed a select few to use her own scrubbing board and mangle as long as they brought their own soap and did our laundry while they were at it. She was particularly proud of her charity when the clean sheets billowed out in the summer breeze or when she had the smalls pinned up on the whirligig. In winter, clothes had to be dried indoors on a 'maiden' which is a word imported from the colonies and refers to one of those wide, grassy spaces used by the dhobi-wallahs (also an Indian word) to dry clothing once they had been thoroughly battered about the ghats. In Yorkshire, the term used to describe the same article was 'a winter-hedge' and it is still widely used in areas yet to be connected to the National Grid.

Since those tough days of the 1970s, the situation has improved immeasurably and all kinds of new technology have been invented and applied to save the fairer sex from dish pan hands and the rashes associated with the harsher forms of carbolic. These include Dry Cleaners, Laundromats, maids and bespoke laundry services. There are also cheap and readily available home appliances to be found in the white goods area of any High Street retailer, Out-of-Town Discount Shopping Village or the Internet. They are simple to use because they were designed with women in mind. This is not to say that a chap can't master them; we invented them after all. Here are a few easy rules to bear in mind.

1. Never put a red sock in with the whites wash. It is a ruse as old as breaking a plate when asked to do the washing up and about as effective. You will *not* be excused duty and you *will* be wearing pink shirts.
2. Everything can be washed on Number 4 unless it is white. Except woollens.
3. Whites are washed on Number 1.
4. Put soap powder in the machine before switching it on. Leave 'Conditioner' to the experts.
5. 'Delicates' means that it belongs to her. Do not wash them. You will ruin them and have to pay for more.
6. Underwear need not be handled with tongues. It is rarely that soiled.
7. If you are unfortunate enough to own teenagers be aware that they are best cleaned outdoors with the pressure washer and yard brush.
8. Never boil nappies unless you want to look poor and 19th Century.
9. Do not do washing on a Monday. Although Monday is traditionally known as 'washing day' in some traditional societies, the practice is to be avoided in the new world of Feminist dominance because she will be so tired from her first day back at work that she won't have the energy or the manners to notice your own sterling efforts to keep the house going.

10. Similarly, always wash bed linen in good time for the weekend. She will be grateful for clean sheets when she wakes up on a Saturday but will scarcely notice the same by Tuesday and will be positively indifferent to anything by Friday.
11. Grow some rosemary and lavender, harvest it, put it in an envelope and stick it in her knicker drawer. You will be forgiven much for this small act of kindness.
12. And finally, adopt the moaning, embrace it and make it your own. Operating a Bosch or Hotpoint is really not that difficult but it will validate her own past whining and that can only add to the sum total of domestic harmony.

Pre-Dinner Drinks.

Fridays can sometimes be both a relief and a despair for the working Spouse and so it is important for the dedicated Househusband to be ready with a little lightener as soon as the *whump* of bumper on garage door announces her arrival. I choose to be in holiday mode on a Friday as there is nothing so dispiriting for your Spouse as to be greeted with a sour face or funereal expression. For this reason, Friday is always Champagne Cocktail and I always use my trusty sword to knock the top off the bottle.

This sword is one of the heirlooms of the House of Harpic having been issued to one of my more illustrious forebears, Captain Havelock Harpic, at the time of the Second Afghan War. He used the 1878 Pattern British Indian Artillery Officer's blade (forged by none other than the greatest of imperial swordsmiths, Roddas of Calcutta) to defend himself against a horde of fanatical fakirs while single-handedly manning a lonely sangar so far up the Khyber Pass and of such vital strategic value that the Colonel of the regiment would trust its safekeeping to no-one but a Harpic.

'Harpic,' he said. 'The rest of the regiment will be retreating to Calcutta, but you will be in command of the Rearguard. Hold on as long as you can. Good luck.'

The regiment cheered to the rafters when they heard that Captain Havelock Harpic had been given this noble duty and many of the officers patted him on the back, wiped tears from their eyes and gave him manly grins as they marched away singing 'The Girl I Left Behind Me.'

Well, despite the odds and pierced by wounds, scorched by the blazing sun and buffeted by thunderous rain, he held the position for the duration of the conflict to the surprise of all. So much so that when finally he was relieved, the Colonel could hardly express his feelings so great was the depth of his emotion and he there and then bestowed on him the nickname 'Bloody Harpic' and posted him to New Zealand as a reward.

I showed the blade to Mehmet, the landlord of *The Hanged Man*. He is of mixed Turkish and Limehouse extraction and has the olive skin and red hair that such a parental alliance was always at risk of producing, but which he insists ensures him a privileged place on the cutting edge of multicultural integration. And who can blame him, given the ups and downs that go with his situation? We are actually old comrades, having first met on the Green Line in Cyprus when I was keeping the peace as part of the UN on that divided isle and he was experiencing one of the downsides of his particular situation. At that time, he was manning the Checkpoint at the Ledra Palace Hotel as a reluctant part of the armed forces of the Turkish Republic. I say 'reluctant' because putting on the noble uniform had not been part of his plan when he had organised a Stag do for all his mates from Limehouse, Stepney and Bow in the cheap but fashionable resort of Bodrum. Imagine his surprise when, on landing at Izmir airport he had been presented with his dual British-Turkish citizenship and informed that as part of his duty to the Fatherland, he owed them two years National Service! No more sun, sea and sand for him! Say goodbye to pastime and play lad! Say goodbye to your games with the girls and say hello to an M16 and hairy Sergeant Major!

Well, to cut a long story short, he was posted to Cyprus and that's where I met him. I had been using my UN marked vehicle to import mildly counterfeit clothing in quantities that could be construed as being for my personal use if the diplomatic immunity of the said Landrover was violated and if my pal's shop in Ayia Napa was counted as 'personal use'. Driving the Landrover was my comrade in arms, Captain Cooper, who shared a similar interest in the clothing industry, and in the interests of not causing a diplomatic incident attempted to run the checkpoint without bothering with the sort of tiresome formalities that so inconvenience the innocent traveller. It was a lovey sunny Mediterranean day and we were keen to get to the ~~nipples~~ beach and it seemed rather a waste of time to be showing passports and filling in Customs Forms when we had been going backwards and forwards so often on the official UN business of facilitating peace through the promotion of trade links. Captain Cooper stomped on the accelerator as he was wont to do when going through checkpoints of whatever nature – he had an impressive collection of speeding tickets in a variety of languages in his collection too – and was only moved to apply the anchors when Mehmet hailed him in a version of the Turkish language not commonly heard in the environs of Istanbul.

'Stop the fackin' car, you fackin' barsteward,' came the dulcet tones of the East Ham Bull. 'Or I'll fackin' fack you right ap.'

Captain Cooper pulled up, more out of curiosity than to respect international law.

'Give us yer fackin' passport or yer fackin' brown bread,' said Mehmet approaching. He was only just beginning his patriotic service and was looking rather more sour than filled with martial pride. 'Fack me sideways, I must be fackin' radio rental. Duckin' an' fackin' divin' darn the Captain Kidd one minute, cream crackered, borassic lint and dealin' wiv this old pony the next.'

Captain Cooper produced his travel document in a state of amazement. Mehmet took it, flipped through the pages until he alighted upon the relevant one and then stood back.

'You are 'avin' a fackin' larf, mate,' he said. 'Captain *Cooper*?

'That is indeed me,' replied Captain Cooper, maintaining his aplomb.

'Captain *Cooper*,' insisted Mehmet, in sheer disbelief. 'Captain *Lee* Cooper? Are you tellin' me porkies?'

'No,' replied the honest Captain. 'It is indeed my name. Captain *Cooper,* Captain *Lee* Cooper, is indeed my name.'

'You're going to tell me you ride for the Berkshire Hunt and live in Hampshire Wick next,' replied Mehmet, going through the passport. 'You've got some Gregory Peck.'

Captain Cooper said nothing but was guilty of emitting a rather desolate sigh.

'Fack me sideways,' said Mehmet, handing back the passport. 'And I thought I'd got problems. I'll never Derby and Joan again.'

From that moment on, we struck up relationship based on mutual respect as soldiers, shared love of England's green and pleasant land and bribery, which enhanced Anglo-Turkish relations, encouraged economic links between the Greek and Turkish Cypriot communities and made us a tidy sum which Mehmet used to establish himself in the Licenced Trade once he was demobbed. This transactional arrangement might be misunderstood as a corrupt form of behaviour unworthy of a British Officer, but as I was officially in the United Nations at the time, it was perfectly acceptable and well within the accepted tolerances for the usual UN practices.

So now, admiring old Havelock Harpic's flashing blade, Mehmet's martial blood was stirred and he became visibly impressed.

'That would certainly fack the facking fakirs, mate,' he said, the distinctive sound of Bow Bells clappers clapping through his vowels. 'Fack 'em right up, it would, gor blimey, mate.'

'If you have a piece of pork belly or perhaps a rolled shoulder of the same,' I said. 'I could show you just how powerful a weapon of war it is.'

'What the fack would *I* be doing wiv a facking piece of belly facking pork?' he replied, scratching his full but unkempt beard. 'I'm a facking vegetarian.'

Debates abound about the correct way to open a bottle of champagne. There are those lovers of the boisterous pop and subsequent frothy emission, while others prefer to remove the cork so that it sighs like a satisfied woman. I am a firm advocate of the sword though. For sheer display it cannot be bested.

How to Open Champagne with a Sword.

Step 1. Ensure you have space to swing your blade comfortably. For this reason it is best to open the champagne outside unless, of course, you are the owner of a barn or Baronial hall.

Step 2. Hold the bottle with your thumb firmly inserted into the dimple in the bottom of the bottle. Using the point of the blade, remove the foil from around the neck.

Step 3. Remove the wire by hand and then hold the bottle in the palm of your outstretched left arm. Make sure your fingers are not on top of the bottle.

Step 4. Place the sword on your left shoulder, blade flat, sharp edge towards the bottle.

Step 5. Sweep the blade down in one fluid swinging motion so that it slides along the bottle to contact firmly with the underside of the lip at the neck. Do *not* chop or you'll end up with splinters, wasted booze and egg on your chin. The strike of the blade will cause the neck of the bottle to detach itself and fly off complete with the cork

Step 6. Bask in the admiration of your friends as you slosh out the fizz. For added interest, note the bearing, elevation and time of flight of the cork, retrieve it smartly and display the clean cut and the collar of glass around the cork to the audience stunned by such brilliance.

Fiesta Friday Champagne Cocktail.

Who can forget the moment in the classic movie *Casablanca* when Victor Lazlo orders 'two champagne cocktail'? Not, you will note *'cocktails'* but 'cock*tail*': I wonder why he did that. Perhaps it was because he was Hungarian. Carruthers thinks it is possible. Denning won't express an opinion on the matter: 'Lies outside my purview,' he says. 'And lies within my purview aren't necessarily lies if handled correctly.'

The classic Champagne Cocktail is a mixture of cognac, champagne, cubed sugar and bitters. Why this should be so is a mystery; champagne and cognac don't need anything else with them at all so I have never bothered with either sugar or bitters and have never been disappointed. The Bellini, which combines champagne and peach juice is an elegant twist on the old Bucks Fizz, while adding *crème de cassis* to the old Shampoo produces the magnificent Kir Royale. In more recent times, pretentious barmen at equally pretentious hotel bars have attempted to pretend that they deserve anything more than the minimum wage by inventing or 'creating' ever more ludicrous variations on the champagne theme. This is like trying to play Mozart on a didgeridoo; green apple liqueur (whatever that is) mixed with whisky and then topped up with champagne is something that I would not wish on Ostrakov.

The price of champagne can sometimes put people off from the enjoyment of this simple pleasure but one of the benefits of the Free Market so derided by Communists is that acceptable substitutes are quickly supplied. The Spanish *Cava*, though a little acidic, is a welcome addition to the Vintners shelves and the Italian *Prosecco* has rightly established itself as a firm favourite for its lightness of touch. French producers have long argued that the *terroir* of Reims is not unique to that region and so have adapted the *method champenoise* to other localities, most notably Saumur, with great success. My heart swells with patriotic pride that the best fizz is universally recognised as being produced in good old England and I look forward to the day when I can afford to try some. The New World, though providing some splendid reds, has not been particularly noted for its sparkling products and it would be my advice to avoid anything labelled with the term 'domestic' when visiting the old colonies of Australia, New Zealand, South Africa and the United States of America. It isn't worth the risk. Similarly, one must never be tempted by Russian or Chinese 'champagne' – it most decidedly is not – or indeed anything made east of the Rhine. If you are the sort of person who enjoys sparkling perry then I shouldn't bother at all although it might help to shift that fake tan, if applied with sufficient vigour and a pan scrub. Stick to proper booze.

The sound of a working Spouse asleep at the wheel reminds me of my duty and I decapitate the Bolly just as she misses the child on the bicycle and glides effortlessly into the driveway of *Chez Nous*.

'Flute or coupe?' I ask, as Louise staggers out of the car.

'Bucket,' she replies. 'And put that bloody sword away before someone rings the police.'

I pour freshly fizzing champagne onto the cognac ready waiting in her choice of stemware and hand her the Friday Fiesta.

'What do you think?' I smile a confidant smile knowing that you can never go wrong with champagne.

'I think I'll have another,' she replies, wiping the back of her hand across her lips. 'And another after that.'

Dinner. Sausage Roll.

This is a recipe for sausage roll which I picked up off the telly.

Step 1. Cut up 400g belly pork, 300g pork shoulder, 150g streaky bacon and 100g pork fat. Combine in a mincer and mince up. You have a mincer, don't you? Everyone has a mincer.

Step 2. Add a handful of freshly chopped thyme, the zest of a lemon, freshly chopped sage, freshly chopped parsley, Maldon sea salt, freshly ground black pepper, nutmeg, 2tsp mustard powder and 1tbsp of syrup from a jar of stem ginger. Mince from coarse to fine and reserve in a bowl.

Step 3. To make the pastry take 225g plain flour and sift it with a pinch of salt. Grate in 170g of very cold butter and combine. Add enough very cold water to turn the crumbly mix into a paste, wrap in clingfilm and put in the fridge for half an hour.

Step 4. Maintaining a positive outlook throughout this palaver, wash up the two chopping boards, seven ramekins, nutmeg grater, cheese grater, three knives, two spoons, two mixing bowls and the mincer. You'll probably have to wipe all the surfaces down too.

Step 5. Take the pastry out of the fridge and roll it out on the floured surface that you have just cleaned. Place the rolled out pastry on one of the chopping boards that you have just washed up and cut it into three strips.

Step 6. Place the meat mixture along the pastry strips in a slightly off centre position and maintaining the will to live, fold over and seal with an egg wash. Slice into 3cm sections and place on a baking tray. Put the baking tray in a pre-heated oven at 220°c for about half an hour.

Step 7. Wash up the chopping board and knife, again. You'll need a stiff drink at this point as you realise that you have just spent at least two and a half hours preparing something that takes thirty seconds to eat.

Recipe: Harpic's Sausage Roll.

Step 1. Take some sausage meat from the butchers and remove the packaging.

Step 2. Take some ready rolled puff pastry from the supermarket and unroll it.

Step 3. Chop an apple and an onion into slices and lay them on the pastry. Put the sausage meat on top and add salt and pepper. You can vary this by chopping a bit of chorizo into it or adding some dried apricots. Roll the pastry over and stick it down with your thumb.

Step 4. Bung it in the oven for a bit. Then eat. It tastes fine, honest. Besides, it's Friday night, for heaven's sake. Who wants to spend time bollocking about with all that crap and spending the rest of your life washing up when the Pub is open?

Friday Night Down the Pub.

'I saw Tabitha Greenwood today, Harpic,' says Louise, finishing off the second pint of Fiesta Friday Champagne Cocktail. 'You may go to the Pub. You are **Allowed** but do not come home in your usual state or you will be sleeping in the garage. Clear, Harpic?'

'Perfectly, my dear,' I reply from the end of the driveway.

My arrival at the end of the cul-de-sac coincides serendipitously with the appearance of Rip-Roaring Rupert, the Slimstead Baggins, in his Hounds tooth jacket announcing the arrival of his little red corvette convertible with an air horn blast of La Cucaracha. He slows to a halt, turns his *Drive Anthems of the 80's* down to a level more in keeping with the quiet suburban standards hereabouts the norm, and gives me a cheery wave with one hand while running the other through his tousled salt and pepper hair.

'Fancy a snifter, Harpic?' he displays a shiny epns hip flask and I catch its merry sunlit glint.

'It would be rude to refuse,' I answer, mounting his modern charger. 'I shall drink to your good health, Roopie.'

'What do you think of the air horns, Harpic?'

'Suitably retro-chic,' I reply, glugging back the electric soup. 'We've got half a tank of gas, it's half a mile to the Pub and I'm not wearing sunglasses. Hit it.'

Rip-Roaring Rupert had been expensively educated in the hope that he would occupy a senior position in the family crime syndicate but turned out to be a sad disappointment to his parents; you do really need a Comprehensive education to succeed in the criminal underworld. Shortly after his First Class Honours, they had him shipped him off somewhere Out East, where he somehow slayed a dragon and, to the disgust of the family, returned with wealth beyond the dreams of men in several different currencies and a variety of financial instruments, all legally obtained. They disowned him and threatened him with a concrete overcoat and a corner of the M6 Toll road that would be forever Roopie if he ever darkened their doors again. Such trauma had forced him to eschew work and for a while he had slunk about in a dejected manner, but the stiff upper lip ethos drilled into him at Public School has reasserted itself and he has manfully overcome his personal challenges. Now he devotes himself to drinking late, long lie-ins, living life to the fullest and being an Object of Admiration to All and Sundry.

'Been reprieved tonight?' he says. 'Let out for good behaviour, is it?'

I show him Bill Gon's £50 note.

'I say,' he says, opening the throttle as if he were flying a Spitfire. 'This calls for a celebration. What d'you say? Shall we collect the Barkingham Adonis and make it a *menage a trois*?'

'Jolly good idea,' I agree, as we roar down the road, top down and *Boston* blaring.

A little further on as the crow flies and a lot quicker as Roopie drives, I spy a gaggle of villagers in Hi-vis jackets hiding behind a hedge at an upcoming bend in the road.

'Speed gun!' I cry over the sound of screaming guitars.

'What?' answers Roopie, stepping on the gas.

'Community Speed Watch ahead!' I shout. 'They've been issued with a speed gun by the Fuzz.'

'Excellent,' says Roopie, stepping harder on the gas. 'Although it is true that I live in terror of getting a non-legally binding letter from anti-car busybodies from time to time. Still got my hip flask, Harpic? Hand it over.'

The verges along this stretch of the Barkingham road are not raised allowing Roopie to fade one wheel remarkably close towards the hedge. This generates a satisfying amount of consternation among the Community Speed Watchers, to which he adds by revving hard, blasting La Cucaracha out of the air horns, waving his hip flask in plain view and shouting 'Does that thing go up as far as a ton?'

I spy Ostrakov among the scattered geese, his nasty Communist face bearing a suitable degree of wonder at the glories of unfettered capitalism, and communicate my glee at his discomfiture.

'Baastaaaaaaaaaaaaaaaard!!!!!!!!!!!!!!!! Hahahahaha!!!'

'Communist, is he?' asks Roopie, coming off the pedal. 'I knew a few Communists out in China. Jolly good businessmen they were, too.'

Only a couple of minutes later the sound of a siren and the flash of blues and twos threatens to bring our innocent revelry to an end.

'Surely this thing can outrun a miserable mobile pig-sty, Roopie?' I ask. 'We can lose them in the country lanes.'

'Never flee from the long arm of the law, Harpic, for they will always catch up with you in the end,' he admonishes and glances in the rear view mirror. 'This thing my father told me and he knew a thing or two about it. It's why he employed lawyers. You need lawyers if you are to escape justice.'

My heart sinks and my opinion of the dashing Roopie diminishes as the revs of the engine subside. I always had him down as a manly sort of man, indeed the square jawed epitome of the mannish Englishman, and not to be deterred by a rozzer or two.

'Don't look so glum, Harpic,' he says, cutting the engine. 'We'll soon be in the Pub.'

The Filth pulls in behind us, puts on his hat and exits his vehicle menacingly.

'Just keep mum and agree with everything I say, Harpic.'

I nod dumbly as the Road Nazi approaches.

'Do you know what speed you were doing, Sir?' he says, a false politeness emanating from his Fascist snout.

'Of course, I do,' replies Roopie, handing him a lawyer's business card, deftly whipped from a concealed pocket. 'What do you think the speedometer is for? But *you* don't know because I suspect the speed gun is presently in the hands of the Slimstead Community Speed Watch and you don't have any witnesses. I *do* - or will have by the time you have filled in your paperwork.'

Undeterred by this all too familiar gambit, the trained eye of the Old Bill's professional suspicion falls upon the hip flask.

'Have you been drinking, Sir?' his tone is mockingly respectful. 'I'm sure that you are aware of the dangers of driving under the influence of alcohol, Sir, and would not want to cause a hazard or endanger other road users.'

'Boozing? Me?' replies Roopie, his voice slurring. 'Absotively not, drinkstable.'

'Step out of the car, please,' says the impudent young sleuth. 'I'm afraid I'm going to have to breathalise you, Sir, if you don't mind.'

'Don't mind at all,' says Roopie, falling out of the car. 'Gimme the bloody thing here and I'll blow it up like a hot bladder. My girlfriend can eat a banana underwater, you know.'

'Indeed, Sir? Well thank you for that,' he replies, propping Roopie up against the wheel and handing over the nozzle. 'Just blow evenly until I say stop.'

Roopie blows. The results are disappointing to the mind of the local constabulary. Roopie hops back into the car and starts up.

'Better luck next time, officer,' he says.

The Babylon is not happy.

'Wizard wheeze, Roopie,' I say as we begin to pull off. 'What's the word on the boozometer bamboozle?'

'Unlicensed Chinese wonder drug,' he winks.

'Serves you right for giving a speed gun to a Communist,' I call over my shoulder to the Blue Meany, as Roopie heads into warp speed accompanied by the revelrous sounds of La Cucaracha on the air horn and La Bamba on the stereo, my faith in him restored. I give a cheery wave and wonder about the costs involved in replacing a stamped upon policeman's hat.

Slaloming on through life's chicanes, we turn up the Annie Lennox, a notable Feminist of the 1970s and something of a pin-up girl for the lads back in the day – though not to be compared with Debbie Harry, of course – and remind ourselves of the joys of motoring.

'*Mad Max*,' I offer.

'*Death Race 2000*,' he replies, clipping a bollard.

'*Genevieve*.'

'*Grand Theft Auto*.'

'*Ice Cold in Alice. The Blues Brothers*.'

'*Frogger. Fast and Furious. Easy Rider*.'

'*Bruce Springsteen and the East Street Band*.'

Roopie is awed into silence: '*Born to Run,*' he says reverently.

'Crank it up,' I reply, punching the buttons. 'And pass the hip flask.'

Mickey Kingdom, aka the Barkingham Adonis, lives conveniently close to the Barkingham Butchers and by the time Clarence Clemens of the East Street Band has announced our arrival by means of screaming saxophony, he is waiting at his gate ready.

'You've dented your bumper,' he says.

'It is but a trifle,' I reply. Trouble yourself not. The insurance will pay.'

'Insurance?' says Roopie. 'Oh, yes...'

Mickey Kingdom acquired his title as the Barkingham Adonis from a comparatively early age when a clear skin, boxer's physique, dreamy grey eyes, narrow waist, wide shoulders, perfect teeth and a winning smile made him something of a favourite with the local milk maids. 'A Horse! A Horse! Half of Kingdom is a horse!' was a piece of ribaldry oft repeated that did him no harm at all and caused an amount of jealousy with the Barkingham male community commensurate with that generated among the Slimstead manhood by the presence of the American airbase.

'Fancy a run ashore, old boy?'

The Barkingham Adonis shakes his palsied head, coughs into a grey rag of handkerchief and wipes his rheumy eyes. He leans against his gate post and scratches the varicose veins that give his bare, thin legs the appearance of a road map to a place that no-one wants to go.

'Don't think I'm up to it, I'm afraid chaps,' he pauses as a spasm racks his frame, his knees knock and his glass eye drops out into his waiting palm. 'Touch of the clap again, I'm afraid.'

'When were you last at the clinic? Would you like me to ring for an appointment?' says Roopie.

'No need, Old Boy,' he replies bravely. 'Since they started the research project I have my own nurse and dedicated hotline. She's upstairs right now.'

I look up and catch a fleeting glimpse of a white uniform, marigold gloves and a strikingly impressive bosom drawing the curtains across the bedroom window.

'You're not...?'

'No, 'fraid not, regrettably,' he gives a wan smile and smiles. 'Days were when I knew the name of every nurse and her mother in Barkingham General. Not so, these days. Can't even manage the gardening.'

It is always distressing to see the decline of a legendary swordsman and so we give him a cheery wave as he totters back up his garden path while we head back towards Slimstead, our thoughts full of regret for the passing years and the depredations of time.

'Shame about the garden,' I venture.

'Too bad, too bad,' says Roopie. 'I hear the only thing he can grow these days is Chlamydia round his back door.'

'Is that a flowering variety?' I ask. 'Where did he get it?'

Roopie looks at me as if something is amiss.

'He got it from the girl at the garden centre, as I recall.'

'I must find out which,' I reply and make a mental note to consult my online gardening encyclopaedia.

'Do let me know how you get on, Harpic,' he says, turning up the *Bon Jovi*.

'Wait,' I say, spying the scattered remnants of the Slimstead Speed Watch limping down the road ahead. 'Slow down.'

'Whatever for Harpic?' complains Roopie. 'They're hardly going to nab us now, are they?'

'Of course not,' I agree. 'I just want to moon at Ostrakov.'

*

Approaching The Hanged Man, after duly and democratically showing Ostrakov my arse, I experience a small frisson of worried anticipation at the reception I might expect after last night's vote in the Slimstead ~~Men's~~ Social Club, but on entering my fears are immediately relieved. There on her normal perch is Miranda McNulty, Queen of the Pub and Slimstead All Comers White Wine Drinking Champion, sprinkling a wave at me with her tinkling be-ringed fingers. She is wearing a sparkly top and beige trousers as usual, but tonight has adopted a turban in a not quite matching mushroom shade, complete with a costume jewellery aigrette. The effect is more Angela Lansbury in *Death on the Nile* than Marlene Dietrich in *Shanghai Express*, but credit must be given for a brave attempt at bringing a dash of the chic to The Hanged Man on a Friday night.

'Well done for last night,' she says, smiling alluringly. The effect is rather disconcerting, but then she has been trying to seduce me ever since I came to settle in the village. 'Let me buy you a drink. For a moment, I thought that Ark was going to be successful in blocking the motion. It took real courage to do the right thing, especially with that lunatic Carruthers discharging his gun like that. I thought he was going to shoot you.'

'Oh, it was nothing,' I reply, graciously accepting a pint of JCB. 'One does what one can, you know.'

She twinkles from beneath her wrinkles, kisses me on both cheeks and breathes heavily and muskily in my ear.

'And how is the lovely Louise?'

'He has buried her under the patio,' says Roopie. 'Finally got tired of her, bashed her over the head with a spade and crazy-paved her.'

'Really?' she says.

'Utter rot, of course,' I reply. 'You know I'm no good at DIY.'

'Don't look so disappointed, Miranda,' says Roopie. 'Jealousy will get you nowhere.'

'You must content yourself with admiration from afar,' I add.

Miranda retires to powder her nose. It is a bone of contention with her that I am already spoken for. She feels that she is diminished because of it and fears being eclipsed in the womanly charm stakes by the massively titted Tabitha Greenwood. Rumour has it that the great breasted behemoth stole one of Miranda's target paramours from right under her wine glass and there has been bad blood ever since. Certainly there was a terrible scrap over who should be in charge of the flower committee at St.Moses the Black when an unexpected vacancy occurred. In this case Miranda won it – heaven knows how, but the Vicar ain't telling – and she can be seen periodically placing posies on the tombstone of Bazooka Greenwood's dead husband (no.2) and dabbing at a tear with a frilly hanky.

The Pub begins to fill up with the village worthies keen to enjoy their well-earned Friday night pints and the jolly hubbub of well met, hail hearty yeomanry and recently liberated women fills the room with fine cheer. Trucker Higgins is there, staring glassy-eyed into the mirror and wondering if what he is looking at is his own reflection or some dreadful vision of the future, while Barney the Builder is popping peanuts into his cement-mixer and wondering if his Missus has done the football sweep yet. I spy Ark Slymstead, whose brow is clouded and await the storm.

'Harpic, you bloody idiot,' he says. 'Thousands of years of tradition has gone into making that club the last refuge of the men of this village. It's the only place where we can go to be away from the constant nagging and whining of all these blasted women. And now you've gone and ruined it by voting to allow women to become members.'

'It wasn't me,' I say, indignantly. 'I abstained. The responsibility for the debacle lies squarely on the shoulders of that weasel Ostrakov who took advantage of the confusion to use his casting vote.'

'Oh,' he replies. 'That's alright then. Pint?'

'JCB for me, thanks.'

'Next one's on the house,' says Mehmet. 'For rolling back the Dark Age frontier of fackin' oppression a little fackin' further. I am an oppressed minority myself. You are a hero, Harpic.'

'Well, that's jolly kind of you,' I reply.

'Since when have women been a minority? They outnumber us,' protests Ark indignantly. 'I see I shall have to take my custom elsewhere.'

'Will you?' enquires Mehmet, quizzically pulling his pint.

'No,' concedes Ark, taking it and handing over the dosh.

A little later, Tabitha Greenwood hoves into view like a battleship taking up moorings.

'You don't fool me, Harpic, you little worm,' she says, eyeing me beadily. 'If it wasn't for your wife, you would have voted for the continued oppression of women, you sexist pig.'

'Oh, well,' I reply, hesitantly. 'Perhaps I can further the cause of liberation and make things a little better by offering to buy you a nice glass of white wine?'

'The days of women having to be bought drinks by men in their so-called Public House sanctuaries are over, Harpic,' she replies with a sneer. 'Now women are free to buy men drinks.'

'Well, mine's a JCB then.'

'Two pints of JCB Mehmet,' she demands. 'And grovel when you serve it, vile oppressor.'

'Two pints it is, inshallah,' he replies. 'Fack me.'

A little while later, I hear the powerful roar of Roopie's little red corvette and peering through the latticed window observe him leaving with the clear skinned, milky-blonde Karolina riding shotgun.

'Early to be knocking off, isn't?' I ask Mehmet.

'Oh no, I had to let her go,' he replies. 'She decided that the fackin' bright lights of Slimstead were no fackin' match for those of the big city. Roopie's giving her a lift.'

'I bet he is, the cradle snatcher. And Karolina! Gerontophilia is not attractive in one so young,' I say. 'But it's a long way to London at this time of the hour isn't it?'

'She's going to fackin' Berkstead,' he replies. 'But don't worry she is being replaced by Aurelija on Monday. She's a Lett.'

'A Lett?'

'Like a Latt.'

'A Lapp?'

'Latt,' explains Mehmet. 'It's a sort of Balt.'

'Ah,' I say. 'That would explain it. What time is it?'

'Time for another?' interjects the Right Reverend Richardson, newly incarnated at my shoulder. 'No need to be abstemious on a Friday, eh?'

'Certainly,' I reply, toasting this great man of the cloth in good Christian JCB. 'Good haul from the Poor Box this week?'

'Humph,' he replies, rather gruffly. 'Charity begins at home.'

'Quite right, too,' I agree. 'Actually, I think I should go home after this one.'

'Why?' asks Mehmet.

'Because I live there,' I reply.

'Well finish that one and have the one that Bill Gon left in the pump for you and then you can go home with a full tank,' he advises.

'Serpently,' I agree. 'Fill her up.'

Going home is no simple matter since the Parish Council voted to switch off the Hope Street lights after 1 am in an attempt to save on the village electric bill. Fortunately, there are white lines in the middle of the road to guide lost lambs back to the sheepcote but I do not need such unreliable navigational aids – you never really know which white lines you are following until you end up where you didn't want to go and then you are faced with the baffling conundrum of deciding whether to trust them to take you back to where you was wenting from as well as what you were back to, even if it's only a bit further.

I prefer to navigate by the stars, which is really simple once you get the hang of it. I simply orient myself in the direction of the Plough, that great Seven Starred Dipper, Ursus Major, which hangs above the village north like the mandate of heaven. Putting my head down, I ~~stagger~~ proceed in an orderly fashion until Cassiopeia appears above the Berkstead Road and thus entices me past the bus shelter towards her embrace. When the pavement runs out, I turn for guidance back to the Plough and head up the cul-de-sac to my own *Dunroamin*, which is where I live, and arrive proud that I can hold my head high in the company of any Columbus, Cook or – my own favourite mariner of yore – Captain Bligh. Up the driveway and to the front door, where I deftly thread the key into the keyhole – this can sometimes be more challenging than it needs to be due to the excessive rotation of the Earth that happens in the early hours - which is something some Astronomers should do something about – and so arrive safely at my home port.

This being *Friday*, when I am naturally at my wittiest, most handsome, nay *alluring*, I ~~stumble~~ gently climb the stairs with the intention of giving the old girl a squeeze and a bit of a jolly. Unfortunately tonight there is a post-it note on the bedroom door which reads 'Garage, Fester.' The Black Gate Is Closed.

Day Six: Saturday I Go Out To Play.

'A woman's work is never done. That's because it consists principally of thinking up jobs for men to do.'

J.Harpic.

This being Saturday, it would be uncivilised to do the weigh-in. After all, everyone needs a break and all work and no play would make Jack a very dull boy indeed. And what better way to start the day than breakfast in bed, curled up and stretched out on starched Egyptian cotton or the best snowy percale?

Breakfast in Bed.

To begin with, it's probably better not to go with the full Monty if you intend to eat in bed simply because you can never get a stable enough platform. One little wriggle or fluffed pillow and the sausages are rolling brown sauce down the duvet and the last time Denning tried eating an egg banjo in bed the yolk ran up his pyjama sleeve and dripped off his elbow. He swore he would never try that again and if a fine legal mind like that is wary of hot breakfast items between the sheets then we lesser mortals should take note. In recent years there have been attempts to solve the stability issue by attaching a cushion to the underside of the breakfast tray but really, like the onesy, it just falls so far down in the style department that you may as well get up and eat breakfast off a dustbin lid. I count myself lucky that for many years I have owned a breakfast tray with fold out legs which had at one time belonged to an Early Ming Emperor and was looted from the Forbidden City in Beijing by the derring-do of Havelock Harpic sometime in the late 19th Century. Since the Rise of the Asian Tigers there have been some questions raised as to the actual legal ownership of the piece but I have ever directed any queries on this matter to the British Museum marked 'Elgin Marbles Department' which seems to have done the trick. I haven't seen any Ninjas lurking in the shrubbery recently at any rate.

The Continental Breakfast of *croissant, pain beurre et fromage avec confiture* is often cited when the matter of breakfast in bed comes up, but I, for one, am not a great fan. To be successful, breakfast must have some interest to it and cheese, or even a slice of ham, doesn't really come up to scratch on this front. Frankly, it lacks the balls that bacon brings to the table.

In this respect I should warn the serious breakfaster against visiting Turkey because the Turkish breakfasts which were inflicted on me during the five days I spent in Istanbul with a Norwegian philosopher were very unsatisfactory. On the first day I was presented with bread, cucumber, tomato, a boiled egg and a very small pat of butter. I do not eat eggs (of which more later) so on the second day the item was not provided and so I buttered the bread and was about to place a slice of tomato upon it when I discovered a small, but very evil smelling worm in the red flesh of the fruit. Not wanting to cause a fuss, I discarded the tomato and made what meagre repast I could with the remainder. The next day, breakfast arrived with neither egg nor tomato and so I had little choice but to put a brave face on and restrict myself to a cucumber sandwich. Unfortunately, the cucumber, on close inspection, appeared to have a pubic hair on it and not being able to pin-point its owner, I decided to play safe. The fourth day dawned and to my chagrin, I was provided only with bread and butter which, everyone will agree, is not much to start the day with. However, I was prepared for this, having already spotted a pattern, and had brought my own Frankfurter-style sausages to the table and thus tucked into something that was a little better than nothing. On the last morning, I got *indeed* nothing and upon complaining was told that the chef had taken my repeated refusal to eat what he provided as a mortal insult and had decamped to Cappadocia. I also got billed for the sausages. 'A barb of sorrow has lodged in my heart,' was all the Norwegian would say, which just added to my low opinion of philosophers.

There was something to be salvaged from this experience though and that lies in the business of the croissant. Many people ascribe the origins of the humble croissant to the French but in reality it was invented by Austrian bakers with no other purpose than to annoy the Turks during the Siege of Vienna in 1689. The bakers produced their bread-like item in the shape of a *crescent* to mimic the Turkish flag and in handing them out to the defending soldiery basically said to the Turks 'Come on if you think you're hard enough. I'm going to have you for breakfast mate'. This is essentially what happened and the Turks were forced to withdraw. How the French got hold of the recipe is beyond me though. However, the mighty croissant remains and in terms of breakfast in bed, it cannot be recommended too highly. Whether supplied plain or with a cheesy topping, whether with or without butter, whether dipped in good creamy coffee, the properly flaky croissant has no peer. My own favourite is the almond croissant, and I have had many spirited debates on the relative merits of its great rival, the croissant stuffed with ham and cheese, which is fine as long as the cheese has melted.

Nor is it necessary to make your own. Most patisseries will supply good quality croissants for a reasonable price and as I understand that Costa and Starbucks can now be found in the North country, our cloth-capped brethren may also enjoy this exotic delight as a welcome change from gruel. Supermarkets sell them too, which is interesting, but I get mine from the local farm shop which supplies them frozen. They go into a cold oven overnight to 'prove' or 'thaw and rise' in layman's terms and then it's just 15 minutes on about 180°C and Bob's your uncle.

Coffee is the ideal beverage to accompany a croissant and presents few problems for those enjoying breakfast in bed; just keep a mat on the bedside table or chest of drawers and no harm will come. Barrista style coffees are very popular but, on balance, I do not think that they are worth all the effort first thing in the morning when, possibly, you may have had a little more beer the previous evening than you had initially planned for. Filter coffee made in the simplest of French Press devices is acceptable but again, it can be messy if grouts are involved. A good cup of good quality instant will do fine in most circumstances; do not be tempted into using cheaper varieties as they just don't do the job. Save them for when unimportant people visit.

So, there we have it; coffee and a croissant makes an excellent, elegant and satisfying breakfast in bed for a lovely Saturday morning. And the beauty of all this lies in its simplicity. She can learn to make it for you in no time at all.

Shopping.

'You have the musk of Miranda McNulty on you, Harpic,' says Louise this bright morning, throwing open the garage door. 'I need not remind you of the consequences should you decide to humiliate me publicly.'

Louise is descended from the Countess Theresa Horthy-Worthy of Borsova and Chop in Sub-Carpathian Ruthenia and Prince Selim Seljuk of the Sanjak of Novi Bazaar in somewhere else on her mother's side; they are proud of having at least one Papal Mistress in their ancestry, and two or possibly more members of the family in the Ottoman Sultan's Harem, depending on whether you count eunuchs. Sub-Carpathian Ruthenia is a small place which used to be stuck on the end of Czechoslovakia until the end of Czechoslovakia itself. It has by turns been invaded by Hungarians, Cumans, Mongols, Habsburgs, Transylvanians, Ottoman, Ukrainians, Hungarians (again), Romanians, Hungarians (again again) and then forced by the French to join Czechoslovakia (how and why is a bit of a mystery), Hungarians (persistent little buggers), Slovaks, and then finally the Russian Communists until that went tits up in 1991. The Sanjak of Novi Bazaar has been, by turns, Serbian, Ottoman, Bosnian, Rumelian (who?), Austro-Hungarian, Serbian, Montenegrin, then Yugoslavian and is now a bit of Kosovo, Serbia and Montenegro. It was the Communists who abolished the titular nobility in both cases of course (bastards). Hailing thus from the theological and political melting pot of Islam, Orthodox Christianity, Balkan Catholicism, Menonite Christianity with a dash of Hussite, Communism, Capitalism, Feudalism and Byzantine rite that is South Eastern Europe, plus murder, Louise's views on adultery tend therefore towards the conservative underlined with sharp knives. Her father's side were horse-thieves and gunrunners, not particularly religious, but religious enough to insist on the practice of arranged marriage and debt slavery; modernity is not for the male members of the Sodality of the Red Bear. They too possess sharp knives and have done ever since I rescued her in a card game in Bosnia back in the 1990s. Louise has the tendency towards touchiness common to dispossessed Countesses the world over and a predilection for historic vendetta that would shock you. She won't speak to the Russians for what they did to her Grandmother's donkey during the retreat from Moscow and mutters darkly whenever a Slovene appears in Slimstead, which is rarely, thank heavens.

'I need no reminding, my sweet,' I reply, giving her my winning smile and freshening up my breath with a spray she has thoughtfully provided. 'Fancy a quickie when you've finished making breakfast?'

'The world has survived the Harpic gene so far,' she replies. 'Let us not push our luck. Get dressed. I will issue orders when you are in a clean and presentable state.'

Up and out of the garage, through the shit, shave, shower routine and then front and centre before the kitchen table, where Louise sits behind her tea set. She is looking jolly presentable herself this morning, all almond eyes, alabaster skin, scarlet nails and matching lipstick with raven hair frothed up like she's had her fingers in the plug socket. To one side is her Tablet Computer, flashing.

'You are to go shopping, Harpic,' she says, without looking up from the electric aide. 'You will cook and prepare an edible meal for myself and my guests this evening. Your presence will *not* be required.'

'Bilderburg Group rules, eh?' I wink and tap the side of my nose with my finger. 'Davos, Omerta, that sort of thing, eh?'

She looks up for a moment and then, as if to see me better, places a pair of half-moon spectacles on the tip of her nose.

'Indeed,' she says, after a pause. 'Andrea Lloyd and Patricia Dalrymple from the Parish Council, as well as Tabitha Greenwood are to be my guests. What we are to discuss is beyond your meagre understanding and certainly beyond your pay grade. While you are catering for this event, I shall be shopping for a new outfit. On the purchase of this outfit you will make no comments unsolicited. Is this clear, Harpic?'

'Aye aye, Ma'am!' I snap a salute off and click my heels. 'Keep Quiet and Cook, it is, Ma'am.'

'Harpic,' she says, removing her spectacles and sighing. 'What did I do to deserve *you*?'

'Come, come, Old Girl,' I say. 'I did rescue you from a fate worth than death with that Royal Flush during that card game in Bosnia.'

'Did you?' she replies. 'Did you?'

To the shops. Berkstead is blessed with two Supermarkets. One is the rather tatty Co-op which I do not patronise on account of its origins in Northern Communism while the other is a household name which is committed to Free Market Capitalism and thus gets my custom. On top of this, there is a traditional baker from which I locally source my bread and pork pies, a Family Butcher (my Carpathian in-laws were much impressed that the English had legalised the vendetta and I didn't have the heart to disappoint them in their hopeful translation) and a Greengrocer who is a right geezer. Sometimes there is a mobile fishmonger, a mobile cheesemonger, some retailers of discount clothing and one or two examples of the entrepreneurial spirit who flog things out of the back of their cars. All in all, there is a veritable cornucopia of produce and product awaiting the careful shopper. I usually work my way round in a strict rotation of butcher, baker, greengrocer and supermarket avoiding the fishmonger because his dull eyed, rubber lipped catch often reminds me of people I once knew and choose to forget. That goes for the cheesemonger too but for different reasons.

This particular fine morning I am gratified to note the appearance of a rare breed pork pop-up shop with an exciting range of gourmet sausages. A free sample of Ginger and Spring Onion whets my appetite and I buy a pound of Old Smokey, a pound of garlic laden Provencal Pork and the more conservative Pork and Chive, which should see me nicely through the weekend. At the bakers I buy the rarely seen Cottage loaf to provide the toast to go with the old bangers and a couple of pork pies for emergencies. It is important to be prepared for emergencies, I find.

So many people under-rate the Saturday morning grocery trip, obsessed as they are by the endless rush of the modern world. Young mothers are possibly the worse, hogging the parking spaces nearest the supermarket doors, loading their mewling chocolate-smeared brats into specially designed trolleys and howling down the aisles as though they owned the place, while smelling of that peculiar milky odour and too much talc. They seem to have no consideration for those who believe that shopping is a pleasure to be taken seriously and unwilling to appreciate the glories of logistics that this temple of modern retail is. They ought to take a moment to consider the effort that has gone into providing the discerning customer with the variety and quality of produce that a Yorkshire peasant toiling away in his humble dale can only dream of. Imagine the look of joy on the face of the Northumbrian yokel were he to be given a choice of Gallia melon from Guatemala or Honeydew from Honduras in place of the tinned prune that is his lot. Imagine the Cumbrian oaf gibbering with delight at the thought of meals created from things that he has not had to hunt down himself. We civilised people really do need to appreciate the good things that are provided for our delicate palates and not shove sharp elbows into those gentlemen gourmets who take pride and time over the task of choosing a tomato.

Similarly, a little patience would not go amiss at the self-service checkout while that same gourmet, a chap no doubt of impeccable taste, who has given service to his country, been a captain of industry and deserves to be treated with a little respect in his well-earned retirement, looks for his glasses. His use of credit cards in strict rotation is to be admired as prudent financial management, as is his careful selection of loyalty card, his attention to the detail of the vouchers bestowed upon him by a grateful marketing department and the 50p parking ticket refund. It is not his fault if he is sprightly enough to require a busy assistant to detach herself from a rushed and demanding customer and make sure he is old enough to buy beer, nor to help him key in the codes of the vouchers that he accidentally dropped in a puddle and so won't scan properly. The fact that some of these may be out of date is a fault of the supermarket marketing department not his vari-focals and no amount of puffing and panting or pointing at the 'eight items only' sign will change this. Finally, he *is* using some of his own bags as his contribution to saving the environment and the fact that this requires the machine to ask him to remove the 'unidentified items from the bagging area' which he bought at another shop is a fault in the system not in his comprehension of it. Chill out. You'll give yourself a coronary and become a burden on the NHS.

Still, the Gentleman Gourmet can enjoy a simple retribution for all the trouble these busy young mothers put him to: go shopping on the first day of the school holidays and see them *really* stressed.

When shopping for a dinner party, it's always best to work out your menu first and then shop accordingly. This is my standard Bill of Fayre for when Louise has her chums round for dinner, which seems to be happening more frequently recently.

A Feminist Dinner Menu in Three Courses.

Cold Tongue and Pig's Ear

Roast Boar with Porcini mushrooms

Hard Cheese

This is, of course, just a postmodern joke meant to be understood in an ironic and fashionable manner.

For The Starter.

Pasta. Every time. For some reason, women think it's healthy and I see no good reason for a chap to challenge this prejudice unless he is spoiling for a fight and believe me, if you start challenging propositions like 'All men are bastards' or 'Equal pay for equal work' or the even more ludicrous 'Women Can Have It All', you will get one. Just stick to pasta, old boy, and then ladle the cream sauce on liberally. I like to set one portion aside especially for Tabitha

Greenwood, adding a clove or two of especially pungent garlic to it. The sweetness of breath generated enhances the solidarity of the Sisterhood no end. Serve it with some finely chopped and wilted spinach. It sticks to the teeth perfectly.

For The Main Course.

Roast shoulder of Pork is an ideal main course for several reasons. Firstly, cooking it is easy; just sprinkle salt on it and put it in the oven for a bit. Secondly, because it is full of fat, it won't overcook and they can natter on long past the time when we chaps would have had the thing out of the oven and jolly well devoured with no deleterious effects. Thirdly - and this is the clever bit – because it is full of fat, women will talk about what it is doing to their thighs and so not eat it all, leaving plenty for a left over midnight snack when a chap gets back from the Pub. I serve this with curried sweet potato and lime, a simple dish easily made by roasting chunks of the aforesaid vegetable in curry powder for about twenty minutes and then sprinkling lime zest on top. Again, reserve one portion if someone is especially sensitive to the hot chilli powder that may be added at the last minute.

For The Dessert.

Cheesecake, Belgian chocolate, Premium ice-cream, cake and *creme brule*, in that order. You will need to triple the amounts that you might ordinarily serve to the chaps.

Saturday Lunchtime in the Pub.

You will want to time your return from shopping to coincide with your spouse's own afternoon shopping trip if you are to get the best out of Saturdays. As a guide, International Rugby tends to kick off around 2pm, but you'll want to be in the Pub a good hour before that.

Today, I choose the Old Queens Head as the venue for sporting pleasure and am gratified to see my American friend DeVon Diego LeShawn already at the bar drinking a lager beer. He is new to England and I have gone out of my way to make him feel welcome. On his first visit to the Old Queen's Head, I drew his attention to the ancient oak beams and invited him to breathe in the scent of our shared historical heritage.

'Shore looks old,' he said, eyeing up a bit of peeling paintwork.

'Ah yes,' I replied. 'The King regularly stayed here on his tour of the country.'

'Elvis stayed here?' he replied, awed. 'Boooooooooooooooooooooolsheeeeeeeeeeee-it!'

Good relations between our two great nations are essential, in the Harpic book at any rate; I do not speak for Ostrakov the Communist. One day I hope that the Americans will see the error of their ways and return to their true allegiance under HM The Queen and in doing so cast off the false promises of George Washington – a man who famously claimed 'Father, I cannot tell a lie' but was happy to break his oath given to the King when he was made a Colonel in the British Army. In pursuit of this lofty aim, therefore, I have introduced DeVon to the noble game of Rugby in an attempt to wean him off American Football.

'Why DeVon,' I say, chafing him. 'Shouldn't you be wearing body armour? I thought that just watching Rugby is a little tough for you weakling Yankees.'

'Booooooooooooooooooooooooooooolsheeeeeeeeeeeeeeeeeeeeeeeeee-it! You Limey fags don't need body armour because you don't hit each other goddam hard enough,' he responds. 'Try getting bitch-slapped by a 6ft 5in, 285lb Defensive End moving at about a thousand miles an hour before you start criticising the old Gridiron.'

He has a point, although I doubt he has much concept of being bitch-slapped by Laurence Dallaglio or Martin Johnson whether wearing body armour or not. The more interesting point lies in how the two different versions of what is clearly a very similar game have emerged. We know, for example, that Rugby was invented at Eton so that the Duke of Wellington could win the Waterloo Cup. Sometime later, the game crossed the Atlantic and was then radically restructured by allowing the ball to be thrown forward - which rather defeated the object - but was then rescued by the introduction of Cheerleaders, which was lucky. It also crossed the Indian Ocean in chains to Australia where it became Football Ozzie Rules, which is a game so formless that it redefines tedium. Gridiron resembles the Northern version of the game known as 'Rugby League' in the matter of the 'down' but is still a bit girly because they don't have scrums and how else are you to get the honourable scars of cauliflower ears and broken noses? Even Northerners have standards when it comes to a muddy brawl on a wet field. In the end though, it shows that we have something in common with our American cousins, though much of the South West speaks Spanish, most of Miami is Cuban, half of the Mid-West in Norwegian, San Francisco is almost entirely Chinese, New York two thirds Irish, two thirds Jewish and half Italian and B-mor speaks rap. Even those who own up to an English heritage declare that they were all on the side of George Washington during the War of Independence, which is quite strange for a civil war, but we can live with it.

Where the most serious divide lies though is in the matter of pies. It is the Great Imperial Divide that separates the culinary heritage of the British Empire from the United States of Independence in America and a matter of indisputable historical fact. To wit: wherever the sway of Empire was to be found, so was the pie. Steak and Kidney, Meat and Potato, Chicken, all are to be found adorning the tables of Britain, Australia and New Zealand. Canada, drawing on its combined Anglo-French tradition has contributed the Pork *Tourtiere*, while the South African Pepper Steak is a magnificent example of the pie-makers art. In Nigeria and Kenya the Meat pie is king and even India, which does not eat much beef for religious reasons, can still offer up the lamb samosa which is close. Jamaican curried patties are excellent and the Egyptian sambousak a delicious snack (though a bit on the small side for my liking). Argentina and the rest of South America, though not formally part of the empire, benefitted from the export of the Cornish miners' humble pasty and the *empanada* can now be found anywhere that cocaine is cultivated. It is one of the great gifts of the conqueror to the conquered and colonised and the foundation of the Commonwealth.

'Its absence from the USA is the cost of independence,' I declare. 'Was it worth it, DeVon?'

'Booooooooooooolsheeeeee-it,' says DeVon. 'Hell man, we got mo' pies than a muthafucker. Ain't nuthin more 'Merican than Mommas apple pie, dude.'

'You are mistaken,' I reply. 'Americans have *fruit* pies and something called Pecan pie, which I'm sure isn't of animal origin. This is the crucial point. America does not have meat pies. For you, the concept is alien.'

'Boooooooooooooooooooooolsheeeeeeeeeeeeeeee-it,' says DeVon. 'Hell man, we got pot pies that got meat in. Hell, down Louisiana way they got 'Gator 'n' Raccoon 'n' all kinda pies like that.'

'Aha!' I say, displaying my superior debating skills by luring him into my culinary and intellectual trap. 'But a pot pie is not really a true pie. It is a pot or dish containing ingredients that is then capped by pastry. The *true* pie is encased in pastry, top, bottom and sides and *never* served with whipped cream.'

'Goddam it! You got me there,' he concedes. 'Damn, you Limey bastards are smart. Let me buy you a beer.'

'JCB, thanks,' I reply. 'Try one of those cold pork pies on sale.'

'Boooooooooooooooooooooolsheeeeeeeeeeeeeee-it!' he replies, as the barmaid hands him one. 'You Limey fags *eat* cold *pork* pies?'

'And Gridiron is still a girl's game,' I remind him, while taking an extra large spoon to the Colman's English. 'Help yourself to a good helping of mustard. And after that you must try a pickled egg in a bag of Cheese and Onion crisps.'

It speaks volumes that though we each have our different ways, we and the Americans still see eye to eye on many things. This was especially the case during the Cold War when I was posted to the Lance Tactical Nuclear Deterrent Missile Regiment on Salisbury Plain where, after a small mishap for which I was not entirely responsible and which certainly did not deserve the degree of panic and subsequent scrutiny, the Colonel of the Regiment was visited by a high level delegation of Americans who came to discuss the matter. It was after serious negotiations took place that he came to an agreement with his American counterpart that I should be put in charge of buttons.

'Lieutenant Harpic,' said the Colonel, his palsied hands clutching at a large cut glass tumbler of whisky. 'You are now Officer Commanding Buttons, do you hear? Buttons.'

'Certainly, Sir,' I replied, cheerfully snapping off a salute. 'Buttons are what holds the Atlantic Alliance together.'

'Harpic,' he replied, agitatedly. 'Should any button of whatever size, shape or appearance ever present itself within range of your blasted finger ever again, you are *not* to push it under *any* circumstances whatsoever. If it is a *red* button, you are to freeze on the instant and call for assistance. Do you understand, Harpic? Do you?'

'Does that go for elevator buttons?' I innocently enquired.

'Sergeant Major,' he replied to the looming presence of the RSM. 'You are to take Lieutenant Harpic out and bury him in the garden.'

This, I thought was rather harsh.

Still, the Harpics have always been indefatigable and when instructed in my new duties as Officer Commanding buttons, I threw myself with unreserved enthusiasm into the role, because buttons are indeed important. Buttons are what holds the army together. The regulation issue combat jacket had at that time seven buttons down the front, four at the cuffs, six at the throat to keep the wind out, five under the collar to allow a hood to be attached, two for the epaulettes, four for the external pockets, four for the internal pockets and four more for which I could never discover a use; 38 in all. The standard issue combat trousers had a similar number, including the all-important ones that did the vital job of holding them up in the absence of braces. Now considering that the army as a whole numbered in the several hundred thousands, imagine how important my job of counting them was! What would happen to the credibility of Her Majesty's Armed Forces if, on the day of battle, an unexpected shortage of buttons meant there was nothing to hold the chaps' trousers up? It did not bear thinking about. No: The Colonel had certainly made an excellent choice in selecting a Harpic for this vital role and in those spare moments between counting out the button supplies for the Regiment and pondering the fate of the Western world should the Cold War go nuclear, I confess I entertained myself with thoughts of the OBE I was likely to receive at some time in the future for my vital service in the defence of democracy and all we hold true on both sides of the Atlantic. I'm sure I would have had it too if Fatty Pang hadn't rusticated me in the Gun Hill Barracks in Hong Kong. Perhaps a Congressional medal may sometime find its way to me.

DeVon regains his composure somewhat as the effects of the Colman's begins to wear off and though he is still in a recognisably distressed state, it is beyond the wit of Harpic to know whether his condition is due to the mustard or the pickled egg. This is a question for later though as the game is about to kick off.

'What makes Rugby ineffably superior to the degraded practice known as 'soccer' over your side of the pond,' I say. 'Is the fact that the referee is respected and arguing with the balanced, even-handed way in which he comes to a decision is simply not done. This is a game unsullied by the bribery and corruption that characterises soccer and the fans are still agreed on the principle that it is not so much the winning that is important, as the taking part. We respect our opponents and give credit where credit is due.'

'Is that so?' he wheezes, a little hoarsely, in reply. 'Booooooooooooolsheeeeeeeeeeeeee-it.'

The game begins with a tremendous display of attacking play by the England side which culminates in the first of a series of spectacular tries, each one more perfectly executed than the last.

Waaaaaaankerrrrrrrrrrrrrrrrrrrrrrrrs!' I cry in jubilation as the England team go through their opponents once more. 'Waaaaaaaaaaaaaaaaaaaankeeeeeeeeeeeeeeeeeeeeeeeeeerrrrrs! It's going to be a cricket score!'

'You for real, muthafucker?' asks DeVon. 'Cricket? Ain't this Rugby?'

'Indeed it is, old boy,' I declare happily. 'It is simply an idiom.'

'Yup, you shore are,' he says, ordering a JD to go with his pickled egg.

By half time, the comfortable lead that England have so far enjoyed is being rapidly eroded by a resurgent opposition. Right on the whistle, they manage to score a disputed try to even the score.

'Typical,' I remark. 'The referee must be South African to give that as a try. It was obviously not a legitimate score.'

'What you talkin' 'bout, dude?'

'South African referees are notoriously biased and underhand when it comes to England. It is an unhealthy trait that goes back to the Boer War when we gave them a damn good thrashing for being unkind to our black brethren,' I explain.

'That so, huh?' replies DeVon, looking at me with renewed respect.

'Indeed,' I declare. 'It is a well-known fact that when a South African referee is involved, England will always be given the bum's rush.'

'Bum's rush?' queries DeVon.

'It is a quaint olde English idiom.'

'You shore are,' he replies, ordering another JD. 'Sheeeeee-it, this pickled egg is goooooooooood. Got any more o' that motherfuckin' mustard?'

The next half begins and is as keenly contested as the first. Scrum follows scrum, ruck follows ruck and maul follows maul as England strive to gain the breakthrough they so richly deserve. Then in the final five minutes, the England scrum half executes a perfect distribution to the winger who tears off like a greyhound towards the try line.

'Hey, this game is just like the old Gridiron after all,' declares DeVon. 'That was a great forward pass.'

'Nonsense,' I declare indignantly as the winger places the ball right under the posts. 'The referee would certainly have blown the whistle if the ball had gone forward. He has a reputation for sharp-eyed honesty second to none.'

'Yo? So what that muthafucker with the flag at the side waving his arms about for?'

'You mean the touch-judge?' I reply, dismissively. 'He is French and so not to be trusted. He is bound to be biased against England.'

The kick goes over and England coast to final and well-deserved victory.

'So what do you think of the noble game then, DeVon?' I enquire, heartily slapping him on the back.

'Fuckin' A,' he replies. 'Got any more of those motherfuckin' pork pies?'

Harpic feels content. He has done his bit to cement the Atlantic Alliance.

Saturday Afternoon Snack.

Saturdays can be quite a challenge when it comes to meals because very often one has to go out for dinner and as one can never be entirely sure as to what time and in what quantities the meal will be served. Whether in a restaurant or a private residence, this means that one runs the very real danger of getting well pissed before the main course arrives and duly disgracing oneself. In the Harpic household, there is also the question of Louise's dinner parties which I am required to cater for but not be present at in person and so run the risk of getting slaughtered by drinking JCB on an empty stomach. To cope with this culinary conundrum, the Saturday Afternoon Snack has quite naturally evolved and the perfect dish for this is bacon and cheese on toast.

Recipe: Bacon and Cheese on Toast.

Step 1. Fry or grill some bacon.

Step 2. Make some cheese on toast.

Step 3. Combine.

Lately I have been experimenting with strong cheeses of the Stilton type and have found them to be very agreeable when toasted and served up with bacon. Cambozola is not really recommended though as it tends to be a little too creamy to retain the desired zingy taste and crumbly texture, but Danish Blue is certainly acceptable in this respect as is Bleu D'Auvergne and even Gorgonzola. Roquefort or Saint Agur is excellent but – and here is a great tip – it is best served *warm* rather than melted. The heat from the freshly grilled bacon will provide the desired degree of melting for the perfect snack. It goes without saying that other condiments are unnecessary for this dish and under no circumstances should you be tempted to add onion or, worse still, onion marmalade.

The early part of the evening is spent in preparing the pasta in cream sauce, the roasted shoulder of pork and the desserts, which I always buy ready made from the supermarket because, frankly, it's too much of a fag to make chocolate gloop. All the while though, my mind is turning to the question of cocktails suitable for a Ladies dinner party. Obviously they will be drinking white wine throughout the meal and this will be done in a controlled fashion unlikely to reduce them to a state of swinish inebriation, so the choice of cocktail is important.

For Patricia Dalrymple, Mistress of Five Chimneys, fearsome dogs and alarming jodhpurs, we will obviously need something robust to thaw her out but a quick internet search reveals that horse tranquilisers are not so easy to come by legally. Nevertheless, something capable of inducing a trance-like cataleptic state characterised by profound amnesia – something like ketamine – would be ideal. Alas, it is too late and I reproach myself for letting international rugby come between me and a trip to the teenagers at the skateboard half pipe by the church. A nuclear G&T will have to do.

Andrea Lloyd, the elegantly coiffured political operator who wields mighty influence in the Brownies and at the Slimstead Horticultural Society, on first acquaintance appears to be a more difficult nut to crack because she is teetotal. Nothing could be further from the truth; teetotallers don't recognise the early onset of spliffication and so can be plied with generous amounts of alcohol quite easily as long as it is reasonably disguised. The trick, however, is not to get them completely plastered as their behaviour will only be forgiven as a rare aberration; they need just enough alcohol to be *unforgivably* rude or indiscrete. A *very* Bloody Mary would be appropriate here.

For Tabitha Greenwood, no effort can be spared. She must be given something so outrageous that the hangover will last well into the next week and be acerbated by flashbacks guaranteed to bring a flush of perditious embarrassment that begins in her toes, fills up her massive tits like bottles of Vimto, then ends at the very tips of her flaming tresses and then repeats *ad infinitum*. The Harpic Zombie will suit her no end.

Recipe: The Zombie Harpic.

Step 1. Combine 2 dashes strong Bacardi with 25mls *each* of white rum, dark rum, gold rum, apricot brandy, orange juice, pineapple juice, a twist of lime and a dash of grenadine.

Step 3. Shake over crushed ice and pour into a large glass. Top up with soda.

Step 4. Repeat.

For Louise, as Chatelaine of the House of Harpic, nothing but the finest low alcohol *frizzante* will do, as she will no doubt want to preserve herself in a state of sobriety which will lend her a superior air and allow her to take notes on the several failings of her guests when they get tucked into the *soupe electrique*. The *frizzante* can be passed off as champagne and thus underscore her stylish credentials and allow her an advantage in the face of her boorish and slovenly companions.

As if on cue, my Darling Dearest emerges from the bathroom in a cloud of steam and Chanel, hair wrapped *a l'imperatrice* in a white towel, fingernails like bloody talons and the rest of her swathed in a towelling robe that would grace an art deco ball. For one fleeting moment there is a glimpse of shapely calf and the merest hint of heaving bosom and then she is gone into the bedroom to drape herself in whatever designer tat she has picked up at Oxfam the Tailors.

'There will be Champagne, Harpic,' calls The Voice. 'And strawberries.'

'There will be *frizzante*,' I mutter in reply, assembling the ingredients for the Harpic Zombie.

From outside the sound of a horse box grumbling heavily up the cul-de-sac announces the arrival of Patricia Dalrymple. She is on time, as usual; Louise is fashionably late for everything and everyone; it drives the Headteacher bonkers. Looking out, I see that the Dalrymple has brought Tabitha Greenwood with her and as she gets out of the cab, I realise that for the Zombie to have any effect whatsoever on the bulk of those titties, the measures will have to be doubled. As the gruesome twosome approach the front door, I make the necessary adjustments to the Zombie and slosh in an extra slug of gin for the Dalrymple Pre-emptive Strike, but am still just in time to be there when the doorbell rings, noble footman that I am.

'Harpic, you sot,' says the Mistress of Five Chimneys. 'I didn't expect you to be here still. Shouldn't you be soused up in some low dive by now?'

'I raise my glass to low standards,' I reply. 'Do come through to the conservatory where drinks will be served momentarily.'

She marches on, the scent of horseflesh and wet dogs only thinly disguised by the lavender talc that hangs about her Burberry body-warmer like marsh gas and leaves a trail of contemptuous stable litter footprints on my recently Hoovered carpet. Behind her appears the massive bulk of Tabitha Greenwood.

'Good of her to let you ride up front,' I say. 'Must make a change.'

'Out of my way Harpic,' she replies through basilisk eyes. 'Every day I pity your poor wife and pray for something vile to strike you down.'

'Straight on through,' I reply. 'And try not to catch your reflection in the mirror, eh? Don't want any more statues cluttering up the place, do we?'

She snorts and moves on, her tits cantilevered three feet in front of the rest of her.

Andrea Lloyd appears next, pulling up in an eco-friendly jalopy that runs on her own carefully harvested methane and comes complete with a variety of badges and bumper stickers proclaiming her membership or support for Brownies, the Caravan Club, the Green Party, the LibDems and Christian Aid. There is a dirty red nose on the radiator grill still, like a worn out joke and a yellow tree air freshener dangling from the rear view mirror to mask the smell of the bio-fuel. It has taken her a little while to get here and as she steps out the vehicle she primps and crimps herself before lugging out a large briefcase, full of tagged and colour coded files.

'How's the empire building going?' I ask, choking a little on the hair spray fumes. 'Annexed the allotments yet?'

'Go away you horrid little man,' she retorts. 'What sort of an idiot is it that is so easily fooled by Bill Gon?'

'I have no idea,' I respond.

'As I thought,' she answers and sails on towards the conservatory.

The homely smell of roasting pork is getting the old Harpic juices flowing just as Louise appears from her boudoir.

'You are still here, Harpic,' she says. 'And I do not have champagne in my hand. Your dereliction of duty is astounding.'

'Coming right up, Sweetheart,' I reply, reaching for the *frizzante.*

'Harpic,' she says, casting her gaze across the tray of drinks I have prepared for her guests. 'I thought I had made my thoughts clear on the issue of drinks. There will be champagne. The gaudy concoctions that you prepare for me in my despairing state at the end of a day at St.Wiccas are not acceptable for civilised company. There will *be* champagne.'

'Righty ho,' I say. There is no point clinging to the raft of a dead stratagem when you face being torpedoed by Cetus himself and so reach for the quality fizz, my visions of reducing the Sisterhood to drunken debauched behaviour dashed. 'I say, what do you want me to do with this lot? Perhaps you might save it for after dinner drinks?'

She looks at my cocktail creations, takes the champagne from me and leaves without further ado.

It looks like I'll have to drink them myself. And then go to the Pub.

Actually, they taste alright.

Day Seven: Saturday Night and Sunday Morning.

'Be drunk and be happy.'

Alan Sillitoe.

Waking up on a Sunday morning can be tricky, especially if one has spent Saturday night in convivial company and is not entirely certain of the exact flow of events and has only a hazy recollection of how one came to be in this particular geographical location. Relax though, you are in good company; the famed actor Anthony Hopkins once woke up in the wrong state while Boris Yeltsin, former president of the USSR got so pissed on a visit to the USA that he was found bumbling down Pennsylvania avenue in his underpants looking for a pizza. Rip-roaring Roopie claimed to have once woken up on an aircraft carrier heading for the Falklands after a particularly bibulous night in Pompey and only narrowly avoided being press-ganged (I think that was the phrase) by jolly Jack Tars, but this is nothing compared to Buzz Aldrin who went all the way to the moon while pissed as a fart. A record of some sort, surely? Nearer home, Trucker Higgins can often be found sheltering under a hedgerow in the early hours while Ark Slymstead is an habitual bus shelter occupant. Denning, with his fine legal mind and geographically mobile features is not to be drawn on this point: 'Habeus Corpus,' is his usual reply. Carruthers is rather more forthright: 'Always carry a compass and a condom,' he declares. 'Then you'll be prepared for anything – except bears.' I feel there may be wisdom in this.

Coming up to periscope depth this fine morning, I sweep the horizon with one eye, the other being gummed down still and note that although I am metaphorically all at sea, and indeed experiencing a touch of biliousness not unlike that experienced by mariners diverse, my mouth is as dry as Gandhi's flip flop and something furry has slept on my teeth. I ponder on Jane Austen and admit the truth of her dictum that it is a truth universally acknowledged that a married man in possession of a hangover must be in want of an alibi. The periscope revealing that the horizon is for the moment free of Dreadnoughts bristling with depth-charges, I decide that I must surface, if only to blow the tanks, so to speak. That done, I can get on with the business of the day.

Younger readers should take note: however unpleasant the immediate consequences, it is always better to be up and at 'em after a night on the grog than skulking in the slough of despond. Headaches can be banished through the application of cures diverse; excuses for behaviour boisterous or amorous may be a little trickier, but a clear head will help you dissemble more effectively and it is impossible to dispose of any incriminating evidence if you are stuck to the sheets as firmly as though you were wearing Velcro pyjamas. Hangovers notwithstanding, on a Sunday morning, I, Harpic, make it a point of honour to be up and about early and off to the newsagents to collect my Sunday papers – or more accurately, Ostrakov's. He being a Communist and so enamoured of that utterly subversive rag *The Observer*, I make sure that I buy all four copies delivered to the village so that he will have to read something else and so open his closed Communist mind. Accomplishing this task means getting up early, however dense the fug.

Out and down the cul-de-sac, I ignore the sensation of wearing a balaclava and give as cheery a wave as can be managed under the circumstances to Chubble the Postie who is coming down the path of Mrs Johnson, the recent divorcee.

'Sunday deliveries from the recently privatised Royal Mail, I see. Ah, the wonders of the free market.'

'You might say that,' he replies, with a grin. 'But I hear you're no slouch on that front either.'

Before I can ask him what is meant by this cryptic comment, he is away on his bicycle, though looking a little saddle sore from this angle.

A little further on, Barney the Builder is emerging from his lair, looking frowzy but still human.

'Magnificent, Harpic,' he calls out. 'Truly magnificent.'

'Bugger me, Harpic,' says Trucker Higgins emerging from a ditch. 'I don't know how you do it.'

'Do what?' I protest.

'You know,' he replies, with an appalling wink. 'Still, what happens in The Hanged Man stays in The Hanged Man, eh?'

I march on, mystified, until confronted by Mehmet and his *Racing Post*.

'Fackin' good effort, mate,' he declares and pats me on the back. 'Pity about the tiger.'

For a moment, I have a fleeting glimpse of a waste paper basket, cheese and bacon on toast, a Zombie Harpic and a ruined tie.

'Whatever do you mean?' I ask.

'Legendary,' he replies, leaving me doubly mystified.

At the Newsagents, I see Miranda McNulty, turban in a delicate state, scuttling off with her copy of the *Mail on Sunday* tucked under her arm. I attempt a cheery wave, but am blanked in reply. Inside, I buy up the available copies of *The Observer* and then pick up my own *Telegraph*.

'I hear you've got a whole section to yourself on the Celebrity pages,' says Mrs. Perry, Chief Gossip By Appointment. She is a large, red-faced woman with a permanent pinched look of disapproval and a froggy mouth. I detect a note of disapproval in her tone.

'I'm sure I don't know what you mean,' I reply.

'Tell that to *her*,' she says, archly, nodding in the direction of Miranda McNulty's back.

A chill goes down my spine.

'Tell *what* to her?' I say.

'You *know*,' says Mrs. Perry, through gimlet eyes.

'I can assure you, I do not know anything,' I reply.

'Well, it's not for me to say, is it?'

'What isn't?'

'You know.'

'No, I don't know,' I insist.

'Well you ought to know better then.'

There seems little point in continuing with this dialogue and so I retreat. Half way back to the cul-de-sac, Denning slows down his car to a practiced kerb crawl and hands me his business card.

'Just in case,' he says, winking in a fashion unlikely to inspire confidence in a man on Death Row. 'Mum's the word. Tricky business.'

I am still in a state of profound ignorance when Carruthers approaches from across the bean field.

'The alpacas are fine,' he says. 'No thanks to you.'

'Is that code for something?' I ask.

'Least said, soonest mended,' he replies and hops over the gate back into the bean field.

'Morning Mr. Harpic,' says Ostrakov, appearing as if from nowhere. 'I see you are delivering newspapers for those unable to collect them themselves. How generously public spirited of you. The village is proud of you.'

'I do what I can,' I answer.

'I see you are a *Telegraph* reader?'

It is a comment pregnant with the sweat of Show Trials, the stench of torture chambers and the chill fear of the Gulag.

'They do have some good writers on their staff, don't they?' he says, through his goatee Leninist beard. 'Although I prefer *The Times* on balance.'

I am not fooled. The *Socialist Worker* is more his style and I move on, comforting myself that he will never besmirch the village with his *Guardian* and *Observer* while I can still afford to buy up all the copies.

'Oh and don't worry about last night,' he adds, from a distance. 'I'm sure your conscience is clear.'

Determined to clear up this mystery, I head home with redoubled energy and upon reaching my garage nesting place, attempt to reconstruct events by assembling the evidence before me. My jacket reveals a wallet empty of Bill Gon's £50 note and, except for a Bolivian Boliviano, devoid of any other legal tender. There are also two tufts of what looks like alpaca wool and an ear-ring, which is unmistakeable as one of a pair commonly worn by Miranda McNulty. My heart sinks.

In the other pocket is a key piece of evidence in the form of a folded piece of paper which when opened reveals itself as the architect of my misfortunes.

The Second Hanged Man Annual Beer Festival.

Tipler's List.

Sample all of them over the Weekend and get a free Tee-shirt!

Golden Rain 3.0%

Pats Gniss 3.1%

Carter's Colonic Irrigation 3.8%

Garden Sprinkler 4.0%

Fat Pig 4.1%

Drunkard Bar Steward 4.4%

Ducky Fuzz 4.6%

Flock of Starlings Stout 4.9%

Farting Fox 5.0%

Bitter Ending 5.3%

Old Scrunge 5.8%

U-Boat 7%

Please note: It isn't necessary to sample all the beers in one session to qualify for the free Tee-shirt. Drink Responsibly.

I note with some dismay that I am wearing a Tee-shirt that I did not own before. I sense an impending disaster. Time for breakfast.

The Weigh-in?

On a Sunday? Barbaric.

I enter the kitchen with a certain amount of trepidation and immediately see that my trepids were well dationed. It looks like a pork shoulder bomb has gone off and I have another little flashback of last night's gaieties. At some stage, I must have decided that a roast pork sandwich was an achievable aim and had made sterling efforts to achieve it; there is a loaf scattered about in varying stages of crummage, crackling gently softening in the sink, salt strewn liberally around, the microwave door off its hinges, a fork standing up in the butter like Excalibur, an opened pot of jam (jam?) and the remains of a noble roast looking like it's been had by werewolves. There is also a bloodied carving knife on the counter; for the first time, I notice several plasters badly arranged about my fingers. On the cupboard door is a Post-It Note from my Dearest: *'Look on your works O Harpic and Despair.'* I take this as an admonishment and decide that I had better wash up before the crisis requires a UN Peacekeeping Force to be deployed. Never let it be said that Joely Harpic cannot see the wood for the trees or is unable to prioritise.

Washing Up: Harpic's Universal Principles.

A chap will need to learn how to wash up if he is to enjoy his retirement to the full, especially if his other half is possessed of such a generous nature as to continue working while he mans the Home Front.

1. Always use Fairy Liquid. Accept no substitutes. Remember that hands that do dishes can feel as soft as your face with mild green Fairy Liquid. This I picked up from my sainted mother who was a dab hand at directing washing up operations.
2. Never use Marigold Gloves or wear a pinafore. They are not masculine.
3. *Hot* soapy water is essential. Washing up in cold water may seem like an economical use of electricity or gas but it does not produce the desired results. Things will remain greasy. Global Warming will have to be risked.
4. Glasses first, then plates and cups, then cutlery. Then change the water for pots and pans and general cooking utensils.
5. It really doesn't take very long and is nowhere near as difficult as Feminists make out.
6. Only wash up once per day. Otherwise it's a fag.
7. An amusing trick when other people are washing up is to place a pig's trotter in the water overnight. Just see their faces when they reach into the water and brandish it aloft!
8. Do not use pan scrubs on non-stick pans.
9. If the hot water takes a long time to reach the sink, collect the cold water as it comes out of the tap in a vase or other receptacle and put it in the watering can for use on the garden later. This will conserve water and thus cancel out your contribution to global warming by having hot water. You can congratulate yourself on this easily achieved carbon-offset measure.
10. You don't need to dry up. Things dry naturally.

Breakfast.

Whatever the challenges ahead, no matter how high the odds stacked agin you are, however strait the gate, one must never neglect the gentle art of sausage eating. It calms the nerves, clears the brain, steadies the soul and goes a long way to ensure that you are the indeed the Master of your Fate. Or if you aren't it certainly helps to cope with probable wrath, bludgeonings, the charge sheet and the possibility of tears. This morning, I turn quite naturally to the Ginger and Spring Onion variety that I picked up from the Pop Up yesterday and what a triumph they are.

There are some people who swear by the Full Monty on a Sunday morning and although I have some sympathy with this view, I cannot really lay claim to being an uncritical fan of this most filling and celebrated breakfast. Named originally after General Montgomery who, according to received wisdom, declared that all the troops should have a full breakfast before storming the positions of the Afrika Korps at El Alamein, the term has recently been confused with a tawdry type of striptease. This was due to a rather depressing film about a bunch of Northern bums who, having been liberated from the tyranny of drudgery that the rest of us were wont to call 'work' and which they were always striking against, decided to put on a male strip show despite being in receipt of benefits and despite the employment opportunities provided by the expanding Financial Services sector beckoning them from the prosperous side of the North/South divide. The only thing it has in common with the true breakfast is the name but it is entirely typical of Communist cultural entrepreneurs that they should want to besmirch a great British institution with schoolboy jokes about exposed genitals; it has nothing to do with sausages at all.

And the Full Monty *is* a British institution; the combination of bacon, sausage, mushrooms, tomatoes, beans, fried or toasted bread, hash browns or sauteed potatoes and eggs has won a place in the nation's heart and far from it be for me to criticise this traditional marvel. And yet still, I confess to harbouring some reservations, but not any that would mark me out as a Communist sympathiser like Ostrakov or Channel 4 or the BBC. My objections are purely culinary.

Take the mushroom; this useful fungus is incomparable when combined with cheese, garlic, a dash of balsamic vinegar, some red onion and then placed under a grill. Similarly, sliced and fried up with bacon and garlic, it makes a fantastic starter for any meal and its addition to stews and pies cannot be challenged by any rational man. Yet when placed on a plate alongside the honourable sausage and venerable bacon, its sometimes slimy texture makes it lose some of its allure. To me, mushrooms are best left until the evening, even though I am aware that dedicated mushroom hunters swear by an early morning chanterelle. It is understandable.

The stewed tomato is something of an abomination really. Tomatoes are wonderful things to eat with salads, are delicious when stuffed with a Bolognese type sauce and baked and their central contribution to Italian cuisine when peeled, de-seeded and reduced to a puree or passata cannot be understated. Where would we be without decent pizza topping? Back in the Stone Age, that's where. However, when boiled and then placed on the plate their appearance can only be described as rather grossly humanoid, redolent of something only recently killed in a very grizzly and painful manner by anthropophagi, then peeled. Best avoided, I feel, on aesthetic grounds alone.

Baked Beans are a staple of the nation and it pains me to level a breakfast criticism at them and yet, like the mushroom, I feel that this is an evening item rather than one for the morning. One need not descend to farting jokes to make this point; would one eat *Saucisson Toulouse avec haricot blanc et sauce tomate* for breakfast? Of course, not; the idea is ludicrous. But one would definitely wolf down beans and sausage for tea, wouldn't one? Of course. In this case, I disqualify beans on the grounds of timing.

Fried bread is a difficult area because in the North country it has been traditional to use lard, which the serious gourmet dieter cannot really condone as an aid to weight loss. In the South, healthier oils have been used, but sunflower oil and olive oil really doesn't have the depth of flavour to compete with this Northern delicacy. Being more highly civilised, we Southerners have eschewed the need to clog our arteries up with cholesterol in order to prevent the early onset of emphysema brought on by chewing tobacco down coal mines. It is why we invented Financial Services.

Hash Browns are a recent development in breakfastology and I confess that I am not at all inclined to give them the time of day. I have no objection on principle to shredding up a potato and frying it, but I do feel that the preparation of this item betrays a certain laziness. Why not turn to the Swiss *Rosti* for inspiration or perhaps roll a little left over mashed potato in breadcrumbs to provide a well turned croquette? These both seem to be admirable alternatives. My main objection though is that the presence of potatoes on a breakfast plate violates the overall health giving properties of this national dish. There are just too many calories in fried potatoes – and that goes for sautéed potatoes too. Best to leave them off the plate or, at best, have Bubble and Squeak instead.

Eggs I will dismiss entirely but as this is a subject which merits deeper investigation, I will leave it until later and content myself with bacon, sausages and the noble toast. After last night, I don't have the appetite for much more.

No sooner has the last bit of sausage toddled off down the little red lane than the sound of Louise's mobile can be heard, ringing like a tocsin. Ask not for whom the bell tolls, I say to myself; it tolls for thee, Harpic and I decide that it is probably a good idea to make myself scarce until such time as I can more securely reconstruct the events of last night. Before the first call is over – and I suspect that the 'call waiting' function might well be taxed to its limits given the eagerness with which ladies are apt to pass on bad news to their girlfriends – I have strapped on my trusty boots and have exited the front door for the second time this good Sunday, O Lord. Church, here I come.

Generally speaking, I try to avoid Sky Pilots and After-Life Insurance salesmen like the plague principally because I can't afford the church roof bills that accrue from lightning strikes whenever I venture within ten yards of a lytch gate. It is also the case that religion and a sense of humour rarely coincide – I make an exception for the great Dave Allen here – and despite much talk of meekness and inclusivity, Roopie and I have been ejected from Midnight Mass on Christmas Eve on several occasions for bringing a little light banter to the proceedings. Admittedly, straying from the authorised versions of the carols being sung is not everyone's idea of wit, but even the most bigoted zealot must admit that sheep do occasionally fart however Silent the Night and that 'In the bleak midwinter' does need cheering up a bit (although possibly not with a kazoo). As for Good King Wencleslas, there is more than enough historical evidence to justify the view that *the silly bugger did fell out/ on a red hot cinder*. There was absolutely no need whatsoever for the un-theological language that followed on that particular Noel. As I say, theology and humour do not make good bedfellows. Think of the Ayatollah.

On this day, I feel the need to consult with the Vicar of St. Moses the Black, mainly because a hazy recollection is beginning to appear as through a glass darkly that the Right Reverend Richardson played some part in last night's events. And if you can't trust a man of the cloth to give an unbiased yet sympathetic narrative of events, who can you trust? Mind you, there have been some dodgy Popes and as I head down towards the House of God, I am reminded of one such Pope and the efforts of the Office of Religious Works back in the 1960s to get lots of black babies into heaven.

It was while my father was doing Missionary work in the North that his attention was drawn to the activities of a Bolivian Catholic Canon in this respect. Basically, the caper was to sell cut out pictures of black babies said to represent the poor benighted heathen in darkest Africa to the children of the poor benighted heathens of darkest England in return for their pocket money. The babies could be coloured in with crayons and I can tell you now that anyone viewing the resultant variety of hues that were said to represent the poor benighted heathens of Africa in the imagination of the poor stunted, be-ricketed brats of the Satanic Mills would have had a fit. Purple, orange, green, blue and mixtures of the above were the order of the day; the Bolivian tried to explain all this away as being representations of the diseases that the poor black babies of Africa were suffering from and so making their way up the Stairway to Heaven in such numbers. Brushing aside all suggestions that perhaps food and medicine should be the object of the exercise if the pocket money tax was to go ahead, the Prelate of Rome promised that the funds raised would guarantee a place in heaven for the black babies who would otherwise have to go into Limbo, which is a kind of waiting room for deceased heathens – or was until a subsequent Pope abolished it (which begs the question of where the residents of the Republic of Limbo went to; if the Heavenly admissions procedure is anything like our immigration and asylum system, they're probably all sat on comfortable clouds, eating ambrosia and strumming on Angel tax-payer funded harps while sticking two fingers up at St.Peter). In reality, the loot went into the coffers of the Vatican Bank after some dodgy Mafia types had robbed the Holy See blind. The cove who thought up the scheme was subsequently found hanging under Blackfriars Bridge with a copy of *The Holy Blood and the Holy Grail* in one pocket and *The Da Vinci Code* in the other, which leaden tomes are just the sort of thing that might lead to a determined suicide attempt.

As you can imagine, my father was outraged by the deception and took to robbing the poor box at the Catholic Church every week in righteous indignation and retribution. He used the money to provide free gruel to mill girls under the banner of Protestant Aid. The Bolivian was so angered by this that he retaliated by banning all the Protestants from attending the monthly dance at the Catholic Parochial Hall; 'no Credo – no disco, mate,' was about the size of it.

The carillon of bells is ringing brightly and loudly as I approach the church of St. Moses the Black, which is a bit of a mixed blessing in my present fragility although I really have only myself to blame for this. Ostrakov lives nearby and once conceded that although he enjoyed the sound of bells, the campanologists could sometimes be guilty of little too much enthusiasm on certain Sundays.

'Troika bells more to your taste, eh?' I challenged.

'Oh no,' he replied, through those shifty Communist eyes. 'It's just that I like to ring my Great Aunt Gertrude on a Sunday morning – she's in a hospice in Bognor – and her voice is so weak now that she is a little difficult to hear.'

At this I snorted with derision. Great Aunts in Bognor hospices, my eye! Keeping up with his KGB controllers more like! I resolved then and there to bung the bell-ringers a fiver for an extra loud effort every Sunday morning so as to scupper his plots. This particular Sunday morning they seem to be hoping for a tenner.

I am distracted from my mission by the appearance of the three venerable gentleman who, though of ragged and dishevelled appearance, appear in fine spirits this morning and I determine to ask them if they have insights into the previous evening that they may wish to share with me.

'Shocking,' says the first.

'Outrageous,' says the second.

'Shouldn't be allowed,' says the third.

'Bark,' says Bark.

This response, though capable of being interpreted as over-judgemental, I take as heartening for if they have not been jolted out of their well-worn groove by any actions on my part then nothing I have possibly done could be *that* shocking, outrageous or worthy of being banned. Unfortunately, the delay caused by this frank exchange of views means that I am too late to make it to the church and though the last cadaverous body slides in only moments before my arrival, the richly be-robed Right Reverend Richardson is adamant.

'I fear for your mortal soul, Harpic,' he says, rather ungenerously I feel. 'Matrimony is a serious thing and not to be corrupted by Bigamy.'

'Unless you happen to be Muslim or a Mormon,' I quip, but he is not to be drawn into a debate on comparative religions, however ecumenical his ministry purports to be. This is disappointing behaviour from a man of the Church of England and only cements my view that the Break From Rome was not break enough and Henry VIII should have gone one further and invented a whole new religion, like the founder of Scientology, L.Ron Hubbard, whose views on the Deity being of Extra-terrestrial origin are worthy of consideration. This aside, it is only when the ancient welcoming door of the church has been barred against me that the full import of his words strike home.

Bigamy?

Oh Lord, now I am well and truly in the soup.

It's worse than Adultery, you know.

Looking up at the church clock I see that it is now 11am and thus at least a full hour before I can fully investigate matters by going directly to The Hanged Man. I see there are a number of freshly laid stems about the churchyard and the thought does cross my mind that a propitiary bouquet may go some way towards repairing relations with the Memsahib but I dismiss it. Spouses can smell graveyard bouquets just as they can instinctively distinguish petrol station flowers. There is also the size of the offence – the magnitude of which is as yet undiscovered - to be taken into account for upon this will depend the size of the bouquet; the basic rule is that the bouquet must be at least twice as large as the bollock you have dropped if it is to be deemed acceptable. Neither option is a possibility because the petrol station is too far away to walk to and the thought of venturing any closer to the old homestead to pick up the car while the mystery of last night's bigamy is still unsolved is about as attractive as putting one's penis in a bulldog clip. I confess; I am beginning to panic.

Roopie roars up in his corvette at just the right moment. He is looking sharp, dapper and full of vital health, salt and pepper hair waving in the wind. He is my rock in a hard place, my umbrella in the tempest, my lifeboat off the Titanic.

'You look like death warmed up this morning, Harpic,' he says, coming off the accelerator and quelling the beast. 'Fancy a snifter?'

'Just the ticket,' I reply, accepting the epns hip flask gratefully. 'Troubles weigh heavily on me this morning, Roopie, old chap. Seems I may have overstepped the mark at some stage last night.'

'Jumped over the broom would be a better way of saying it,' he replies. 'Miranda McNulty thought all her Christmasses had come at once - until the Vicar stepped in.'

'Ah,' I say, taking a second pull on the flask and appreciating the arse-hair shrivelling properties of the fiery cordial within. 'That explains a great deal. Question is; what to do about it.'

'I daresay the telephone hasn't stopped ringing all morning?' says Roopie.

'We'll need to put in another line I think,' says I.

'Ah well then,' he replies. 'Time for the application of *Muti*.'

'*Muti*?'

'Muti,' confirms Roopie. 'Got the wheeze from Carruthers. It's what Zulu warriors give their official wives before telling them about the *unofficial* ones. Softens 'em up a bit and mutes the reaction somewhat.'

'Excellent,' I say. 'Where do I get some?'

'South Africa.'

'Bit of a long way to go on a Sunday morning, Roopie,' I remark.

'Very true, old boy,' he agrees. 'Fortunately the kids at the skateboard ramp usually have a fairly reliable supply.'

'It is *morning*, Roopie,' I remind him. 'The skateboarders will not be up before the late afternoon at the earliest.'

'Perhaps Carruthers has got a bit spare?' Roopie suggests.

'Not sure I'm in his good books right now,' I reply. 'Something to do with alpacas.'

'Yes,' agrees Roopie. 'I'd forgotten about the alpacas. Magnificent that was, Harpic. Never forget it.'

'What did I do?'

'Best let Carruthers enlighten you there, old chap,' he says. 'But trying to teach them to recite *om mani padme hum* was inspired.'

'*Om mani padme hum*?'

'You had mistaken them for Llamas, apparently.'

'Was that the worst of it?'

'Not at all, Harpic,' he says ominously. 'Not the half of it.'

I hand him his hip flask back.

'Drinks later?' he says, before opening up the throttle. 'If you are still in one piece?'

Roopie my rock has turned into a hard place, my umbrella has turned inside out in the storm and it's women and children only in the lifeboats. I have had better Sunday mornings, though by the sound of it, not many better Saturday nights. There is nothing to be done except to return to the scene of the crime and seek the full unexpurgated version from the landlord of The Hanged Man.

I repair there, heavy of heart and doomed by evil forebodings and only slightly buoyed up by the thought of a restorative JCB and yet I am denied even this small solace because I am early and the place is not yet open. I sit on the bench by the tavern door and look up at the sky. There is a possibility of rain, perhaps even squalls and a thunderstorm. I have come out without my umbrella and seem to have developed a tick in my left eye. I also seem to have developed a very warm left foot and looking down I see that a very small dog of indeterminate breed is lamp-posting me. I shake it off, remove my sock and shoe and roll my trouser leg up in an attempt to limit the damage. Can Harpic be reduced in circumstance much further?

I look up and discern the looming, massively titted Tabitha Greenwood approaching through a sulphurous fog of her own exuding. Her green eyes are glittering, her flaming hair looks like the fall of Nero's Rome and she has the smile of the blade stilletoing across her face. She is looking down her nose and through her cleavage at me as I bend over the bench wringing urine out of a sock.

'Joining the Masons, Harpic?' she says, taking in my rolled up trouser leg. 'Well, I suppose they might pay for a decent burial – if they can find the bits.'

She moves on, like a massively-titted landslide and I realise that I have met my Waterloo, sunk to the depths of my plumb, reached my nadir and then been run over by the Wheel of Fortune. I am well and truly shafted.

'JCB, Harpic?' says Mehmet, unlocking the sacred door.

'Mate,' I say. 'You are the dog's bollocks.'

Inside the beamed sanctuary, I see my sins lined up against the wall, each with their cooling jacket, distinctive label and tasting notes. I shudder at the thought of what *U-Boat* might have done to me.

'That's £3.50 mate,' says Mehmet drawing the foaming pint of JCB.

I pat my pockets, pull out my wallet and realise that I am temporarily distressed.

'Look in your inside pocket, mate,' insists Mehmet.

I follow his instruction and am amazed to find that the bulge in there is not a misplaced pair of underpants but a comforting wad of tenners atop of which is Bill Gon's £50 note.

'How...?' I mouth, goldfish like.

'You don't remember winning the sweepstake then?'

I shake my head.

'You came in fackin' first in the Inaugural Slimstead Alpaca Stakes Cup.'

'First?'

Mehmet nods.

'Who came in second?' I ask, counting out what amounts to a tidy sum.

'No-one,' says Mehmet, with a twinkling smile. 'The other alpacas were fackin' un-jockeyed.'

'How come I won then? Wouldn't the other alpacas have been faster without having to carry a jockey?'

'You put chillies up its bum,' says Mehmet gleefully. 'It went like greased shit off a fackin' shiny shovel.'

'Was this before or after I married Miranda McNulty?' I say, handing over a fiver, and gulping half the JCB.

'Just after; but before the divorce came through.'

'Divorce?' I gulp.

'Yes,' says Mehmet. 'You got divorced just after your Missus rung up. Fack me she was fackin' furious.'

'Oh Lord,' I say, finishing off the pint. 'Louise knows. That's me for the high jump.'

'Another JCB?'

'Better ought to, I suppose,' I reply. 'This being my last day free and at liberty on God's good Earth.'

Sunday Lunchtime in the Pub.

Sunday lunchtime in the pub is one of the great civilised rituals of England. It is a time for the community to meet up and mingle, the experienced topers rubbing shoulders with the weekend occasionals, the cheery churchgoers, dog walkers, cyclists and those whose labours through the working week have qualified them for the pleasure and luxury of having a traditional meal laid on by a cheery landlord all in the company of old friends, family and the odd unwelcome aunt. In summer the cricketers add their happy banter to the hubbub of conversation, while tails wag contentedly as hands reach down to pat wet noses and glad hand the porky scratchings to the canine members of the community. It is one of the great morale builders of life and, if you are in a bit of a pickle with the bailiffs, in arrears with payments on the mortgage, facing an unwelcome redundancy or being posted to a war zone then one can do no better than have a good old Sunday roast to help perk the old pecker up. It can certainly be recommended for those with unforgiving spouses who might be feeling a little glum at the prospect of an uncomfortable interview with the said loved one over an indiscretion that may need the application of some creative thinking to be survived. Being no slacker in the creative thinking department myself, I still believe that I perform better after a face full of the old roast beef and Yorkshire pudding to help boost and stimulate the old grey matter.

'Mehmet,' I say.

'Coming right up,' he replies.

It appears we have been here before.

Roast beef and Yorkshire pudding.

Beef is, of course, central to the psyche, health and well-being of the British nation (apart from the Hindu bits). Ever since King Charles I knighted that loin of beef, the Sirloin has been a favourite of the table whether served up as a steak or, for them's that can afford it like King Charles, as a roast. Topside is probably the most common fayre for the beefy yeomen of England, although there are those who prefer the more grainy Silverside – excellent for sandwiches when eaten cold. Boiled beef is not so common these days outside certain hackneyed cockney enclaves like, well, Hackney, where it is consumed traditionally with carrots and shrill tunes sung by Pearly Kings gor blimey. In this case the cut of beef is usually brisket, which can be tough. Sometimes, salt beef attracts the attentions of the chattering media classes, but it really isn't worth the fuss involved in boiling it out two or three times; the chattering media classes eat it because they have servants to prepare it for them. By far the best cut for a Sunday roast is rib and although there is some debate over whether it is better on the bone or rolled, I choose to go for rolled rib because it is easier to carve. But feel free to differ if you must.

Good beef is unavailable from supermarkets because the miserable, scrivening little bean counters who run those soulless emporiums refuse to have their capital tied up in warehouses when it could be speeding up the cash flow. Beef needs to be hung up for a minimum of 28 days for it to achieve the correct tenderness. For you squeamish Townies who think the countryside consists of nothing more than cuddly badgers, fluffy bunnies and yokels in smocks and who imagine that meat arrives from a magical place where animals are never killed, 'hung up' does not equate to a fashionable neurosis that you catch from reading Women's magazines. It means 'rotting' and it has to do this for a minimum of 28 days to get the right flavour and texture. Supermarkets rarely hang beef for more than 14 days and make a big noise about their *Rubbishest but Eye-Wateringly Expensivest* ranges hanging for 21 days but it still isn't enough. I know a chap who likes his hung for 52 days or until it glows in the dark; this might be a bit excessive to some minds and it's probably a good idea that the Health and Safety Nazis don't know anything about it but each to his own, is what I say. I once asked the Butcher of Barkingham for his professional views on hanging: 'You or the meat?' he replied, churlishly I feel, but then, after he had stopped laughing and put the meat cleaver down came out wholeheartedly on the side of 28 days or better. Which Proves It.

The rearing of the beef is of prime importance too. It should be grass fed outside and then brought inside for fattening, ideally on a diet of barley and treacle fortified with the odd mangel-wurzel if the Northern peasantry haven't eaten them all. This will give the meat a deep purple colour, a sweet taste and impart a creaminess to the fat. It should not be force fed in a feed lot, packed into a cutting shed in Ireland for slaughter and then encased in plastic wrap for the freezers of large supermarkets. If possible you should always know the farm from which the animal came so that you may be assured of its local, sustainable credentials. You don't need to know its name though; it won't have one; you don't give food names.

Roasting the beef is a surprisingly easy art form to master. For the beginner, one need only remove the meat from its packaging, sprinkle a little salt on it and then place it in the oven on 180C for about an hour and a half. Any fool can do this but the experienced beef lover will keep a trick or two up his sleeve for the amazement of his guests and the delectation of his tongue. Some people like to spike the meat with slivers of garlic; this means cutting up a clove or two and then stabbing the joint with a sharp knife and inserting them. It's a jolly nice way to eat roast beef, if you can get past the French connotations, but a word of warning needs to be added here – it doesn't taste so good cold, so make sure you invite lots of people - or few very fat ones - to make sure you haven't any leftovers. Other culinary masters use the same technique but employ rosemary instead; this too is good, but rosemary can be a bit bitty and so I prefer to infuse the flavours of the rosemary into the gravy rather than directly into the meat. For Topside, I like to rub a spoonful of Madras curry powder into the fat alongside the salt; it does not make the beef taste of curry, but the spices do something delicious to the juices that go to make the gravy. At other times, I might sprinkle an Oxo cube onto the Topside for the same reason. For Rib, however, only salt is needed; a well hung joint of rolled Rib needs nothing else. When cooked, the fat will turn from a creamy white or pus yellow into a delightful crackling – and you don't get crackling from supermarket beef.

Yorkshire pudding is something of an oddity. For many years, when my father was doing missionary work in the North country, I thought it was an insulting term used to describe the leaden temperament of the lumpen proletariat rather than a traditional accompaniment to the noble Sunday roast. I never equated the golden crunchiness of the batter and its luscious slurp when it mopped up the gravy with the grimy masses who would sometimes push their stunted noses up against the windows of our modest mansion on the outskirts of somewhere dreadful.

Looking back, however, I do now recognise the similarity in shape between the Yorkshire pudding and the flat caps of the heathen and I confess to feeling a surge of humility. Think of what the inventor of the Yorkshire pudding endured all those years when he was forced to reside among the clogged slatterns of dark Blackpool, depressing Blackburn, grim Hull or scummy Scunthorpe in pursuit of his Civilising Mission. Think of the years of misery as he kept the flickering candle of hope of relief lit in grim Grimethorpe, the arse end of Ramsbottom, funereal Wakefield or the well-named Grimsby, desperately praying that he might one day be posted back to the civilised South, perhaps to a parish in bright Brighton, sunny Somerset, tuneful Finchingfield or colourful Saffron Walden. Imagine him trying to make the best of grey Bradford, sooty Birmingham, bloody Batley or toilety Bogthorpe and then, his hopes almost gone amidst the desert of rickets, ringworm, dense Trade Unionists and Dark Satanic Mill girls, determined to do one last thing for humanity before his death bed claimed him. To this great man, the Reverend Digby Potterton-Smythe of the Parishes of Sandown and Sevenoaks, we owe the gift of the Yorkshire pudding the recipe of which was bestowed on a grateful nation, written down in a hand palsied by tripe and cowheel on the only piece of parchment that the natives of Brigg had not eaten. It is said he is buried in Bury, behind a black pudding and clog shop. If you want really brilliant Yorkshire puddings, add sage to the mixture.

Roast potatoes are an essential part of a Sunday roast but Slim Hipsters like us have to be aware that they do contain calories – not many, but enough to encourage us to treat them with respect. Six is probably enough but it does depend on the individual size. Again, there are as many theories on the construction of the perfect roast potato as there are people who go to the effort to make them. Let us rule out from the beginning, however, the readymade articles found in supermarket freezers; they are a disgrace to the national cuisine and are really only fit for cattle food or famine relief in Newcastle.

The construction of the perfect roast potato is immeasurably complicated because of the wide variety of potato available from your grocer but it is possible to narrow the field down by removing such obvious contenders as new potatoes or Charlottes – they cannot be roasted with benefit. Similarly, I would avoid overly waxy potatoes - but this is only a matter of taste – and very big ones, which are best used for baking in their skins. Ospreys and Whites aren't that good either, nor are Cyprus or Egyptian varieties and Desiree are probably best avoided. Generally speaking, I'm a King Edward or Maris Piper fan but, as I say, each to his own.

To cook the good old spud, peel and parboil for about twenty minutes until you can push a knife in about half way. Remove from the heat, drain and then rattle them round the pan a bit to rough them up. Some people like to add a bit of cornflower at this stage but I can never be arsed to be honest. Next, put them into hot, clean sunflower oil and deep fry until crispy and golden. This is my favourite way but there are those who swear by goose fat and oven roasting after parboiling; they are noble variations and ought to be tried. In recent years the Fibre and Roughage Brigade have been pushing the idea of *unpeeled* roast potatoes. My views on this are simple; get 'em, peeled, you idle bastard. The only time peel stays on a spud is when it is baked.

Into the Yorkshire pudding must go good gravy. Good gravy is made from the water from the boiled vegetables, salt, pepper, herbs and spices to taste, plus Worcestershire sauce combined with the juices from the roasting tin. Oxo cubes *must* be used; any other item purporting to be stock is a pale imitation and until I see a building on the South bank of Old Man River Thames named the Knorr Stock Pot Tower, I shall remain unpersuaded. Some people like to add red wine or beer – both good options – while others like to add a spoonful of Horseradish Sauce, which is a good tip. However you have your gravy and Yorkshire pudding remember good old Digby Potterton-Smythe who looked into the begging bowls of his Northern charges and saw only the inspiration for this masterly creation. He deserves reverence indeed.

Vegetables are served with a Sunday roast and one must just make the best of it. Peas, though bright green, are really a bit of a waste of time and cabbage is best served with lamb and mint sauce. For beef, carrots mashed with plenty of white pepper are the best option while artichokes are – well, what *are* artichokes? Some people like to mash carrots and turnips – acceptable, certainly as long as one realises that a turnip in the North is orange and called a Swede while a Swede in the South is white and called a turnip, if that makes sense. In all circumstances avoid Sprouts – they are the Devil's Bogies. Broccoli is OK, if a bit girly. Parsnips roasted in the oven are good but not until the first frost has been on them and not after Christmas, otherwise they are woody and floury and, like ready-made roasties, fit only for cattle feed and famine relief in Newcastle.

But what to drink with roast beef? There can be only one answer to this: a South African Pinotage of 14.5% strength. Believe you me, this vintage has no equal and certainly nothing as insipid as a Beaujolais Nouveau or Burgundy can compare. The Italian Barolo sometimes has pretensions in this direction but we may dismiss them as much as we may dismiss the related but still inferior varieties of Hermitage or Cote de Rhone. The Spanish Rioja is not in the same league (although the Toro is not to be sniffed at) and pouring any of that revolting Ozzie Shiraz down one's throat is an insult likely to bring the ghost of the cow back to give you a bloody good goring and serves you right. Australian Shiraz used to be used for make jam and they should have continued on this path. I suppose you could serve it to plebeians at barbecues and I understand that it is popular in some of the grimier parts of Middlesborough, but there is no reason to inflict it upon civilised society. A Chilean red might substitute in an emergency but, in this day and age, we should be reluctant to compromise. You may save yourself the trouble of Argentinian Malbec by pouring it straight into the gutter or Manchester. Good beef deserves good wine and the Pinotage is its acme. So pop the cork – or undo the screwtop – and enjoy its deep berry flavours, the smokiness of its nose and the long, dry peppery sweetness of its finish as the staff prepare your well-earned Sunday lunch. And anyone who even suggests white wine or – God Forbid! – a soft drink should be rusticated forthwith.

'There you go, me old mate,' says Mehmet, producing as fine a piece of rolled Rib as ever graced a table south of Watford. 'If that don't fackin' sort you out, I don't know what fackin' will.'

Looking out through the window at the rose gardens of Slimstead, I tuck in to this undoubtedly effective brain food and by the time I have got through two goose fat roasted spuds and half the Yorkshire pud, the first green shots of recovery have pushed through the intellectual undergrowth and germinated the stalk of a solution. That's the thing about us Harpics: we are never down for long.

Take my grandfather, Captain Havelock Harpic who served with distinction throughout the First World War. He was known as 'Sap' Harpic because of his ability to dig trenches forward towards the enemy in record time and so was always given the job, especially when times got tough. During the Ludendorf Offensive of 1917, he was unanimously chosen by the officers and men of the 3rd City of London Regiment (the Sewage Works Pals) to man the forward position known as the Forlorn Hope in the sure knowledge that he could be trusted to bear the brunt of the German attack. This was an honour that he had been hoping to avoid, having been asked to man similar positions on several other occasions and, truth be told, he was feeling a little glum from all the shell shock. He obeyed, of course, and trudged off with his tin of bully beef and leaky boots and the best wishes of his comrades to do his duty for King and Country. Despite the fact of being shelled by his own side several times due to a break down in communications early on in the battle, he stuck to his position – which became known as 'Harpic's Folly' – until over run by several regiments of fierce Bavarians, among whom was a grotty little corporal with bad teeth, a Charlie Chaplin moustache and a horrible hair-do. I well remember him telling me that he had the blighter in his sights and was ready to squeeze the trigger and consign him to kingdom come when he was seized by a sudden rush of Christian charity and mercy. Considering that such an ill-favoured little sausage-eater couldn't really do the world much harm, given that he had enough to do contending with so many personal grooming issues, he forbore to splatter the brains of the diminutive Hun over a sizeable portion of the battlefield. Instead, he let him go and shot the bloke next to him (there are limits to charity).

This made the old Harpic feel a little happier and impressed on him the truth of the saying that every cloud has a silver lining, which perked him up a bit, and he manned the machine gun and went on to mow down large numbers of Frenchmen, who got in the way a bit, which was irritating but not something to be really concerned about. All in all, he felt a little more chipper as the day wore on and the bag grew. Later on, when the British counter-attack drove the boche back to his own trenches, Sap Harpic was found intact, smiling and indefatigable, atop a pile of empty cartridge cases and bully beef tins, much to the wonder of the Sewage Branch Pals.

'You are a true shithouse rat, Harpic,' said the admiring RSM.

'I have killed all known Germans,' he replied, proudly. And the Sewage Branch Pals were known as the 'Shithouse Rats' for the rest of their regimental existence. (They were disbanded a year later when the war ended and most of them were dead).

So now, by the time Mehmet has tooled up with the sweet trolley, Joely Harpic, the longest serving Lieutenant in the British Army and Consultant to Large Corporations, has moved on from the stalk germination stage to the full blossoming of the springtime bloom of his considerable, highly focussed intellect.

'What's it to be Harpic?' he says. 'Fackin' cheese or fackin' cheesecake?'

This is a conundrum that has puzzled me for many years. Does cheesecake really have any cheese in it? I am convinced it does not; I have never once seen a Stinking Bishop or Lincolnshire Poacher cheesecake; they have always been varieties of fruit – often strawberry or blackcurrant and sometimes coffee or chocolate, but never cheese.

'What kind of cheese do you put in a cheesecake, Mehmet?' I ask, thirsty for knowledge.

'Fackin' cheesecake cheese,' he replies. 'Wot d'you fackin' fink?'

'I think I'll have the Stilton,' I reply, rather crestfallen. Mehmet is not so much of a fount of culinary knowledge as I had hoped, but more of a long arid stretch of dessert.

'Fackin' good choice, mate,' he says, in a genuinely congratulatory tone. 'We buy the cheesecakes in anyway and they taste like shit.'

He cuts the cheese and then retires as is his wont, leaving me to ruminate not just on Stilton but on Stilton and Port and whether one should combine these two wondrous products. As you will be aware, there are those like Carruthers who absolutely refuse to countenance Stilton without an accompanying glass of port while still others consider it as much a sacrilege to mix the two as to have Pussy Riot give the Christmas Day sermon in St.Basil's basilica. I confess I have no strong feelings either way; the noble Stilton is versatile enough to cope with both options, especially if it comes with a nice bit of crunchy celery. I like those Hovis biscuits with it too.

Finally, my repast complete, I come to the full fruition of my donnish ruminations and settle on the perfect way to placate my dearest wife Countess Louise.

'Put the bill on my tab, Mehmet,' I call, the scent of victory clear in my nostrils. 'But give me a double snifter of brandy first, eh?'

'You sure, mate?' he says, ever the responsible landlord. 'You look a bit pissed to me and that missus of yours is a bit of a fackin' dragon, I hear.'

'Nonsense, Mehmet,' I say, with all the sincere gallantry at my disposal. 'If you only knew her like I know her, never a bad word would ever dare cross your lips.'

'I can fackin' believe that,' he says, obliging me by tipping the snifter into a balloon. 'Too fackin' right, I can.'

Half an hour later, thoroughly restored by a good lunch and the moderate consumption of alcohol, it is time to return to the homestead and win back the love and glowing admiration that Louise has only temporarily put into storage. A thorough reconnaissance tells me that she is not at this moment of the late afternoon in residence and this accords with my plans. Slipping in through the front door and heading for the kitchen, I note that she has cleared up the aftermath of the pork bomb and apart from a post-it note requesting me to tidy up the vomit in the shrubbery, all is ship shape and Bristol fashion. This is a point to note, chaps: she will *always* clean up if you leave it long enough. Women are programmed by evolution for it. As I say, it is something to do with their vaginas.

I head to the fridge and prepare a repast that will have her melting into my arms just as she almost did on the night that I rescued her from the card game in Bosnia.

Recipe: Bacon Roses.

Women love flowers and they love bacon so this is a sure fire way to rescue any bollocks that you may have dropped along the way. There are those louche recently privatised postmen who claim that the way to a woman's heart is through her stockings, but we Harpic gentlemen know that the real secret lies in the stuffing. And for this, Sage and Onion is best. The recipe is a piece of piss too, so you don't even have to make very much of an effort.

Step 1. Get some streaky bacon and roll it up very tightly around some Sage and Onion stuffing before placing it in the sort of tray you would use to make individual Yorkshire puddings in.

Step 2. Bung it in the oven until the bacon is done. You might need to drain the excess fat from time to time.

Step 3. While the bacon is cooking, get some celery stalks and cut them at the top so they branch out.

Step 4. When the bacon roses are cooked, stick them into the celery branches at the top. The bacon will look like roses! Voila! Your bacon will be saved.

'Harpic,' says Louise, placing a piece of celery on the plate and dabbing at her satisfied lips with a linen napkin. The candle flickers warmly in the gloaming, spreading a softening light across the dinner table. 'There is a strange and uncertain charm about you that would not be believed were it not experienced directly. Some might say that there is genius in your madness, others that your madness is of the fey variety possessed by sprites, goblins and faeries. Whatever, it is, it has served you well. Your execution has been stayed on condition that I, and only I, am the sole person to whom you will serve this delicacy. Do you understand, Harpic?'

'Perfectly, my sweetness,' I reply, beaming with joy.

'Miranda McNulty is never, repeat *never*, to taste this dish. Do you understand this, Harpic?'

'Absolutely, my Angel,' I say, giving her my special wink. By Jingo, she looks ravishing tonight; all high colour and lips as luscious as a scarlet petunia. 'Fancy getting under the duvet?'

'Do not push it, Harpic,' she replies, a tad icily. 'This is merely a stay of execution, not a reprieve. Now bring me a drink.'

'Two champagne cocktail?'

'It is Sunday evening and I must be among the screaming brats of St.Wicca's early tomorrow, Harpic,' she replies, with the merest hint of a smile playing across her lips. 'I shall require four.'

Day Eight: Stormy Monday

'Revolutions always start on a Monday. The American Revolution began on Monday 4th July 1776. The French Revolution began on Monday 14th July 1789. The Russian Revolution began on Monday 25th October 1917. People should be more awake to the possibility of a revolution happening on a Monday than on other days. It isn't only Kings, Queens and Tsars who need to pay a bit more attention than they normally do on a Monday. This is why coffee is important.'

AJP Taylor.

No one likes Mondays. This is a Fact. Even God fumbled for the light switch on the day he decided to get out of his celestial bed and fill the void with work-related activities. It was the same horrible depression at waking up in the chill light that made him so cheesed off with Adam and Eve over their apple scrumping that led him to expel them from the Garden of Eden, which was an over-reaction in my opinion and probably wouldn't have happened if he'd had a coffee and a bacon sarnie before he found out about the missing Forbidden Fruit. He was so grumpy about being rooted out of bed that he went further and decided that if He had to put up with bloody Monday mornings then there was no reason at all that all bloody mankind shouldn't do the same. This was the famous Curse of God: women would bear their children in pain while men would always have to work for their daily bread. Note, Dear Sisterhood, that this is clear proof that God was not a woman; if he was he wouldn't have gone for the whole PMT bit at all, would he? Fortunately though, he is not an unforgiving God and has ensured that Feminism has triumphed to the extent that not only do women have to do the whole screaming in pain and eating the placenta thing, but they also get to go out to work to earn their daily bread too.

The only way to cope with the sheer misery of Monday morning therefore, is to stick to a routine and just get it over with. When I was in the army, Monday mornings were much like any other morning. Crawl out of sleeping maggot before the crack of sparrow's fart, shiver in the pre-dawn light 'Standing To' in case the Soviet Union should choose to unleash the Communist Horde that morning and then, when thoroughly convinced that Ivan was still in his comfortable feather bed having his tea made for him by buxom Siberian peasant girls, 'Stand Down' and get a brew on, two sugars and powdered milk if lucky. As a Consultant to Large Corporations things were a little easier as I was rarely required to sleep in a hole in the ground – although some of the hotels I did stay in might meet the brief – and there was always time for breakfast and no chance at all of being gunned down by an AK-47 (except in Nigeria).

The Weigh-in.

You will no doubt have lost weight over the weekend simply because your exertions at disco dancing/alpaca racing/walking home on Saturday night because you missed the last bus and the bloody miserable bastard of a taxi driver couldn't fit you in until Tuesday week/whatever will have expended all the calories you have consumed through the consumption of roast potatoes. This is pretty much guaranteed, although I make no firm promises; I don't know exactly *how many* roasties you pigged, do I? This can make a difference, but if you have eaten and drunk in moderation like the old Harpic here, you won't have gone far wrong. To breakfast.

Breakfast: Some New Perspectives on Bacon.

As the longest serving Lieutenant in the British Army, I have had a great deal of experience with a staple of Tommy Atkins' rations known as Bacon Grill. This is a bacon substitute that resembles in some ways the American Spam, but maintains its own distinctive characteristics. It is not pink, for example, and is not accorded the same patriotic status here that it enjoys over the pond in democracy's greatest daughter. However, it does come in cans and is made in a similar fashion, containing cuts of pork shoulder and cured ham combined and flavoured to taste like bacon. It is something of an acquired taste because when fried or grilled it forms a sort of skin which gives way at the bite to an odd layered consistency which, though not unpleasant in itself, can be a novelty for the new recruit. Adaptation is not much of a problem, however, and the young man-at-arms soon follows the grizzled veteran into a shared appreciation. Whether eaten on a cold morning on the North German Plain, enduring the icy blasts of the polar wind in Northern Norway, sweltering under the blazing heat of a Mediterranean sun, in the constant pissing rain of the Falklands or the drear misery of Benbecula in Ultima Thule, its bacon like saltiness is always welcome. Unfortunately, if the bread ration hasn't turned up again because the Quartermaster has just fenced it to a cattle feed lot, it can be a bit of a disappointment; the British Army provides biscuit as the main form of staple and it just isn't the same as a butty.

Not that there is anything wrong with Spam, in small doses, if grilled or fried. It is not a substitute for bacon at all but we may still be grateful for the part it played in sustaining the nation during the Second World War when the Germans conquered Denmark and so cut off supplies of the vital ingredient of an acceptable breakfast. Even today, Spam sustains the grimmer parts of the *Tartanic* where it forms the main source of protein for the benighted and be-kilted Celt and is an essential part of the regular famine relief efforts needed in Newcastle. My Uncle, Jedediah Harpic, certainly has Spam to thank for surviving a torpedo from U-97 in the mid-Atlantic during the dark days of 1942. He was the Captain of the tramp steamer *Harpic Star* carrying Spam and bullets on the Boston-Liverpool run and had unfortunately become separated from the rest of the convoy and armed escorts after a dispute over the exact location of the North Star with his First Officer, who insisted it was in a different place to that which Uncle Jedediah was used to finding it. Being torpedoed unexpectedly and holed right on the waterline, the First Officer suggested that lightening the ship would save it, a plan to which Uncle Jedediah rapidly acceded. However, when the First Officer proposed throwing several tons of tinned Spam overboard, old Jedediah bridled; he had seen famine in Liverpool before the war (moral and intellectual as well as physical) and could not bring himself to see food wasted thus. Nor would he allow a single bullet to be jettisoned as he rightly regarded those precious machine-tooled items from the Arsenal of Democracy as central to Churchill's strategy of winning the war. The First Officer began to tear his hair out as the ship began to founder and the U-97 came on in quick pursuit hoping to slam another tin fish into the sturdy *Harpic Star* and so send her straight down into Davy Jones' locker.

Uncle Jedediah had not been chosen to rescue the vessel from the knacker's yard and breathe new life into the old rust bucket for nothing though. Taking in the dilemma in an instant, he ordered the crew to eat as much of the Spam as possible, washed down with lashings of 190% Proof Navy Grog. Thus, he reasoned, when the laxative properties of the Navy Grog took effect, the process would lighten the load without wasting food and buck the ship's company up into the bargain. Tins were broken open without reserve or ration book, forks issued and the cooks got to work frying, grilling or serving the pink marvel up *au naturel.* The crew set to with gusto; many of them were Scouser First Voyagers who had never seen such bounty – they had been confined to the ship in Boston in case they stole it - and they rose to the task of gobbling the lot with all the enthusiasm of car thief in Toxteth. There was a minor hiccup when the heads proved unequal to the Herculean task of coping with the demands laid upon them, but then old Jedediah had the crew hang their arses over to leeward and thus bypass the block in the plumbing.

Not only was the plan remarkably successful in lightening the load of the ship to the point where the hole was now clear of the waterline, it also frustrated the attempts of U-97 to put another torpedo into the *Harpic Star* because it had to keep surfacing to clear the shit off the periscope. Each time it did so, Uncle Jedediah issued another ration of Navy Grog and the resultant broadside of depth charges forced the crew of the surfaced U-97 to do their jobs with pegs on their noses. Eventually, the beastly Hun decided to attack the heroic freighter for freedom with gun fire but on manhandling the gun into position found that the firing mechanism had been fatally jammed by the key used to open the Spam tins. On top of that the barrel was stuffed with turds, so they just gave up and went in search of easier and less odiferous prey. Uncle Jedediah came home safely (via Bristol, Shannon and Cork due to a renewal of the doctrinal differences on navigation between him and the First Officer) and was proclaimed a hero. He was sunk by the Bismarck later in the year though, but was rescued and rose defiant from his dinghy claiming that it was the Spam tin he had chucked at it that had jammed the steering gear of the Nazi battleship and thus allowed the Royal Navy to sink it. Unfortunately, his claims were never given the credence they deserved and he never got a medal for his heroism purely due to Admiralty spite.

As we're talking about the Atlantic, this seems a good opportunity to mention the bacon that is available on the American side of the pond and I should say at the outset that Americans have a veneration for bacon similar to our own. However, they are not so well versed as their older cousins in this matter and many of them have never really known a proper rasher. I feel there may be an export opportunity for a forward thinking entrepreneur if EU regulations and the Tax man permit. Americans prefer their bacon to be streaky and it can be a challenge to find any other variety at all. They also like to grill or fry it until very crispy and serve it as an accompaniment to eggs, which is a bit of a waste of time if you ask me. This is a cultural difference though; Americans have eggs as their main breakfast item and serve them up sunny side up or on waffles or as something called Eggs Benedict, which sounds alcoholic to me. We Brits, of course, have bacon as our main breakfast item, with sausages coming a close second. Eggs are optional to the Brit, but essential to the Yankee Doodle.

Smoked streaky bacon is known in America as 'Canadian Bacon' although this term can cause confusion because real Canadian bacon is not bacon at all but is what both Brits and

Americans would recognise as loin of pork and is not smoked at all. Similarly, many Americans call Ham 'Canadian Bacon' and fry it for breakfast in a dish known as 'Ham and Eggs' which is nothing like bacon at all. Someone should introduce some EU style regulations here, I feel, as this is just sowing confusion. Still, both – indeed, all – these products are superior to Chinese bacon which is made without salt. I spent some time in China as Consultant to a Large Corporation and can attest to the sheer tastelessness of Chinese bacon (I shudder as I write). There was some relief in the availability of air dried and cured hams which was where all the salt had gone, I presume, and these were perfectly acceptable (although a little sweet, perhaps) when fried. I also knew a Chinese-American chap out there who called it 'bacon' but really it was closer to what Australians and Germans call 'Speck', which just added to the confusion. Fortunately, I was able to buy Canadian ham, which made an acceptable substitute when lightly fried.

Today's Exercise Regime: A Lovely Walk.

There are those who are of the opinion that old Joely Harpic can sometimes be a bit lacking in the sensitivity department. I know this is hard to believe, but I have heard it whispered from several quarters from time to time. This may or may not be the case, but where old Joely Harpic is not lacking is in the computing department and although the gears may creak from time to time, the cogs still roll around and keep the mental abacus turning. So it is that as we set out on our lovely walk, I cogitate on something that Andrea Lloyd let fly at me on the night of the dreadful dragons' dinner party.

'What sort of an idiot is it that is so easily fooled by Bill Gon?' she had said, and though I had not fully understood her meaning at the time, Harpic's own Bletchley Park apparatus had been steadily gnawing away at the enigma of that statement throughout the weekend. Whatever could it mean?

The answer is on the tip of my tongue when I am distracted by an ecological dilemma for there, just where the path passes a lone oak on the way to the Nature Reserve, is a badger being worried by a fox. On closer inspection the badger is revealed to be suffering from TB, while the fox appears to be a toothless old vixen on her last legs. I am paralysed by indecision. Should I take firm hold of a lusty rock, beat the badger to death in an attempt to put it out of its misery and risk the wrath of the anti-cull Fluffy Bunny and Brock the Friendly Badger Brigade? Or should I take that same rock and beat the sad old vixen to death, knowing full well her teeth will never get a good killing grip on the badger's throat thus prolonging the agony of Brock and condemning the vixen to the long slow lingering death of starvation? That might risk bringing the smelly anarchist anti-Hunt lobby down on me though. Perhaps I should rain death down on upon them both? For a moment my vision is filled with the delightful prospect of T.Blair Esq being hounded down by a pack of knackered old foxes and given a dose of TB by a pissed off posse of terminally ill badgers but there isn't much prospect of that dream coming to fruition as long as the bastard is jetting around Central Asian dictatorships in his private yacht. In the end, my dilemma is resolved by Bill Gon, who comes speeding around the corner in his new 4x4, runs both of them over and flies on without stopping. He is a real countryman is Bill Gon and has none of the Townie's false sentimentality about the mewling of terminally injured but not yet dead roadkill.

A moment later and Old Timeon steps forward as if from nowhere, surveys the scene of animal carnage and without more ado despatches both wounded and aged animals with a clean sweep of his scythe as efficiently as any Swiss clinic would wish. Next, he turns slowly to me and, swaying only slightly, fixes me with a sincere stare alarming to the uninitiated.

'Bill Gon is up to something,' he says, slowly and full of portent. 'I can feel it in the water and in the air. The trees are screaming.'

'Really?' I say. 'Screaming is it?'

'There are old trees felled within the sacred precincts,' he says, straightening up and raising his eyes to the sky. 'The Horned God weeps.'

'No, no,' I say. 'Bill's just removing some invader species from the Nature Reserve to preserve the native bio-diversity in a sustainable way. Nothing for old Horny Head to get upset about just yet.'

'Harpic,' replies he. 'The earth convulses beneath my feet. It fears. It groans. Its secrets are violated. I can feel it in my water.'

'Better get that checked out,' I reply, helpfully. 'Could be a touch of the clap from when you had all that Free Love back in the 1970s.'

'Bill Gon,' he mutters. 'Bill Gon. The bowels of the Earth will resist you.'

'Chickadee,' I say to his daughter, who I am distressed to find has loomed up behind me unannounced complete with chainsaw. 'Do you think the old chap is everything he should be today? Perhaps he ought to go home and lie down for a bit.'

'Harpic, you plonker' says Chickadee, a purple painted fingernail clawing away a stray frond of hair. 'Bill Gon is installing a fracking plant in the Nature Reserve.'

'What!' I cry. 'It's the first I've heard of it. How can this be true? How can our green and pleasant land be despoiled by the black talon of industry? Are we so far gone that we must stoop to the level of Yorkshire and dig up hydrocarbons to feed the flames of unsustainable global growth and population explosion? How could this happen to us?'

'Because you're the one who voted it through, dickhead.'

'Me?'

'Last Thursday at the Parish Council meeting,' she says. 'When Bill Gon was going through the planning applications.'

I am appalled, distraught, distraught *and* appalled at my folly and run through the whole gamut of emotions from 'G' to 'T' as the cogs on the Harpic Bletchley Park suddenly clunk into place. So *that* is what Andrea Lloyd was referring to! I thought that she was testing my general knowledge of people with low intelligence! (Technically, an idiot is someone with a mental age of less than three years old or has an IQ of less than 30; both 'dolt' and 'dullard' are synonymous). This is why I was confused; I thought she was talking about someone else or perhaps just making philosophical cocktail party conversation.

Distraught and appalled, I begin to pull at my face and grab chunks of my hair. There is a possibility that I might rend a garment in my despair. Oh what a fool I have been! Great Crested Newts! Invader Species! Fifty Pound Notes!

I make my farewells as quickly as decency allows but eschew my normal characteristic cheery wave as inappropriate behaviour at this time and head off in the direction of the church that stands, like an ark of redemptive hope amid the waving seas of corn about to be despoiled by the monstrous hand of the fracking industry. Visions of Middlesbrough chemical works assail me; stark, visions of twisted metal tortured into the gas works of Bradford appear where once the Old Queens Head slumbered in grace. The sheepfold and green vale of England where sheep may safely graze is torn up and covered in the horrible slum dwellings and affordable housing of lolling dullards (see above for a definition) drawn to the Mammom of industry. Where once fair milkmaids fluttered chaste hankies at honest ploughmen at their honest, noble labours there would now be foul Trade Unionists hauling wheelbarrows full of coal across blighted slag heaps shouting obscenities at factory drabs. No longer would the gentleman angler sit under the sighing willows in the silver morn catching his honest breakfast of tickled trout but he must make way for the shrieking of fishwives piddling in a foul, stinking mire of a seething poisonous canal. Oh fields of Southern England! What terrors of Northern grime have I brought down on you?

Approaching the lytch gate, I spy Ham at his trade, digging a hole in the churchyard to take the revered bones of Cooper the Cooper, recently deceased. Perhaps his long years of honest toil have granted him wisdom? Can he be persuaded to pause in his stately task and share some nugget that might alleviate my mental strife? I find a spot by the churchyard wall and nonchalantly lean over it. Ham has a face like a rusty rivet on a Baltic icebreaker and hands that look like Arctic Hake. His back is broad but stooped from his industry and he rubs it from time to time as though he might massage the years of stretch from its knotty warp and weft.

'Ham,' I call. 'Lend me the knowledge and wisdom of your years. I must know how big a fracking site is.'

'Eight foot,' he replies, without pausing. 'Eight foot by two and a half.'

'Ah, I fear you have misheard me,' I persist.

'Eight foot by two and a half foot,' he repeats.

I decide to rephrase the question.

'How deep does a fracking hole go?'

'Six foot,' he says, without looking up.

I detect a pattern here and decide to test if my instinct is correct.

'How tall was Cooper?'

'Six foot,' comes the reply, with a scoop of earth to emphasise it.

'How wide is the church tower?'

'Two and a half foot.'

'How long will it take me to walk to Barkingham.'

'Eight foot,' comes the reply.

Abandoning all hope of wisdom from this quarter, I turn my back and head for a place where I will be guaranteed the answers to my questions and perhaps be granted the solace I seek: the Pub.

(Wildlife spotted. Not counting the road kill, four rabbits, two muntjac, a pair of pied wagtails and a jay).

Lunch.

No time for Lunch today. Harpic's on a mission. A quick snifter will have to suffice.

The Old Queens Head is run by Perky Pete who had pretentions to poetry before his wife proscribed them and pointed him towards the profession of publican, for which are all mightily grateful. Although he can sometimes be a little mournful at the loss of his vocation and apt to be terse with those legions of parasitical officialdom who wax fat on the imposition of needless taxes and regulations on the honest, self-employed wealth creators of the nation, he maintains a generally sympathetic mien towards those who come to his counter in search of solace and wisdom. This is, of course, the chief function of a publican; no social worker, churchman, doctor or soothsayer can ever match the Tough Love Counselling of the publican and Perky Pete is a master of his profession. His method is not the insipid, arm patting empathy of the 'We Feel Your Pain' brigade but rather the older 'stiff upper lip, pull-yourself-together' variety. Not for him the over-feminised weeping of a faux-guilt ridden wet liberal society! 'How far would that have got us in 1940?' he rails, sometimes to the stars, outside the back of the Pub after closing time. 'Just how successful would Churchill have been if he had confronted the panzer hordes of the Third Reich with nothing more than a load of namby-pamby social workers armed with advice leaflets on getting in touch with your feminine side? No mate,' is his considered advice. 'I don't feel your pain – I make *you* feel your pain. So Man up and grow a pair.' It is remarkably effective, I must say. We don't get many weepy, softy Cecils in Slimstead since he took over.

Maureen, his Missus, is of much the same opinion. She grew up in the North country and is credited with the defeat of the Kray Twins' attempt to expand their business operation there. The story goes that she was working as a bouncer at her father's nightclub in Burnley to supplement her income from the paper round and so finance her dreams of escaping the extreme poverty and general grimness of her surroundings. On one particular evening, just after she had beaten three drunken proles to a pulp with a claw hammer for daring to question her femininity, the Kray Twins turned up on a day trip from the Blind Beggar. Demanding entrance at a favourable rate (free), she defied them in a spirited manner.

'Do you know who we are?' said Ronnie, as Reggie loomed threateningly.

'No,' she replied, truthfully.

The two criminal masterminds looked at each other in mild disbelief.

'You don't know who we are?' said Reggie, as Ronnie loomed threateningly.

'Are you fuckin' deaf, you Cockney wankers?'

Ronnie looked at Reggie and Reggie looked back at Ronnie and then both, in sibling harmony shook their heads despairingly.

'If these Northern monkeys are so ignorant as to not know who we are, it will take years to educate them,' said Ronne.

'And looking around this dump,' replied Reggie, stepping over the malleted proletarians on the pavement and heading back to the car. 'It probably wouldn't be worth the effort.'

'So it was,' declares Maureen when she relates the story. 'That the invincible ignorance of the North triumphed over the entrepreneurial instincts of the South.'

She moved South the moment she reached her sixteenth birthday and married Perky Pete while waitressing at the pub round the corner from Basingstoke Art College, where he was studying ~~drinking~~ poetry.

'Pete,' I say, entering the half-timbered fastness. 'What terrible things are happening to our village? Is it true that Bill Gon is about to frack us and ruin our Arcadian idyll? Give me the counsel of your years, I beg.'

'Didn't you know?' he says, raising an eyebrow in his stern but avuncular face. 'I thought everyone knew.'

'But...but...the Great Crested Newts?' I say, my world reeling. 'I understood he was the guardian of our protected status as a Site of Special Scientific Interest?'

'It's just a few newts,' replies Pete, dismissively. 'And it'll bring business to the village. JCB, is it?'

'It is,' I reply. 'But aren't there larger principles at stake here? A whole way of life? Aesthetics?'

'As long as he spends some of the money he earns in here, I've got no problem with it,' says Pete, handing over the pint.

'But surely, not everything is about money? There must be room for truth and art and beauty, surely?' I hand over my £50 note.

'You got anything smaller?' asks Pete.

'Put it on my slate,' I reply, replacing the note alongside my alpaca racing winnings. 'Surely, we must organise a protest?'

'Go ahead. Be my guest,' says Pete, enthusiastically. 'You can use the Tap room as your base. Shall I contact the media? They're a thirsty crowd by all accounts. But no smelly hippies with no money. We want good quality middle class protesters or none at all.'

'Is there any other kind?' I ask.

'Great,' he says. 'As soon as you've assembled the Boden rent-a-mob I'll get on to the brewery and double the order.'

'Fantastic,' I say. 'Thanks for your support.'

'Another JCB?'

'Well,' I say, weighing up the pros and cons and squaring up to the possibilities that I may just become the Saviour of Slimstead. 'Just this once, then. We Eco-warriors appreciate the natural health giving properties of a pint of good English ale.'

As I say, a bit of Perky Pete's Tough Love Counselling always makes me feel chipper and a couple more JCBs finish the job.

Thank God Monday is Over Drinks.

Never one to shirk my duty, I am home in time for the return of the bread winner and though eager to outline my plans to raise a media storm and fly high the banner of protest against Bill Gon's plan to frack us back into the industrial Dark Ages, I make sure that drinks and dinner are ready preparing for when my dearest returns from her day at the chalk face. So, as soon as the grinding of a slipping clutch indicates her presence on the driveway, I am ready with a soothing drink, served over ice. Today, I'm serving a white wine spritzer.

Recipe: The Stress Clinic Special.

I have always found it amusing to be given advice about moderating one's alcohol consumption by nurses who in my experience have never shown the slightest restraint in this matter once out of the confines of their uniforms (and oft times when still within them). When I was a Lieutenant in the British Army, nurses were regarded as a sort of perk of the job and whenever the Colonel decided to hold a cocktail party in the Mess, those officers of manly appearance were despatched to the Nurses Homes to advertise to the good ladies resident there the prospect of prompt transport, free booze and a good rogering afterwards. I was almost chosen for the duty on several occasions, but the officers of the regiment always insisted that I was more valuable deployed in other ways. Usually, my role was to nip down the Cash and Carry for stuff suitable for a Mickey Finn Guaranteed Knickerdropper, a role at which I flatter myself I excelled. Certainly, I never saw a nurse go home sober from the Regimental Cocktail Party; actually, I rarely saw a nurse go home at all. They were absolutely game for it and all should have been awarded campaign medals for the repeated Battles of Bacchanalia that they so gloriously distinguished themselves in. On one occasion, the RSM found two student nurses had moved in to a sort of annex in the Officers Mess, so impressed were they by the gallantry they had experienced and it was only the fact of a complaint from a disgruntled matron that they had missed two vital classes on surgery that they were ever discovered at all. And shortly after they were returned to their rightful abode the RSM was found in a cheap gin shop with the matron herself kicking up a can-can. I tell you, PMT in a nurses home stands for 'Pissed Most of the Time' rather than anything to do with the intricacies of the female reproductive system. And as to their behaviour when in any sort of proximity to a Mediterranean holiday resort, one need only peruse a tabloid on a Sunday to discover a picture of debauchery, orgiastic glee and reckless abandon; the Ibiza Tourism Ministry opened its own office in the Nurses Home in Colchester while Magaluf is twinned with the Florence Nightingale NHS Teaching Hospital, or so I am led to believe.

The only time I have ever heard anything approaching sensible advice about alcohol consumption from a nurse (sober) was at our own Emily Pankhurst Memorial Clinic in Berkstead where I attend the Stress Clinic every once in a while and I reproduce it in a slightly modified form here. I modified the advice because, although positive in the area of actually treating alcohol as though it wasn't the most dangerous thing since the Black Death, it was still bollocks.

Step 1: Empty a cold bottle of white wine into an ice bucket. The originally advice given was 'pour a spoonful of low alcohol organic vegetarian white wine into a glass' but we can safely ignore this; it wouldn't be worth the effort of walking to the fridge.

Step 2: Reduce the relative proportions of alcohol to non-alcoholic ingredients by adding ice. No brainer, that one is it? Is this what we pay billions in taxes for?

Step 3: To further reduce the relative proportions of alcohol to non-alcoholic ingredients, add frozen grapes. This, I thought, was a wizard trick and gave the stony faced health harridan hiding behind her gold plated pension full marks. You have to have fruit in a cocktail; that's the whole point; it disguises the alcohol from Prohibitionists. You can put a slice or lemon or lime or both, if you're feeling adventurous.

Step 4: Add 50% soda water. Actually, she said add 250% soda water, the spiteful little puritan, but we can safely ignore this as merely unwelcome state funded nannying.

Step 5: Ignore the rest of the bollocks about units and repeat as necessary.

Louise emerges from the car like a bear leaving a cave and grumbles across the lawn towards me.

'Louise, my dear,' I say, handing her a gallon of spritzer.

'No jokes, Harpic,' she says. 'Not today.'

'Today is not a day for jokes, dearest,' I say, adopting a serious tone. 'Did you know Bill Gon is fracking us?'

'Harpic,' she replies between glugs. 'I am no mood to discuss Bill Gon. That little beast of a daughter of his has joined my already over-crowded classroom today and if she is not expelled by Wednesday, she shall surely be murdered by Thursday and I convicted by Friday.'

'No Bill Gon, it is,' I say, as she sweeps past. 'Discretion is the better part of valour.'

'Dinner, Harpic,' she says, heading for the wine rack. 'And no weeds, understand?'

Recipe: Tuna Surprise.

Fish has gained in popularity over the years, though it has always been a major part of the British diet. In times of Yore, fish was usually dried and pickled or in the case of the herring, kippered. A medieval king declared that all Butcher's shops should be closed on Friday to give the fishing industry a boost, a practice thoroughly approved of by the Pope who forbade Catholics from eating meat on Friday and so it became traditional to regard Friday as 'Fish Friday' – which is not what that louche fellow Chubble the Postie means when he uses the term. When Sir Walter Raleigh invented the potato, the ideal accompaniment to a fish supper was born and the humble chip made its first appearance in the newspapers of the nation.

This was one of England's greatest gifts to the world and any suggestion that the French invented the 'French Fried Potato' is no more than a base attempt at culinary imperialism by a people with an inferiority complex gained as a result of coming second to us in the Great Game of Empire. Some deluded people ascribe the intention of chips to the Belgians, but this too is nonsense and is only another example of EU culinary imperialism to be placed alongside straight cucumbers and metric measurement. As everyone knows, the Belgians ended up even further down the imperial medal table than France.

Since the 1990s, there has been an explosion in the varieties of fish eaten. While before one had to do with cod, plaice or perhaps a bit of rock salmon – which is really dogfish – with your chips, now it is possible to go into a restaurant and order things like Mahi-mahi or Red Snapper or other exotic varieties. Furthermore, the celebrity chef culture has led to fish being served *without batter*, a development that I cannot wholly hold with. Indeed, it is rumoured that whole towns in Devon and Cornwall have been commandeered by 'incomers' masquerading as cooks, displacing local pasty shops and turning whole swathes of seaside heaven into pretentious bijou eateries where fish is served with *sauces* and *without* vinegar. It may be fine for vegetarians and for those with made up food allergies, but for the upstanding Briton there can be no other way to eat fish than to wrap it in batter, deep fry it and surround it with chips. All else is mere frippery.

The exception to the batter and chips rule is tinned salmon, of course, but this does actually adhere to the strictures of our culinary standards because it is usually mashed up with vinegar. Placed between two pieces of buttered brown bread with a slice of cucumber, it is a truly heavenly creation. When holding back the Communist hordes as the longest serving Lieutenant in the British Army, I was once issued salmon that had been tinned in 1945 and asked for my professional opinion of it by a curious Quartermaster. It was perfectly fine and a stout testimony to the preservative properties of the canning process. I drew the line at carrots bottled in 1917 though; they had gone white. Smoked salmon is an acceptable exception too – a dab of horseradish, delicious! And caviar eaten off a willing maiden's thigh is a treat indeed. I suppose we might also add prawns to this, although they aren't strictly fish in the accepted sense of the word. Lobster too, and it goes without saying the oysters served over ice with a squeeze of lemon or a dash of Tabasco are acceptable variations on the fish supper too.

During the 1970s, a new addition to the tinned fish family began to appear on the nations sandwiches; tuna. Originally considered to be an inexpensive salmon substitute, it was extensively marketed in the North country where tinned salmon was regarded as an undreamed of luxury and rapidly caught on. I first tried it there and was agreeably surprised by its properties. It is now a staple of my kitchen arsenal and I serve it in several ways. The simplest way is to add vinegar to it in the same way that one would do with salmon but adding mayonnaise also produces a substantial and tasty dish. In the North country, the fishwives would sometimes club together to buy a jar of what was known as 'Salad Cream' to add to their communally held tin of tuna, which just goes to show that Communists can never get anything right. Mayonnaise has, I believe, since been introduced to certain parts of Yorkshire but without any great success. My mother used to add tomatoes to the mix sometimes but this can be tricky; I once knew a chap who almost cut his finger off while trying to slice a tomato one night after a visit to the local hostelry, so it's best to exercise caution. Here then is my recipe for Tuna Surprise – a truly good Monday night meal.

Step 1: Take two slices of bread and butter them.

Step 2: Put some tuna on one piece of bread.

Step 3: Add salt and vinegar to taste. Some people like to add lemon juice, Tabasco or indeed mayonnaise either with or without the vinegar, but tonight I'm sticking with the traditional.

Step 4: Put the second piece of bread on top of the piece of bread with the tuna on.

Step 5: Serve with white wine spritzers or anything else you fancy.

After Dinner Drinks to Boost the Old Grey Matter.

One of the most offensive pieces of propaganda pedalled by the over-paid, feather-bedded NHS Diet and Health lobby is that booze is bad for your brains. Why they should expect any sentient being to accept this nonsense is beyond me. I always feel sharper after a couple of large ones and am convinced that a drop of the good stuff allows me to think more clearly, analyse a problem more incisively and come to a creative solution to whatever problem life has dropped on me as from a great height. *In vino veritas* is how the ancient Greeks put it; it translates literally as *the truth lies at the bottom of your wine glass* and there's no arguing with the truth of that pearl of wisdom. All this stuff about booze destroying the brain cells can only have come from someone so far down in his cups as to be seeing the real world as if he was peering up at it from the bottom of a very deep well. It is clearly and obviously a load of old cobblers. 'Beer is proof of a benevolent God' said Someone Famous and I believe him. The great Edmund Burke, castigator of the French Revolution and general brain box was of the opinion that booze is there to strengthen the morale of those of us struggling with the mortal condition. During WW11, Churchill ordered a ration of two bottles of beer per man per day to be issued just to piss off that mad, bad teetotaller Nazi, Adolf Schicklegruber and thus leading to Victory in Europe. Plato – no mean smarty pants himself – said it was 'a wise man who invented beer' so when you stack all this *proper* evidence against all the scientific bull that you get from those shrivelled up, pinchfisted, miserable naysayers, it's easy to see which side you should come down on. No: the best thing for a case of nerves is a case of Scotch, as WC Fields once said, and the best thing to get the old grey matter working on a situation like Bill Gon's fracking plan is a bottle or two of good red wine.

But which to choose? A quick trip down to the supermarket will reveal such a cornucopia that one could easily be discouraged and go for the tinnies instead. I understand that there may be an inclination to simply start at the top left corner and work your way steadily along the shelves until you reach the bottom right hand corner - just as you would read a book - but this, though tempting, is no way to get the best out of your incipient oenophilia. Instead, a little research will enhance your drinking pleasure and provide you, hopefully, with a life time of interest.

Firstly, it is important to note that there is more than one type of grape used to make wine. For beginner's purposes we can point to four main varieties which we can confidently identify as Shiraz, Cabernet Sauvignon, Merlot and another one which I can't remember the name of just now. Shiraz is spicy and tastes of blackcurrant while Cabernet Sauvignon tastes of blackcurrants but is not spicy. Very often these two grapes are combined, but for the life of me I don't know why; it matters not. They still achieve the desired effect of enhancing the natural curiosity, analytical prowess and powers of memory of the dedicated imbiber. Merlot tastes a bit like the other two, but can be a bit thicker on the palate and bit like the last one as well.

Secondly, the age of the wine is important. This is because the taste changes as it gets older and, I'm told, if it is stored for a long time it acquires several different layers of flavour and a thicker consistency rendering it a bit like chocolate. You can tell the age of a bottle because the year it was made is usually written on the label. If you are buying it in a bag, it means you are supposed to drink it quite quickly, which is helpful. I once suggested to a producer of bag wine that for the sake of convenience they should put a hole for a straw in the top of the box it is supplied in as is common for children's fruit drinks but the idea has not been taken up.

Thirdly, when opening a bottle the true connoisseur will sniff the wine to see if it is drinkable. Sometimes the wine reacts with the cork to produce a rather musty taint and this is known as 'corked' wine. The chap who sniffs the wine coming out of a bag or a screw top clearly does not understand that you can't have a 'corked' wine unless it has been bottled with a cork and is thus a pretentious wanker.

Fourthly, wine comes from lots of different countries in the world but it is generally classified in three rough ways. 'Old World' refers mainly to the major European producers of Italy, Spain and France. Of course, the Germans make wine but it is usually horrible, as do the Austrians who are a bit better at it and the Bulgarians who used to make something called 'Bulls Blood', which was a flaming lie. 'New World' refers to wine made in the colonies of New Zealand, Australia, the United States and South Africa, and to wine made in South America too. Amazingly, wine is made in Canada but I'm not sure why. Wine made in the rest of the world is usually known as 'wine made in the rest of the world' and is usually as rough as a bear's arse.

Amid this system of classification, it has to be admitted that there is room for a certain amount of chicanery. Take for example the varieties known in France as 'Wine from the South'; when they mean 'south' they mean a bloody long way south ie, Algeria. Similarly, wine from the Holy Land might dream up visions of happy Israeli viticulturists dodging Hamas rockets as they go about their daily business with the big vat and the bare feet, while in fact it comes from Jordan and is so shockingly low in alcohol that it is closer to Hell fire than Heavenly wonder. Even when wine is supposed to come from a specific region, the boundaries can prove surprisingly elastic; there are plans afoot to add 35 extra villages to the Champagne region to cope with the buoyant demand for fizz from Chinese Communists and Oil Sheikhs. I once asked a South African chap where the wine he produced came from. 'Stellenbosch,' the lying bastard replied. It was made in a town about five hundred miles north of this Viticulturist's Mecca. Mind you, it tasted alright after the second or third bottle.

So now, armed with a bottle of good bottle of Chilean Merlot or whatever, I am in a good position to approach the knotty problem of fracking. I leave Louise slumped over her marking and head out into the garden to listen to the bird song and ponder on Bill Gon's machinations. Two or three glasses in, the nature of the problem reveals itself thus:

1. Bill Gon is fracking.
2. Bill Gon is Chairman of the Parish Council Planning Sub-committee so he must have had the backing of the Parish Council for his activities.
3. Ostrakov is Chairman of the Parish Council and is a Communist.

4. Bill Gon is not a Communist.
5. Ostrakov is a Communist.
6. Ergo, it must be Ostrakov's fault.

Pleased with this penetrating analysis, I open another bottle just in case more inspiration is needed to reach some concrete conclusions and a plan of action which, fortunately, it is. After further deep thought and another couple of glasses, the solution presents itself thus:

1. Fracking must be opposed otherwise our dear, fair, fair, fair Slimstead will be turned into something horribly polluted and Northern.
2. Ostrakov must be overthrown by People Power.
3. Such a talented and generous person as Bill Gon has obviously been led astray by the Communist Ostrakov and will need to be welcomed back into the Slimstead fold through constructive engagement.
4. There was something else on the tip of my tongue, but it's gone.
5. Oh yes. Quod erat demonstrandum; which means a big demo with lots of banners, singing, chanting, civil disobedience and police-baiting culminating in a big riot which will get us on the Six O'Clock News. No smelly hippies, though.

Pleased that Harpic's own Bletchley Park has performed so well, I toast it with the remains of the bottle and then, so as not to disturb Louise who is still displaying the dedication to education that she will indubitably one day become famous for, go for a piss in the shrubbery. Actually, it's such a lovely evening with all the lovely, lovely stars shining up in the lovely sky that I think I'll just sit down with my back against this tree for a moment and ponder on the glories of the firmament.

Day Nine: Famine Tuesday

'Go to work on an Egg.'

Fay Weldon

The Weigh-in.

Weigh-in? After the morning I've had it really is not necessary, I can tell you. Sleeping out most of the bloody night *sans* sleeping bag burns off calories faster than a blow torch liposuction. One minute I was staring up at the star spangled banner of the celestial states of the universe the next I'm being shocked awake by two foxes at it like knives on the lawn in the dawn's early light. Talk about a rude awakening? It was worse than the first time I was woken up in Basic Training by the rattle of a tin mug in a steel bucket and the RSM's rousing cry of 'Hands Off Cocks. On Socks!' Where's the local hunt when you need them, eh? Bloody Bollocky Blair and his bloody bollocky Trot fluffy bunny brigade put paid to them, he did, the bastard.

Ye Gods, it was cold. The dew had soaked through my trousers, my ears felt like they were about to fall off and the rest of my body had turned blue. By the time I made it to the back door I felt like Captain Oates and when I found it locked and bolted against me it there were more than a few references to Vivian Fuchs expressed. I had to spend the night in the garage, shivering me timbers off and praying for the moment when Louise would finally rouse herself from her slumbers and take pity on a poor humble waif by opening the bloody door and letting me get into the shower to warm up.

When she did finally allow me access to the old soapy swamp and I was able to massage some life back into my exposure-racked frame, I was disturbed by Chubble the recently privatised postie who felt it important to deliver the gas bill personally and at that particular moment. Apparently, he claimed, it was company policy now to deliver gas bills by hand at the least convenient moment possible. And what a bill! Honestly, all I want is a warm shower in the morning and enough even heat to keep Jack Frost at bay but the bloody bastards seem to have charged me for enough gas to inflate a Zeppelin. What is the world coming to? Here we are at the beginning of the 21st Century and we're still paying through the nose for a commodity as cheaply and readily available as natural gas. Have the Russians put an embargo on it in a crude attempt to get their own back for losing the Cold War? It really doesn't bear thinking about.

And if that wasn't bad enough, I got to the fridge only to find a Post-it note informing me that it was Food Bank Collection Day at St.Wicca's and Louise had taken all the bacon to feed the starving of bloody Up-Northernshire. There wasn't a single sausage to be had either. But – and this really was the last straw – she'd left the bloody eggs intact.

Eggs: The Spawn of Satan.

Chicken abortions. Foul fowl things that smell of Hydrogen Sulphide. How on Earth anyone back in our deep distant prehistoric past came up with the idea of eating the revolting things absolutely beats me. Snakes and lizards eat eggs so why a human should wish to emulate them is absolutely beyond me. In the Philippines people eat *fertilised* eggs. That's right! A half formed chicken omelette! In China, they wait until they are a thousand years old before eating them! A thousand year old egg! In America, Eggs Benedict are only eaten to remind Americans that there are traitors in their midst as they are named after General Benedict Arnold who deserted to the British during the Revolutionary War (or returned to his lawful allegiance, depending on your point of view). Pickled eggs in a bag of cheese and onion crisps – an abomination. *Curried* eggs! What satanic fartmeister invented them? Think about poor old Humpty Dumpty having his head bashed in with a spoon and then - horror! – his honour guard of honestly recruited, well-trained and expensively paid soldiers forced to dip their heads in his brains! It's horrible! It's a Freudian nightmare or something like that and quite possibly grounds to call in the Child Protection Agency. Whether fried, boiled or poached the result is the same horrible slimy ectoplasm wrapped around a yellow blob of life-threatening cholesterol that no seeker of the svelte can ever countenance anywhere near a decent breakfast plate. It's the reason why Italy is in such a mess: the national dish is pasta which is basically eggs hidden in flour. It's easily available, simply grown peasant food and thus a hindrance to economic development. If old Farmer Giuseppe is happy munching his pasta, he's hardly likely to put in the extra effort required to produce bacon or beef is he? And what happens to the economy when you remove the incentives to hard work and innovation? That's right! You get Italy. Would there be a Berlusconi or a Mussolini if Italians had been brought up on a diet of bacon and beer rather than pasta and Vino Collapso? It cannot be imagined.

Sophisticated readers will remember the fine scene in Alan Parker's 1987 classic *Angel Heart* when Robert de Niro, playing the devil, meets Mickey Rourke, a hapless gumshoe PI in an empty, all white restaurant. 'Some cultures regard the egg as the symbol of the soul,' he says, while cracking the shell of a white boiled egg on an equally white plate of bone china with a perfectly clean, white fingernail. Mickey Rourke is mystified, as well he might be, and not a little shocked when the devil proceeds to bite into the egg with equally white teeth. The *Eater of Souls* is another name for the devil, in case you hadn't guessed and what is the devil's favourite food? Eggs: I'm not at all surprised.

If this isn't enough to convince you that eggs are just not the thing for a chap then one need only think back to the 1983 Feminist novel *The Life and Loves of a She-Devil*. This was a terrible tale of horrid revenge, body sculpting and mushroom soup told by a jilted woman with a moustache who could have avoided all the trouble she put herself and her ex-husband through by just losing a bit of weight and investing in some electrolysis to get rid of the moustache. Disturbing enough, I'd say, but when you take into account the fact that the book was written by Fay Weldon who also worked for the Egg Marketing Board to popularise the advertising slogan 'Go to work on an Egg' the worry factor goes through the roof. This pretty much proves a satanic connection in my mind and if old Matthew Hopkins, the Witchfinder General, was still around, he'd be all over the lot of 'em a rash. Be advised: avoid eggs, even if it means a meagre breakfast.

Just wait until she gets home. This has not been a good start to the day.

Today's Exercise Regime: Raising the Flag of Rebellion.

Obviously one cannot be expected to organise an anti-fracking protest on an empty stomach so I hop into the car and head for the Red Bus Transport Café on the Barkingham Road. This venerable institution has been serving fry-ups and bacon sarnies ever since the vehicle itself coughed its last splutter of oily black exhaust fume during the Winter of Discontent in 1979 when the idle Trade Unionist bus driver who should have maintained it declared that there was 'sumfink up wi' differentials'. He was referring to the unfair difference in pay rates between him and a heart surgeon; the bus was referring to its gear box and so the old Atlantean came to a halt in its present position, a leafy lay-by much abused by members of the dogging community, and was bought up by an entrepreneurial professor of physics, who turned it into a highly successful and thoroughly well regarded greasy spoon. I leap aboard my trusty steed – which Louise has mysteriously eschewed for the day – and head for breakfast Nirvana. I have not reached the end of the cul-de-sac before I see the Post-it note fluttering from its attachment on the glove compartment.

'Gear Box, Harpic,' it says. 'Get it fixed. Do NOT attempt to do it yourself.'

That's it with women isn't it, eh? As already noted, a woman's work is never done, but that's because it consists mainly of thinking up jobs for men to do. This is Harpic's Corolary; women think up jobs for men to do, *then* tell them how to do it, *then* insult them by casting aspersions on their ability to fix a simple problem like a slipping clutch. It really is infuriating.

Fortunately, it is not far to Professor Birch's Barkingham Road Red Bus Transport Café and the clutch performs adequately enough to get me within range of a bacon sarnie and a good squeeze of brown sauce. I pull up and bound aboard this temple to industrial fortification and give a cheery wave to the three truckers who are already elbow deep in baked beans and good, healthy fried bread. There behind his counter is the rotund, opaquely-bespectacled figure in a heavily stained apron that has given his name to this excellent eaterie.

'How many rashers, Harpic?' says Professor Birch, returning my wave with a dripping spatula and stubbing his cigarette out.

'As many as you can get between two pieces of a standard white, medium sliced loaf,' I reply, brandishing a fiver. 'And I'll have a chipped mug of instant coffee, two sugars and milk from the bottle that has not been chilled to death in the fridge.'

'Lashings of brown sauce?' he asks, with his sympathetic smile. He really is a decent old cove, much wasted in academia, I'm told. Still, it is always pleasing when a man finds a metier to match his talents and his girth.

While the hiss and spatter of fizzing frying bacon fills the firmament and reminds me of why I am still alive, a thought occurs to me and without pausing to assess its worth, share it generously.

'I say, you chaps,' I declare. 'Would you be interested in joining my anti-fracking protest group? None of you are smelly hippies so you automatically qualify for the selection procedure.'

'You one of the Greenpeace dickheads?' says a trucker in a red plaid shirt and lime green Hi-vis jacket.

'Certainly not,' I reply indignantly. 'We don't want any of that environmental nonsense here.'

'Good,' says Trucker #2, slurping builders tea from a pint mug. 'Greenpeace are bollocks. Have you seen the size of my gas bill?'

'You don't need to tell me about gas bills,' I reply. 'I had mine this morning. It's outrageous.'

There is something of a pause, broken only by the sound of masticating, two farts and a monstrous burp.

'You sure you've thought your protest through Swampy?' says Trucker #3, wiping up the last of the tomato sauce and egg with a slice of industrial white.

'Of course, I have,' I reply. 'We can't have hydrocarbons being fracked into the environment willy-nilly though can we?'

'How did you get here?' asks Trucker #1.

'By car,' I reply.

'How did everything you own get delivered to the shop you bought it from?' asks Trucker #2.

'In a van,' I reply.

'How do you think Professor Birch here runs his cooker and his fridges?' asks Trucker #3.

'With electricity from a power station,' I reply once more. 'But what's all that got to do with fracking? I am a little confused by your line of argument.'

'That's cos you're a knob,' says Trucker #1, getting up to leave.

'Seconded,' says Trucker #2, handing a tenner over to the Prof.

'Motion carried,' says Trucker #3, with a postern blast.

I am cast down. Here are three members of the self-employed, self-reliant backbone of England; the men who keep the country running; the men of common sense and sturdy purpose; the yeomen of England and yet...they seem indifferent to the industrial horror about to blot out the sun above the Red Bus Transport Café. I turn for solace to the Professor who, as an educated man, must surely support my principled stand.

'Harpic,' he says. 'Do you know what fracking is?'

'Well, admittedly, I'm a bit hazy on the details,' I confess. 'But isn't it something to do with earthquakes, pollution and industrial catastrophe?'

'It's a way of reducing your gas bill with minimum disruption to the environment,' he says.

'No it isn't!' I decry. 'I saw those chaps from the university on telly saying that it will bring about fire and flood and devastating climate change and we'll all have to bunk up with Noah or go the way of the unicorn.'

'Harpic,' he replies, tenderly slapping the rashers on the economy margarine spread. 'Those aren't scientists, they're geographers. There's a whole world of difference. Now shut up and eat your breakfast.'

'But I thought the science was settled?' I protest.

'No, the grants have been settled,' replied the Prof, waving a fish slice around the bus rather menacingly. 'And the jobs have all been divvied up. The science has been banished to a dogging lay-by outside Barkingham.'

I am not convinced; but a bacon sarnie is a bacon sarnie.

It has to be said though, that we Harpics are not natural revolutionaries. It is true that a distant ancestor declared for Parliament in the Civil War, but the massed ranks of the Harpics were generally to be found commanding the King's Armies. During the French Revolution, the French branch of the family (since executed) led by Henri de la Harpique held the patisserie monopoly and Henri himself was briefly a speech writer for Marie Antoinette: 'Let Them Eat Cake' was grossly misinterpreted both at the time and later. As to those unfortunate events in Russia during 1917, the best that can be said is that Second Cousin Once Removed Fyodor Harpicksky, a famous swordsman, did his bit for counter-revolution by giving a bit of support to Fanya Kaplan (actually a good rogering) just before she attempted to assassinate Lenin but failed conspicuously to cuckold the murderous old bastard himself by giving his wife Krupskaya a friendly squeeze: she looked like the back end of Professor Birch's bus apparently, and his motivation failed at the crucial moment.

More recently, Uncle Binky once wore a blue coat to a hunt ball and I have been known to don a slightly rebellious pair of taupe trousers from time to time. Auntie Eleanor invested heavily in the counter-cultural movement of the 1960s but lost her shirt attempting to bring in a less brutal form of capitalism by investing in the Woodstock Festival. Fortunately, she was able to get it all back through a lawsuit claiming damages to her bank balance resulting from the organiser's shoddy approach to the principles of good financial management. She used the money to invest in the harder edged anti-capitalism of punk and did rather better; she made a killing out of the Miner's Benefit gigs and retired early to a post-punk, New Age spa in the New Forest where she remains to this day. She was always a generous soul and a free spirit unfettered by materialism. She's on the board of RBS too.

Anyway, its back home with the clutch hardly slipping at all and I begin to wonder what old Louise is so worried about. I mean it's not like she's been entered in the Le Mans 24 or the Paris-Dakar or anything. I doubt she gets into fourth gear at all between home and St.Wicca's. I make an executive decision to leave the clutch alone on the principle that if it's only a bit broke, fixing it will only make it worse. Unfortunately, my executive decision is executively rescinded by the time I get up the cul-de-sac because there's a bloody big tow truck waiting on the driveway, which is again typical of women. They give you a job to do and then just as you are about to get stuck in, decide to do it themselves. I give a friendly toot to the mechanic because it's not his fault and by being polite I might enlist him to my anti-fracking cause.

'Don't be bloody silly, Harpic,' he says, hooking the old chariot up. 'Bill Gon's given me the contract to service the Gazpacom trucks when they come to pick up the frackin' gas.'

I sense a problem. There seem to be quite a lot of people who are actually in favour of this fracking business. On the positive side though, they are all working and so wouldn't have time to come to a protest anyway, so they don't really count when it comes to the sort of riotous direct action that I am hoping for. I decide to make a list. All good revolutions begin with a list.

Entering the hallway of my own dear *Pilgrims Rest*, I note the military prints and the Chesterfield in the lounge and then look at my watch. They'll be open soon and decide that no revolution was ever successfully plotted in a suburban cul-de-sac; revolutions are plotted by candlelight in eerie taverns and secretive rooms hidden away in the back of sooty wine shops. We don't have any eerie taverns or sooty wine shops in Slimstead, although it is true I've seen some strange happenings in both The Hanged Man and the Old Queens Head, but I suppose they'll have to do. Given the family connection to Marie Antoinette and the subject under discussion, the latter hostelry seems the more appropriate venue and, as the tow truck has departed, the walk down there will aid in our weight loss regime.

Lunch.

Just a quick snifter again today. We Revolutionaries need to prioritise as well as lose weight.

Perky Pete is in his accustomed place behind the beery battlement of this fortress of civil resistance to the unbridled forces of the unacceptable face of capitalism.

'Pint of JCB, is it, Harpic?'

'What could be better,' I reply.

'Two.'

'Absotively bang on,' I say, as he pours the first of a thousand kisses. 'Put 'em on the slate.'

'How's the demo planning going,' he asks.

'Well, actually, I thought I'd enlist your help in drawing up a suitable list,' I say, taking the top off John Barleycorn's beard. 'Can't have a revolution without a list, what?'

'Impossible,' he replies. 'I'll get a pen.'

While he rattles around the drawers and beer glasses, his lovely wife Maureen appears. She is a fine woman who by leaving her North country origins early avoided the scourge of rickets and took up aerobics shortly after Olivia Newton John invented them in the 1980s. This has given her the sort of hour glass figure sought after by barmaids since barmaids themselves were invented and is certainly able to rival the clear skinned Karolina of The Hanged Man though her charms of the more mature variety. Still, that's what Wonderbras and reinforced lycra are for, aren't they? Despite the blonde being bottle-assisted these days, it is still attractively groomed and her teeth remain in good shape should Newmarket require her. All in all, she's a fine fettled filly with more than a passing resemblance to Dolly Parton.

'Stop looking at my tits, Harpic,' she says. 'And when are you going to pay your tab? It looks like the National bleedin' Debt.'

'Here, I say,' producing Bill Gon's Fifty Pound Note. 'This should clear my account.'

'It'll do for a start,' she replies, tucking it into her till. 'Have you got any more?'

'Honestly, Maureen,' I protest. 'Don't you think it a bit harsh ripping off a poor and vulnerable chap like myself?'

'Who's interested in ripping off the poor?' she protests in her turn. 'The poor haven't got any money and if you think they're vulnerable, try walking through a Council Estate in Bolton after curfew and see if you get out *with* your wallet and *without* stitches.'

'You paint a depressing picture of our Northern cousins which I find hard to believe is justifiable.' There is no doubt I am picqued a little by her insensitivity to those of us OINKS who have to scrape by on a meagre fraction of what a publican earns.

'Cousins?' she replies. 'We're related to them?'

I can see that this conversation is likely to be of fruitless result and am grateful for the reappearance of Perky Pete, who is of a more reasonable disposition.

'I'll handle Harpic,' he says to her. 'It looks like he's going to be making a major contribution to re-floating the local economy. He's organising a demo against fracking.'

'No smelly hippies, Harpic,' she says, trotting off towards the kitchen. 'And anti-globalisation protestors are welcome only if they pay for the wi-fi and don't complain about the coffee not being from Starbucks.'

'Indubitably,' I say, and then taking another kiss from John Barleycorn, decide it's time to get down to business. Perky Pete produces pen and paper and scratches his head. 'Right then, who shall we recruit? Denning?'

'Perfect,' I reply. 'We may need legal representation when our case for wrongful arrest goes to the European Court of Human Rights.'

'Carruthers?'

'Perfect,' I reply. 'We'll need his knowledge of weapons when we move to the guerrilla stage of the revolution.'

'Anyone else?'

'What about Shocking, Outrageous and Should Be Allowed?' I posit.

'They strike me as being more of the fence sitting type,' says Perky Pete. 'What about Trucker Higgins and Barney the Builder?'

'They'll both be at work,' I say.

'Ark Slymstead?'

'Ditto,' I say. 'Plus, he has too much respect for the workings of the democratic process to be trusted to take direct action.'

'Tabitha Greenwood?'

'Absotively not,' I declare. 'We can't have women getting mixed up in politics. Look what happened to the Slimstead Men's Club! And can you imagine the trouble poor old PC Plod would have manhandling her tits into the Black Maria?'

'Very thoughtful of you Harpic,' he says, scratching out her name. 'Very liberated.'

'Thank you,' I say.

'*No women or smelly hippies*,' he writes. 'I suppose that rules out Old Timeon and Chickadee?'

'He isn't smelly.'

'He is a hippy though and Chickadee is definitely a woman.'

'Put them on one side,' I say, being the good committee man I was when I was Consultant to a Large Corporation. 'We'll decide on them later.'

'Ostrakov?'

'Certainly not!' I cry. 'We can't have Communists coming here and taking over! Why, there'll be a revolution in no time!'

Pete gives me a strange look and pours the second pint.

'Tredegar?' he suggests. 'Are Ukippers in favour of fracking?'

'I believe they are,' I reply. 'As long as it's not done by unskilled immigrant labour.'

'That rules out Stefan and Lucas, I suppose,' he says. 'You know Harpic, we're getting a bit thin on the ground here.'

'What about ringing up Friends of the Earth?' I suggest. 'They'd probably be interested in this sort of thing, wouldn't they?'

'Actually Harpic, I'm sorry to have to disappoint you here,' says Pete, shaking his head. 'I phoned them up this morning but they haven't got anyone available for the next few weeks. They say there's a big anti-aviation pollution conference on in Tahiti and they're all flying out for it.'

'Isn't there a British Anti-Fracking Alliance or something?' I fish.

'There is,' he confirms. 'But it's sponsored by British Nuclear Fuels and they say they can't get bogged down in environmental issues in the present commercial environment. So it looks like it's just down to you.'

'*Us*, surely?'

'*You*,' replies Perky Pete with emphasis. 'I'll be running the bar, won't I?'

'Hmm,' I agree. 'Looks like we're on a bit of a sticky wicket.'

'Perhaps you might want to relax your ban on female participation a little?' suggests Pete, tentatively. 'I mean, all those Yummy Mummies up at St.Wicca's have got money and probably wouldn't want to see little Jasper and Jemima gassed by the fracking fall out.'

I ruminate on this for a moment.

'You're right, Pete,' I say, displaying the pragmatism for which we Harpics are renown. 'I shall canvas the Yummy Mummies. I shall ply them with Cadbury's Milk Tray and feed lollipops to their offspring in pursuit of their good opinion and dedicated support for my campaign.'

'You're going to give sweets to children in a playground?' says Perky Pete. He pauses. 'You might want to think this through a bit more, Harpic.'

'Not at all,' I reply. 'Bribery is the essence of any political movement. Lend us fifty quid for campaign materials, eh? You can put it on my tab.'

Harpic Enchained.

When I was stationed at Benbecula in Ultima Thule, my Commanding Officer volunteered me to undertake parachute training.

'Lieutenant Harpic,' he said. 'The British Army needs to stay ahead of the curve when it comes to new battlefield technologies.'

'Yes, Sir!' I agreed, snapping off a salute so smart it sounded like a whip crack in a bordello.

'Well, Harpic, there's a new kind of parachute being developed and the Army is unanimous in thinking that you're the best man to test it,' he said. 'You'll be jumping with troops using the old, tried and trusted way but you'll have the honour of being on the cutting edge of airborne warfare.'

'Yes, Sir!' I cried, excitedly. 'When do I start?'

'The plane is waiting.'

Well, as you can imagine I was into the gear and aboard that aircraft as fast as the old legs could carry me. Once aboard though, I confess that I experienced just the merest twinge of anxiety and wondered if the two minutes training I had received would be enough to see me through the ordeal ahead. When we got up to 20,000ft, the old red light started winking and I felt a tad less enthusiasm for this particular wheeze than I had originally experienced and hoped that I might perhaps just sit this one out this time or, at the very least, go last so I could see how it was done. Unfortunately, the Jumpmaster insisted that I go first.

'Why?' I shouted against the noise of the engine tearing through the slipstream.

'So you'll be out of the way of the rest of the lads if it goes tits up,' he said with a grin.

That's the Tommy Atkins sense of humour for you and I felt the triumphant return of the temporarily absent Harpic spirit. I gave him a thumbs up and turned to the chap behind me so that he too could benefit from my hearty courage. To my dismay, he looked rather glum.

'What's up, old chap? I asked, putting a manly hand upon his shoulder.

'I'm fucking scared,' replied the grizzled yet wary veteran.

'Surely not,' I cried out as the Jumpmaster drew back the sliding door. 'Why would a chap like you be scared at a little parachute jump?'

'Because it's fucking dangerous,' he replied, to which I had no answer because I was hauled backwards and unceremoniously pushed out of the aircraft, the sensation of which was rather like being ejected from the upstairs window of a brothel.

Now the reason I relate this story – good enough as it as a stand alone – is that the fear I felt that day was nothing to that which I experienced when I was brought *mano a mano* with the Yummy Mummies of St.Wicca's and their perfectly horrible children. For a moment, I even felt a twinge of sympathy for Louise. No sooner had I collected my campaign materials from a disapproving Mrs. Perry and walked smartly up the drive in an overcoat borrowed from the abandoned clothing stand in the Old Queens Head – it looked like it might come on to rain - and approached the first group of school children in the playground than all Hell was let loose. First off, an alarm bell fit to wake all Berlin to the danger of a Thousand Bomber raid went off, which was immediately followed by the squealing tyres and racing engines of two unmarked blacked-out 4x4s which shot out of the car park, decanted eight screaming harpies virtually into my lap who proceeded to beat me about my person with designer handbags while a horde of their orcish children pillaged me of my campaign materials while gibbering, squealing and drooling continually and in equal measure. Shortly afterwards, Police and Social Services arrived, handcuffed the old Harpic and carted him off to the Barkingham nick with dire admonitions about having the right to remain silent and if I didn't bloody well shut up I'd be stuck in Brixton jail and buggered left, right and sideways until Christmas.

So here I sit, nicked and under caution in a very small cell pondering on the bollocks that old Oscar Wilde chuntered about four walls not a prison making. He must have been in Ford Open Prison because I can absolutely guarantee that they do otherwise I'd be out of here like greased shit off a shiny shovel in no time at all. Harpic enchained! Where's Steve McQueen's motorbike when you need it? It doesn't bear thinking about. And there's no booze allowed here either. Just how does anyone survive the ordeal of prison without a quick snifter to steady the nerves and fortify the soul? I've only been here an hour and a half and already it feels like I've been banged up for life in the Chateau D'If. Poor Harpic. All washed up.

There is a rattle of keys and a bolt is thrown back and The Heat is standing four square in the doorway with a face like a long stretch in Alcatraz.

'Well Mr.Harpic, we've carried out some preliminary investigations and background checks and the consensus of informed opinion is that although you are a plonker- not my choice of terms, Sir, you understand – you are not a paedophile.'

'Paedophile?' I shriek. 'Whatever do you mean? This is a fit up! A miscarriage of justice! A dirty trick by the Fracking Fraternity!'

'No, Sir, it isn't and you're not being charged with anything,' replies Five-Oh. 'But you might be advised to refrain from handing out lollipops in a school yard in future.'

'Lollipops! They were my campaign materials designed to establish a dialogue between sacred motherhood, the innocence of childhood and the anti-fracking movement!'

'Whatever, Mr. Harpic,' continues the Nark-meister. 'And I should get that coat of yours dry cleaned if I was you. There's rather more DNA on it than is consistent with good hygiene.'

'How dare you!' I cry. 'That's Dennings' overcoat and he is a barrister of no mean reputation.'

'He is indeed, Sir,' says the Plod. 'You should also thank the Deputy Chair of Governors at St.Wicca's for the character reference he gave you. Chap by the name of Ostrakov? Ah, you know him I see. Well, pick up your belt, laces and other belongings – Mr.Ostrakov has reimbursed you for the loss of your – ahem – campaign materials – and don't hesitate to come again. Have a nice day.'

Harpic is released into the community.

(Wildlife spotted: two rabbits on Cane Lane, several squirrels and I thought I caught a glimpse of a roe deer but it might have been a muntjac).

Returning home, heavy hearted, my blameless and spotless reputation ruined and no doubt an easy front page headline for the reptiles at the Barkingham Gazette and the *Slimstead Insinuator*, I muse on the reception I am likely to get at the hands of my Dearest Louise. I trudge up the cul-de-sac as though I am wearing deep sea diver's boots, every step heavier than the last, each stride a weary mile on my *via dolorosa*, each doomed pace bringing me nearer to the Wrath of Khan. I reach the driveway, take out my key - that wretched reminder of my incarceration – thread it into the mortiss lock as though I were shoving a camel through the eye of the needle and prepare to be weighed in the balance and found wanting. The door of Harpic's own Fortress of Solitude swings back on its hinges with a creak crying out for a dab of WD40 and I prepare to meet Smaug herself, face to face.

To my surprise, the house is full of female shrieking. I don't mean the type of shrieking a chap meets when he runs through the Ladies Hockey Team changing rooms after a match, but the type one encounters when the gels have been on the chocolate and are telling each other dirty stories of their abandoned youth after Lights Out. I go through to the conservatory and there, amidst a volley of champagne corks, am greeted with raucous laughter and a huge cheer from a goodly part of the assembled St.Wicca's staffroom.

'Magnificent, Harpic!' says Miss Ward, her blue stockings all a-flutter. She is a Roman-nosed Goddess fallen to Earth for the express purpose of leading the little ones to a kindly light and I worship her for it. 'Absolutely magnificent!'

'Tremendous! Jolly Dee!' cries Miss Pound, a sparse, pale woman in a black pointy hat, waving what looks like a bottle of my secret stash of fizz around. 'A moment I shall treasure to the end of my career!'

'I'm sorry, I don't seem to understand,' I say, baffled at this unexpected turn of events. 'I rather thought I'd be in the soup over this.'

'Nothing could be further from the truth, Harpic,' declares my own Dear Sweet, cackling. 'It was worth every moment to see Labiaplasty Nolan bag you with her Donna Karan!'

'Old 'Nip and Fuck Tuck' certainly packs a punch,' agrees Miss Ward, delightedly sloshing my fizz into an outstretched glass. 'That stiletto heel to the groin was worthy of the Karate Kid. Can you take my husband with you next time you go campaigning?'

There is a further and unpleasant outburst of cackling while I recall the bruises inflicted on my private area.

'And I particularly enjoyed the way that Social Worker slapped you around the back of the head,' adds Miss Pound. 'We had a fantastic view of that one from the Staffroom window. I nearly fell off my chair laughing.'

'You saw it all?' I gasp like a landed fish. 'Yet did not seek to come to my aid?'

'Are you joking Harpic?' replies Miss Pound. 'We teachers never get in the way of a Social Worker, don't you know. All it takes is a smidgeon of a hint that you may once have belted a misbehaving brat a little way towards Kingdom Come and that's your career over.'

'No more Gin and fizz for you once the Social gets you on their rack,' agrees Miss Ward. 'They're all recruited from the Nazis, don't you know.'

'Still, Harpic,' chips in Louise. 'I do admire your nerve...'

'Lollipops! Campaign materials!' hoots Miss Pound. 'Masterly!'

'...in choosing to open the anti-fracking debate by approaching Madeleine Gon...' continues Louise, slurping my fizz in a very uncharitable gulp.

'...and telling her that her father is...' adds Miss Pound.

'...Ostrakov's dupe! Did you really call Ostrakov a Communist, Harpic?' cries Louise through tears of laughter.

'Did you see the look on that beastly little Madeleine Gon's face when she pressed her personal panic alarm?' shouts out Miss Ward, in a crescendo of mockery. 'Pure venom!'

'Did you see the way 4O went for him?' shrieks Miss Pound, mopping at her mascara. 'That fat kid I like to put in the corner with the Dunce's cap on all day fairly guzzled those lollies.'

'And *Harpic's* face when the Policeman reminded him about speeding traps!' blared out Miss Walsh, a woman for whom I am rapidly losing my earlier good opinion of. 'The colour it went should be registered with the Royal Academy as a whole new colour! What would one call that particular mixture of puce and purple?'

At this point, the room is full of that odious witch-like cackling for which ladies in a certain mood are famous for. Harpic must retire or face a further reduction in his self-esteem.

Drinks for a Sojourn in the Slough of Despond.

For those of you not blessed with an adequate education because your parents did not care enough about your future wellbeing to send you private, the Slough of Despond is not a trading estate near Eton but a state of mind brought on by despair. It comes from a book – again, you'll need to have gone private to know what one of those are – called 'The Pilgrim's Progress' by John Bunyan and is not to be confused with 'A Rake's Progress' though the subject matter might be said to be related. Rake's Progress is, however, all downward from the moment he inherits to the point where he ends up in the Looney Bin from pissing it up, gambling and consorting with bad company (lawyers and whores). By contrast, the Pilgrim's progress is all upward to the Celestial City, but we don't really get much detail on the sins he has committed but do note that in his search for deliverance he abandons his wife and kids, which is a funny sort of way to go about getting into God's good books, if you ask me. Anyhow, the Slough of Despond is a horrible bog and Harpic has found himself up to his ears in it, so what he needs is a bit of a pick-me-up.

Now there is a lot of NHS propaganda about drinking making one depressed but we can safely ignore those miserable, bloody Jeremiahs. Drinking does not make you depressed; this is putting the cart before the horse as any idiot with any sort of experience in the real world can attest; depression makes you drink, not the other way round. And, in many ways, it is a good thing it does. How many times has a little snifter cheered you up again and restored you to your witty, charming, good-natured self? Lots of times. And how many times has your broken heart been mended by a bottle of vodka, a duvet and a pile of old records? Lots of times – and you can ask Tracey Emin to back me up on this one. How many times has the transition from a state of employment to a state of 'resting' or 'being between jobs' been eased by a serious piss up? Exactly. Everyone goes through their own Slough of Despond from time to time and though it is true that what does not kill you certainly makes you stronger and that heartache makes you wiser and more determined Not To Get Fooled Again, as The Who put it, booze makes you forget all about the crap for a while.

This, of course, was what Paul Newman was talking about in *Cat on a Hot Tin Roof* when he spoke about drinking until he got 'the click'; 'All of a sudden, there's peace,' he said and I know just what he means. It's like turning the volume down on TV for a while and just looking at the pictures. It's only then that you realise that what you are watching is really a load of crap that you don't need in your life – although you do need the volume up if you are watching *Cat on a Hot Tin Roof* mind, otherwise, it would be pointless because there are no car chases or spectacular explosions in it – there is a bit of a thunderstorm but nothing to write home about. What you shouldn't do when searching for 'the click' though is become suicidal drunk and drink bleach. This is a bad idea and though it may indeed bring you peace, it is of the RIP variety and even then only acquired after a lot of horrid stomach pumping mullarkey. No; drinking bleach is a no-no.

I knew a Suicidal Drunk called Scrivens when I was holding back the Communist Hordes in Germany during the Cold War. He was a scraggy little object of no discernable use and how he had managed to pass Basic Training was a mystery; he couldn't pass wind without someone to show him first. No one liked him, it is fair to say, though several people tried to befriend his wallet over a game of cards. It was said that he was covered in spot bruises where the rest of the regiment had jabbed him with a bargepole for bets but this was just friendly banter. However, it was true that the hookers on the Reeperbahn in Hamburg refused to take his money and sent him back to the barracks with sympathetic notes about hygiene and proper nutrition addressed to the CSM. It was only when it was decided one day that he might possibly be trusted with a rifle under the close and personal supervision of the instructors that we were alerted to his remarkable abilities as a marksman.

I remember being given the job of holding up the targets – a responsible position that the Colonel had decided could be entrusted to no-one other than I – and watching as he put bullet after bullet into the Bulls Eye. It was amazing. It was as though Dead Eye Dick had married Calamity Jane and from that point on the Suicidal Drunk was riding the crest of a wave to becoming the Regimental Shooting Champion. He was given leave to go down on the ranges with me as his guide every day and all day, though he hardly needed the practice. The Colonel even encouraged him to learn some fancy trick shooting and put the apple personally on my head. Bang! Bang! Apple crumble for tea, no problem. Even when the Colonel insisted he do it blindfolded, the result was the same.

'Bally Hell, Private Scrivens,' he said. 'Don't you ever miss?'

'Never, Sir,' grunted the Troll Scrivens.

'What, never?' asked the Colonel.

'Nope, never, Sir,' insisted Scrivens.

'Blast,' said the Colonel, who in my opinion had rather grown tired of apple crumble.

The day came when the Regimental shooting competition was held and he wiped the floor with the whole field, so to speak, with weapons large and small, of every conceivable calibre and bore. Then on the Colonel's insistence, he repeated his apple off my head trick while riding blindfold, backwards over a ploughed field on a Landrover driven at high speed. I never doubted Scrivens' skill for a moment and when the comforting crack of a bullet parting my hair and splattering Eve's folly came, I rejoiced at the thought of scooping the pool in the sweepstake that the Colonel had organised for the further entertainment of the regiment. Scrivens was triumphant too and the odd squinting cast of his features that I had come to recognise as his version of a smile played over his features like a knife slash on a lump of liver. Two weeks later he repeated his triumph at the Divisional shooting contest and followed it up by knocking a cherry off my bonce at three hundred yards while parachuting from a passing helicopter all to the amazement of the General and the further enrichment of my bank account.

But then tragedy struck. Out of jealousy, the vanquished champions of the other regiments in the Division demanded their pound of flesh in revenge and so prevailed upon the chap engraving the cups to render his victory as *Scrivens: A Prize for the Small Bore.* When Scrivens realised what they had done, he went puce and attempted to murder them all with a machine gun, but was restrained. I attempted to console him and went to visit him in the gaol just after I had banked my winnings and prevailed upon the Duty Officer to release him into my custody.

'The bloody bastards,' he grunted, as he accepted the bottle of whisky that I thought was his due. 'The bloody bastards.'

Well, I sympathised with him, gave him a fiver and sent him off to the canteen to drown his sorrows secure in the belief that alcohol solves everything. That night though there was a bit of a commotion and the guard was turned out, which necessarily meant me being turned out too as he was, technically speaking, in my custody.

'Harpic,' ordered the Colonel. 'You let the bloody man out, so you can get him back in the glasshouse.'

'Certainly, Sir!' I said, snapping off my snappiest salute.

'He's got a gun,' said the Colonel. 'And as you're the only bloody thing he's missed this last fortnight, you can go and get it off him.'

Well, there he was, poor old Scrivens, sat in the middle of the parade ground with several empty alcohol containers around him and in his hands a pearl handled pistol worthy of Patton himself, which he was waving around in an abandoned fashion.

'Have you got the safety catch on, Scrivens?' I fearlessly called.

'Not now,' he slurred in response. 'Bloody bastards. I'm going to kill myself, I am.'

'Now just hold on Scrivens,' I said. 'You might be an ugly little chap without much going for you, but you shouldn't let a bit of a joke get to you this way.'

'Shooting. Only thing I've ever been good at,' he slurred. 'Bloody bastards ruined it.'

'Well, that's true,' I counselled. 'But look on the bright side – I made a fortune betting on you.'

He was not to be assuaged though and without further ado, he put the revolver to his head, pulled the trigger and...missed. How he managed to miss something as close as his head was a marvel but just to prove that he could, he did it again, twice more. After that, I applied a bit of common sense in letting him get it all out of his system and just waited until he had emptied the magazine.

'Bloody bastards,' he wailed, as I took the gun off him and handed him over to the guard.

Once he'd been banged up and given another bottle, everyone thought that that would be the end of it but to the disappointment of the regiment, it was not. From then on he refused to compete in any shooting competitions and every time he got drunk he tried to shoot himself and failed. No - suicidal drunks are such a bore; they never seem to get the bloody job done however many times they try and just end up ruining everyone else's evening. I suppose Ernest Hemmingway might be the exception here, but he was a dab hand with a shotgun and succeeded on the first attempt.

In much the same vein we can draw on another sterling performance from Paul Newman to illustrate some things that are best avoided when drinking in the Slough of Despond. In this case, his role as the Cool Hand Luke in the eponymous film has him getting drunk and then put in jail for ever. This is not a good idea as there is no booze allowed in prison despite the number of rum coves to be found there and although you may well widen the circle of your acquaintances if you are rough enough and that way inclined, you are much more likely to get your circle widened by acquaintances that you may wish you had never made. Prison: best avoided. A couple of hours in the Barkingham nick was enough for me; pondering on what it must be like to be banged up sober was probably the worst part of the whole experience.

So now, down to business. The proper drink for a sojourn in the Slough of Despond depends on how deep you want to go down and how quickly and how long you want to remain there. Assuming that you want just an evening of self-pity rather than a week of it, I'd go for something in a big jug. There is something reassuring in being able to see your progress downwards and to some extent measure it, so always go for something in a big jug. In America they call big jugs of beer 'pitchers' and although American beer can sometimes be very weak, the capacity of the jug can be adapted to any sort of binge-bomb depending on your personal choice. Don't start with shorts though; you cannot drink a jug full of spirits however hard you try without ending up in A&E with a tube down your throat and a lot of vomit smeared about your person, so use mixers to dilute them. Traditionally beer has been the starter of choice, fortified with a chaser or 'sidecar' as they say in America. Indeed, the great Bluesman Rudi Toombs went further than this and swore by 'One Scotch, One Bourbon, One Beer' - this is a perfectly reasonable way of easing you into a profound and melancholy drunkenness but you will need to repeat the mixture several times. The volume of the beer can also mean several trips to the toilet, each of which will get progressively harder and if your choice of boozer has smelly bogs, then this can be unpleasant. You may want to try wine as a halfway house between beer and spirits; it has good alcoholic properties but with only a tenth of the volume of beer. A jug of wine can be expensive in a bar though, so best stick to this if you are aiming to get plastered in the familiar surroundings of *Chez Nous*.

The stages of the Slough of Despond may be roughly described thus; first off there is the glorious and golden release afforded by a good slug of the good stuff. This will allow you to sigh a lot, stretch out your neck and fingers and generally release the tension that has been building up in your shoulders. Secondly, and this will come around the two-drink mark, you will make a serious attempt to analyse the cause of your discomfiture and come to a balanced and reasonable conclusion about your situation. This is a dangerous point as you may well decide to just say 'fuck it' and get on with your life. The serious Slougher will work through to the four-drink mark when you will decide it is all the fault of that bastard in Accounts who's had it in for you for ages. The five-drink mark is where things start to get really interesting though because at this stage you will have entered a higher plane of reasoning, one not bound by the chains of logic, and have concluded that it wasn't your fault at all but that the bastard in Accounts was only one small, piddling part of a much wider conspiracy that goes all the way up to the government or that nebulous thing known as 'the system'. At seven drinks, we have entered the nebulas themselves and you may find yourself outside, whether voluntarily or not is not really relevant, with a fist raised and challenging the stars themselves to do their worst. Nine drinks brings you down from your fine high-flown rhetoric and onto the sofa where the music of your choice will demand to be played at what your neighbours may consider to be an inconsiderate volume. The music will reduce you to tears with its profound sense of understanding just who you really are and just how things have never gone your way and how no-one really understands what it's like to face the everyday challenges of yesterday and the future and all that sort of weird and random shit and pass the bottle it's time for another.

You are now well into the Slough of Despond and can indulge yourself in a bit of nostalgia if you like; if you are of Irish heritage, this is when you get the Daniel O'Donnell out and start singing *Danny Boy* on the back lawn. If you are English, it means photo albums. If you are American, it means a call to your therapist. If you are Russian it means another two bottles of vodka. If you are female, it means cigarettes and smudged make-up. If you are under forty, it means dribbling on Facebook. If you are over forty, it also means Facebook but in this case it means looking up that girl who dumped you at your first disco when you were twelve and proposing marriage. Fortunately, by now you are completely incoherent and incapable of typing anything legible; you will also find that you have been un-friended by a lot of people who did not know you as well as they thought they did and have now no wish to find out more. You have made it to the bottom. Well done. Now go to bed. And hold on tight.

Day Ten: Wednesday. Humpday Revisited.

'Anyone who thinks that honesty is the best policy has never met a Tax man, a journalist, a socialist politician or a thief.'

J.Harpic.

The Weigh-in.

Some mornings can be worse than others although, in general, the whole concept can be a bit on the bloody side. If you have perhaps imbibed a little more liberally than was wise under the wholly understandable circumstances, then it is possible that your eyesight might not be functioning to its original specifications. If you wear contact lenses then you might find that they have stuck to a part of your ocular equipment that they were not designed for and so introduced a novel but disconcerting variation on your normal focal length. Spectacles are notorious for losing themselves and so confining the wearer to a more blurred version of the world at large than one might be comfortable with and all this can add up to a little difficulty when it comes to the morning weigh-in. This can lead to disappointment because if you have been following the basic principles of this diet, you will already have lost nine or possibly ten pounds and you would want to celebrate this. It's essential therefore that you are able to see the scales with sufficient clarity to establish the exact level of your triumphant weight loss but this might not be possible if your vision is blurred. Never fear! Harpic is here! And after many years of studying the problem, he has found an answer.

If your jaded eyesight is not up to the job of looking down between pendulous breasts or over a convex tum to focus on the dial between your painted or broken (as the case may be) toenails then a simple trick will make up for your lack of abstinence. Simply lower yourself down on to your knees, place your hands on the scales and leaning forward to reposition your weight from your knees to your hands, slowly lift your legs off the floor. You may wish to extend your legs into a vertical position as this will help with your overall balance but in any case, you will be able to lower your nose towards the dial and so get an accurate reading of your weight. Yoga enthusiasts may consider adopting the 'half downward dog' position but I can't recommend it; it really is just showing off and a straightforward handstand really does the job with a lot less fuss. The 'rabbit' or 'half tortoise' is useful for if one needs to contact God on the Great White Telephone while you are in the bathroom of course but any of the 'wind relieving' positions are completely unnecessary; if you need to do Yoga to fart there really is something wrong with you.

Cheese for Breakfast.

It isn't very common to see cheese on an Englishman's breakfast table but there are times when it is a perfectly acceptable breakfast item. The cheese omelette is popular with those enamoured of chicken abortions but usually omelettes are reserved for vegetarians, who deserve no better, and the virtuous quality of the cheese croissant has already been discussed. Sliced cheeses are a major part of the Germanic breakfast and can be found in a place of honour alongside the schinken and the wurst; I have eaten this for breakfast on several occasions and can recommend it, especially when on holiday. Of course, the type of cheese served on a Teuton's breakfast platter is different from our own Cheddar or Lincolnshire Poacher; look for Bergkase, which means 'Cheese Mountain', made popular by EU subsidies and over-production by inefficient continental farmers growing fat on the taxes of hard working Britons; it has a creamy texture and is quite nice. Smoked cheese is good too, but on the whole Germans avoid stronger cheese varieties for breakfast because, at bottom, they lack backbone. Italians, of course, don't have breakfast and instead have fiercely strong expresso coffee which makes them bad tempered all day and even worse drivers which is a pity because actually Mozarrella can be served on toast with bacon and pesto as quite an unusual but tasty specialist breakfast. In recent years the Australians have been experimenting with breakfast in a rather forlorn attempt to out-grow their image of Pig Iron Bob in a string vest and corks dancing around a disreputable hat; there may be some mileage in Cheese and Bacon croquettes- but not for breakfast obviously – but Blue Cheese and pine nut focaccia is hardly going to get past the University of Woolamoloo Philosophy Department, is it?

The exception to all this is Halloumi, which is a Greek or Greek Cypriot firm sheep's milk cheese which is designed for grilling. Greeks use it at barbecues but alongside bacon it can give an interesting Hellenic twist to breakfast. Just squeeze a little lemon juice onto the cheese, bung it under the grill and Bob's your uncle; better than the Elgin Marbles (no, you can't have them back).

The main problem with having cheese on toast for breakfast though is that toasted cheese makes you sleepy and so impairs your ability to operate machinery or keep awake through the Health and Safety briefing. Louise has been spearheading a campaign for cheese on toast to be provided free at breakfast time at St.Wicca's, with further portions served at regular intervals throughout the day to 'keep the children's Calcium levels up'. Frankly, if the Ritalin that Miss Pound puts in their morning milk isn't doing the job then it's probably not worth going to the bother of getting the grater out.

Today's Exercise Regime: Shopping for more Bacon.

Due to the Louise's misplaced charity in giving away all the comestibles necessary for the harmonious existence of Harpic to a bunch of dole scrounging, starving benefits cheats in Up-Northernshire, it is necessary today to re-stock the larder to something approaching civilised standards. This will entail a trip to the shops but as she has also given in to an astounding lack of fiscal restraint in the matter of a mildly slipping clutch, old Harpic is grounded due to lack of transport.

But not to worry! We can simply combine our shopping trip with a lovely walk and then justify a return by taxi on the grounds of Louise's unwarranted charity extravagance. So stepping out down the cul-de-sac, we give a cheery wave to Don the next door neighbour as he puts half an hour's work into his garden, leap out of the way as Chubble the recently privatised louche Postie roars out of the driveway of the recent divorcee, Mrs Johnson, and then scatter some seeds of the humble *Bellis Perennis* sure in the knowledge that they will flourish even on the obsessively manicured Astroturf lawn of Norman, doyen of the Slimstead Horticultural Society and a man who needs to get a more moderate perspective on life. Then we take a sharp turn to the left and briskly walk the two miles into Berkstead where there are shops.

In truth Berkstead, like many other fine English market towns has been suffering over the past few years. More and more of the artisan outlets have been driven out of business by big supermarket chains and out of town retail parks and their premises taken over by dodgy charity shops that seem to afford big salaries for Chief Executives while relying on the slave labour of retirees. Add to this the constant demands for taxes by local and national government, endless strikes by grasping proletarians egged on by multi-millionaire union barons, the tick box titans of the Health and Safety Mafia and it's a wonder that the butcher and the baker haven't already gone the way of the candlestick maker.

And then there is the internet, which has wiped out the profits of the newsagent who can no longer sell enough porn off the top shelf to make a decent donation to the Church roof fund anymore, and decimated the video shops, the music shops and the book shops. The only retail sector not to have felt the squeeze of technology seems to be clothing. This is, of course, due mainly to the fact that you should never buy trousers off the internet. Harpic's own favoured yellow trousers came off the internet, only when I bought them they were supposed to be something called 'taupe' which is like khaki, I believe. Also, you should never buy anything off the internet while drunk but it is perfectly safe to buy things from the High Street while drunk because you are reminded of your purchase by the constant need to carry it around. This is not at all like the internet where one-click buying does not produce immediate consequences but rather drip feeds them into your house on a day by day basis, which can be both embarrassing and problematic. I once ordered half a ton of bricks off the internet in the intoxicated belief that Chubble the Postie would have to lug them all the way up the cul-de-sac on his back. It would have been a great joke to see him labouring along under the hot sun but instead a big truck with a crane turned up and dumped them on my flower beds, which wasn't at all the thing.

For women, shopping is close to religion and like their obsession with excessive cleanliness, something to do with their vaginas. For us chaps, all that designer tat is best avoided unless you absolutely do enjoy hanging around changing rooms and being asked to pass comment on articles of clothing that you have absolutely no opinion on whatsoever. And the answer is 'Yes, Your Bum Does Look Big In It' but you must never say it however tempting it may be. When I was Consultant to a Large Corporation in China, I was once asked to apply my formidable intellect to the problems faced by small clothing firms in a part of Tibet only accessible at certain times of the year. 'Whatever you do Harpic,' admonished my boss, when I set out on the Air Mali flight to Lhasa. 'Don't risk venturing back down those mountain passes if you are in any doubt at all. The Company will just have to get by without you if you get stuck up there for the duration. It'll be tough, but we wouldn't want to risk your safety.' Once up there, I identified the problem immediately; the clothes were too well made and reasonably priced so I quickly re-engineered the process to create the sort of shoddy rags that Geordie girls camouflage their bulging bodies with, added an Armani label and tripled the price. They sold like hot cakes and the company did very well for a while until it was forced to cease trading over some footling detail buried deep in a very dull legal footnote about Patents Pending or whatnot. But it just goes to show that just because some slick Italian has written his name all over one's garment, the rag trade is just what it has always been; a stitch up.

On to the more pleasurable aspects of shopping, such as deciding which kind of bacon to buy. This brings me to the delicate subject of Turkey Bacon. This is not *Turkish* bacon but a bacon substitute made from the turkey bird. It is made from chopped up and reformed bits of turkey meat, flavoured, cured and smoked using the same method as in the production of real bacon and is supposed to be a healthier alternative. Don't let this put you off though; the main disadvantage lies in its tendency to stick to the pan when frying and its general unsuitability for grilling. Now if substituting bacon with strips torn off the Xmas treat seems unlikely, as it did when first I came across it, I would urge you not to dismiss it out of hand even though it really is no substitute for the real thing. This is because under certain circumstances, you might have no alternative as I found out when I was Consultant to a Large Corporation in Dubai.

Knowing how keen I was on bacon, and because I had returned unexpectedly early from Tibet, the boss sent me to investigate the possibility of opening up new markets for pork products in the region. Of course, I knew this would be a challenge because Muslims don't eat pork - never mind bacon!

'You're just the man for the job,' he said, handing me my ticket for Oil Bling Air. 'And as it's July, enjoy the sunshine. It'll make a change after Tibet. See you at the end of September.'

It was with a heavy heart that I undertook this task. Imagine three months without bacon! However, duty always comes first with Harpic and so I repaired to the nearest canteen in Gatwick and ordered all the bacon that my last English tenner could buy. There I sat with twelve other chaps breaking bread and drinking tepid coffee, a last breakfast before the coming trials and tribulations, and did my sullen best to enjoy the exquisite saltiness of the magnificent smoked back. 'This is my bacon sandwich,' I said, mournfully shaking out the old HP. 'When two or more of you are next gathered together, do this in memory of me.'

'Amen to that, matey,' said one chap, to general agreement.

'Can anyone lend me thirty pence,' says another, who looked a bit shifty to be honest.

Well, as the plane ascended to the heavens, the taste of that last bacon sandwich reminded me of the difficulties ahead and I wondered if it might be possible to somehow get out of this job.

'Will you miss bacon and Blighty and all things bright and true in England's green and pleasant land?' I asked the excessively tattooed chap next to me.

'No chance, matey,' he replied. 'I'm alright. There's no extradition treaty where I'm going.'

'What about you?' I asked, of the chap on the other side of me. (I did ask for a window seat but was told there was none available). 'Will you miss England, home and bacon?'

'No, mate,' he replied. 'Though I am a true patriot; I'm leaving my country for my country's good.'

'He means, he's skipped his parole,' explained the excessively tattooed gentleman.

Several hours later after a fitful night's sleep dreaming of smoked and streaky, unsmoked, spam, sausages and mustard we landed back on terra firma where amid the melting tarmac and 45°C heat of Dubai airport, I waved my erstwhile companions off and wished them well in their adventurous new lives. Unfortunately, I later discovered that I had also waved my wallet, watch and passport off with them. It wasn't a great start.

On arrival at the Camel's Hump Hotel, things got worse. Breakfast consisted of a watery pile of rubbery omelette adorned with a chicken sausage about the size of a baby's penis and toast that had been toasted to destruction. The coffee hadn't so much been passed through a civet cat but shoved up its arse and the milk had odd lumps of oily fat floating in it. On top of that there was a dab of snot in the sugar bowl and a fat kid was howling at the top of its voice at the next table. I passed, but then noticing a chap furtively munching on what definitely looked like a slice of good streaky, I beckoned the waiter over and asked him what the caper was with the illicit pork.

'I beg your pardon, Sir?' he said, in an impeccable Indian accent. 'To what caper are you referring?'

'You know, mate,' I said, winking. 'The under-the-counter, off-the-record, informal economy meat candy.'

'Please, Sir,' he replied. 'Are you perchance suffering from jet lag? Would you like me to fetch you a soothing glass of water?'

Clearly, he was playing hard to get in the hope that he could extract a premium price for the smuggled-in premium breakfast product. I would have produced a tenner at this stage if I still had my wallet but all I had to bribe him with was an IOU. I wrote one out.

IOU £10. Bring me the bacon.

Joely Harpic, Consultant to a Large Corporation.

'I understand fully,' he said, tapping his forehead and motioning the Head Waiter over. 'Can I get you a doctor?'

The Head Waiter appeared after a moment so, knowing just how hierarchical smuggling networks can be, I immediately handed over the IOU to the Gang Lieutenant.

'You want some bacon, Sir?'

'I see we speak the same language,' I replied, tapping the side of my nose.

'Indeed we do, Sir,' replied the Gangland Kingpin. 'It is a colonial relic but a convenient one for when one sells one's labour in the international market. One rasher or two?'

'Make it two,' I said, not wanting to push things too far too fast.

'The IOU will not be necessary, Sir,' said the Cheese. 'I'll simply add it to your bill.'

'You have the caper all wrapped up,' I said admiringly. 'I dare say you can do a bit of money laundering too?'

'Indeed, Sir,' replied the Peeler Dodger. 'There is a *Bureau de Change* in the lobby.'

'Hookers?

'There is a smoking area just by the bar, Sir,' said the Big Man. 'But if you are new to Dubai you may wish to stick to cigarettes or cigars until you get used to things.'

This last comment baffled me for a moment, but at that moment the bacon arrived and all else was forgotten as my whole being rebelled at the taste of Turkey bacon.

'Turkey?' I squealed in disbelief.

'This is a Muslim country, Sir,' replied the Head Waiter. 'So it is either Turkey or Beef bacon.'

'Beef bacon?' I reeled in disbelief.

My mind was made up. I went straight back to the airport and hailed the first plane home (notwithstanding an unseemly incident with an unpaid taxi driver), which was a pity because I subsequently found (when the boss sent me straight back) that you could buy Hungarian bacon in a special section of the supermarket. Well, you live and learn and if push comes to shove *any* bacon is better than no bacon at all.

Now, in the here and now, coming out of the butcher's with my pound of streaky, pound of smoked back and a pound of green middle, I spy that rat-faced little Communist Ostrakov coming out of the Conservative Club where no doubt he has been listening at doors and spying on the party of free enterprise, freedom and the free world. He is loitering by the bus stop, undoubtedly waiting to contact his KGB controller so he can pass on the secrets that he hopes will eventually lead to the toppling of the capitalist system and the enslavement of the British people in a gulag outside Doncaster. It is time to confront him with his outrageous plans to frack the village and destroy all the hard won freedoms of our two thousand year old realm. Harpic gets up a head of steam and starts down the hill towards the Slimstead Leninist and is about to cross the road when three Gazpacom trucks come out of a side street and temporarily snarl up the traffic. By the time I get across the road the bus has arrived and Ostrakov has mounted it in an attempt to rub shoulders with the underclass.

'Ostrakov!' I cry.

He turns, his eyes wide with wonder at being caught in his subversive act.

'Ostrakov!' I cry again. 'What the devil are you up to, eh? Admit it! Out with it! You're in favour of this fracking business.'

'Mind your language,' interrupts a fat old biddy with a frump of a face and a fearsome terrier folded across her chest like an RPG.

'What?' I say, distracted.

'I said *Mind your language*,' she says. 'And it's *pardon* not *what*. Where was you dragged up?'

'Pardon?' I say, mystified.

'That's alright then,' says the old biddy, marching off.

By the time this intervention has been dealt with, the doors to the bus have closed and the vehicle is moving off. Ostrakov is moving smartly towards a seat with an odiously smug expression plastered across his Communist features. I am undeterred.

'Admit it!' I shout. 'You want to frack us up!'

As the bus gathers momentum and then disappears in a cloud of blue diesel, I catch a glimpse of him nodding and saying 'Why yes, of course….'

I am about to add an epithet but find myself dismayed by a terrier attached to my rump.

This is what is known in modern American slang as 'a wake-up call'. It is time for old Harpic to confront Bill Gon and find out the full story from an honest upstanding member of the community who has been led astray by the Communist Ostrakov and attempt to bring him to his senses and see the error of his ways.

(Wildlife spotted: a couple of scabby pigeons).

Lunch.

Whenever I feel drawn to challenge my own assumption that Lunch is an unnecessary indulgence for the sylphlike among us, I turn to perusing the Sunday newspapers in search of the culinary enlightenment handed down to us, like Commandments, in the columns written by food critics. These lucky chaps seem to have been dealt a pretty good hand of cards by Fortune in that they are required to do very little but go to restaurants, indulge themselves in all manner of delicacies washed down with the best sauce on offer, all paid for by their Editors and then write something acidic about the experience. It is remarkable though – in the same way that travel guides are remarkable – that what you read of the place never, ever matches the reality when you yourself tool along for a bit of nosh and a couple of cheeky ones. It is as though they have been written without the benefit of actual experience – which in the case of travel guides is very often the case, now that the 'cut and paste' function has been mastered by pretty much everyone, (myself excluded) in the inky bullshit trade. And this is when they do actually write about the restaurant that they have alleged to have visited, for most of the time they seem to write about the first vapid half-thought that they downloaded from the internet or go through a sort of mock dilemma about which underwear is most restaurant appropriate or some such nonsense. After that there is usually some hyper-ventilated hyperbole about the freshness of the fish caught that morning by some scrungy old trawlerman in a woollen sweater and a Scottish accent and then helicoptered down all the way from Lossiemouth in a specially chartered, refrigerated RAF Sea King just so that you can munch it down alongside a few chips and the *Huffington Post.* You know full well when you read this old pony that the bit of whitefish off-cut that you'll get on your plate comes in from Tesco and has been in the freezer longer than the chef's ex-wife. How else is the owner going to pay his unreasonable heavy local and national taxes except by charging more for less? As to wine critics, well: if it tastes good, it is good and if you're paying more than £20 max for a bottle, you're either pissed, on expenses or completely mad.

Recently, there has been a development in culinary criticism that is often the only lie bigger than the writer's expenses claim and that is that there are restaurants of note in the North of this Sceptred Isle. I say this is patently unbelievable because all restaurant critics live in London and although they are licensed to travel outside the realms of the M25, they are strictly confined to certain places in the Home Counties, Glastonbury, Glyndbourne, sometimes Aldeburgh, but never anywhere above 52°N and rarely anywhere beyond 3°W. This results in them making up stories about exotic places that don't exist – much like travel writers indeed – in an attempt to gain a Northern readership, which they believe will improve their 'inclusiveness' credentials. This is, of course, all baloney. The idea that Michelin ever went near Manchester in anything other than tyre form is plainly risible and unless it is now possible to be awarded a star for a soup kitchen, extremely unlikely to happen before the Day of Judgement. The same might be said of Liverpool, where Michelin would not only have any stars awarded stolen within minutes by striking workshy Scousers, but also find that his tyres would have been slashed and his car fenced before he'd finished writing out the certificate. Obviously there are exceptions; it is true, however hard it might be for the reasonable man to believe, that there is a Harvey Nicholls in Leeds and that one star has been awarded to a restaurant in Scotland but there is no need to get carried away. Apparently, only one star has ever been awarded north of the Severn-Wash line as compared with several hundred awarded below it; it is hard to win plaudits for gruel, however creatively the offal has been rendered. That it is possible to eat anything decent at all in those blasted heaths is only due to the Missionary work done by Essex-boy Jamie Oliver, who frequently goes bankrupt in his attempts to persuade Northerners to put down their clubs and become civilised over something they need cutlery for. Trying to persuade Rotherham to eat anything but industrial grade slop during his *Ministry of Food* TV programme was a noble undertaking, but doomed to failure. He clearly hadn't done his research. So now, if you are still feeling peckish, I would encourage you to view the aforementioned series and consider a meal of doner kebab and cheesy chips, eaten off the floor, as your special Rotherham treat. A doner kebab. No alcohol allowed. Not discouraged?

The same goes for Wales. In April 2014, a kebab 'restaurant' in Wales was fined for serving lamb kebabs that contained beef and chicken. When charged, the owners claimed that they did not know exactly where the meat came from but from now on would only use 'whole meat' (what were they using before?). In June 2014, another Welsh kebab-meister was fined for serving up beef and goat in his lamb kebabs and, likewise, could not say where the meat had come from. Both of these cases originated in Cardiff. Cardiff, Wales. Wales. Where Sheep Come From. If they don't know where the meat comes from, how will that dodgy place down the High Street know? And you're still eating it? Sober? Add more chilli sauce; it might kill some of the beastly things that are about to start grazing ravenously on your intestinal flora. And put the toilet roll in the freezer.

To My Date With Destiny.

When I was Consultant to a Large Corporation in Northern Saskatchewan, it fell to me as being the only one of our party to have the honour of having served as the longest serving Lieutenant in the British Army, to be in charge of guarding the encampment against Polar bears.

'Harpic,' said the Boss. 'This is an important and responsible job. The future of the Oil Sands industry depends on the safety of our exploration experts and protecting them against Polar bears is central to our corporate strategy.'

'Absolutely right, Sir,' I replied, enthusiastically pulling on an extra pair of socks against the icy blast and permafrost. 'The geographers and geologists may sleep safely in their warm centrally heated beds sure in the knowledge that they are safe against the rampaging beasts that are sure to be about during this terrible blizzard.'

'Harpic,' he said, manfully patting me on the shoulder as he led me to the door. 'You'll need to be out all night if we are to achieve the central aim of our corporate strategy.'

'You can count on me,' I said, pulling my mittens on and reaching for the blunderbuss.

'Harpic,' he said, finally. 'Please make sure that you shoot *away* from the complex – that's if you have to shoot *at all*. Remember our commitment to the environmental sustainability of Polar bears and remember also the cost of bullets. It wouldn't look good on the Balance Sheet if we wasted bullets, would it?'

'Certainly not, Sir,' I replied, stepping out into the flinty sleet of the black Arctic night. 'The environment and the Balance Sheet must come first if we are to save the planet.'

The sound of a door slamming cut off the last of my remarks but I knew that my input into management strategy was valued and, as I stood under the great canopy of storm wracked mountains, watching the clouds fly across the stars like tattered banners under a scatter of silver stars and thinking of the frozen lakes and rivers before me, I felt the thrill that only comes with effective corporate motivation. As I heard the clink of bottles and hearty laughter from within, I felt heartened that I would fulfil my role to the best of my ability and secure the goodwill and fine opinion of my superiors. Looking across the bleak, shattered tundra towards the forbidding iron bound mountains and endless dark forests of the night, I took in the snowy landscape and felt at peace with the world. It was so beautiful, so vast, so serene that I knew instinctively that there could be no danger in it and so I dug myself a snow hole in a handy drift, climbed in and snuggled down for a nice comfortable night.

How I slept through the resultant commotion, I have no idea, (as I told the Commission of Inquiry later), other than the fact that I usually sleep pretty soundly, being possessed of a fairly clear conscience. Of course, it could have been the effects of Exposure, but I doubt it, and this being a disease unworthy of the hardy Harpic, I could hardly use it as an excuse while retaining my self-esteem. Anyway, it seemed that sometime in the night, a large body of Polar bears had attacked the geologists' encampment and eaten most of them, returning in the early morning to finish off with a dessert of geographers, leaving Harpic here as the sole survivor. What was perhaps more serious was that the bears seem to have acquired a taste not just for Oil Sands prospectors but for their communications equipment as well, which meant that old Harpic was stuck up the Tundra without the proverbial paddle and would somehow have to survive the winter or the duration of the storm, whichever came first. Even worse still was the fact that the bears seem to have made off with all the can openers and bottle openers, so I faced the prospect of starving and freezing to death without even a snifter to ease my passing.

We Harpics are a hardy lot though and taking in the situation in an instant I knew that the only answer was to eat the bears. It is, perhaps, not such a Well Known Fact that you can eat every part of every fur bearing mammal as part of a healthy and wide ranging diet and suffer no deleterious effects, with the exception of the liver of a Polar bear which, though rich in Vitamin A, is so rich in it that it will poison you. (And Haggis, which is made with sheep offal but only ever eaten in Ultima Thule by the kilted crew of the SS Tartanic, who don't know any better. Our American cousins have rightly banished the blasted bag of filthy guts and suet, as deleterious to civilisation as to health). Shouldering my trusted blunderbuss, I therefore set off into the wilderness down the trail of bloody spoor and bits of left over geographer in search of my bear salvation. This wasn't such a big job as only a little further on I found the first of several large Polar bears strewn about the place and looking like Dublin on the morning after St.Paddy's day. It appeared that they had acquired a taste for *Geologiste Au Vin* and as they preferred their meat blue and, not having opposable thumbs or discovered fire, were unable to burn off the alcohol with a quick *flambe*. Result? Pissed as Polar bears on Penguin shots.

The first beast was groaning horribly, rolling in its own vomit and pointing to its stomach in a heart-rending display of distress. Next to it, a particularly big, yellowish specimen was holding its head in its hands and complaining just as loudly, so in the interests of humane environmentalism, I blew them both away with my blunderbuss. This brought forth a protest from another couple of *Ursus Maritimis* and so reluctantly, I despatched them too. By the time items five and six had decided that they would like to top off their excesses of last night with a breakfast of Consultant to a Large Corporation, I had reloaded and let the buggers have both barrels with brio and panache. The others buggered off in double quick time so all I had to do now was to skin my new wardrobe, carve up the steaks and hope that there was a bottle opener in the stomach contents. Luckily, one of the geographers had a Swiss Army knife in his pocket when he had been consumed, so all was well with the world. Shrugging off any suggestion of cannibalism – the geographers had not been digested long enough to have entered the meat of the bears – I got the meat and skins back to the encampment, rigged up a shelter, made fire and got down to the serious business of breakfast.

Recipe: Polar Bear Stew.

It isn't ideal as a breakfast meat but faced with the question of Arctic survival sometimes you just have to make do with what is to hand. Avoid the temptation to bbq the steak or even grill it simply because there are no facilities to hang the meat, it's too cold for the maturing process to really get going and, more to the point, it will attract angry relatives. Stick to stewing because long and slow cooking will kill off all the parasites in the meat that in civilised places are sorted out by pumping antibiotics in.

Step 1. Get a big pot and light a fire under it. Put some ice or snow in it to melt. You will need a lot more than you think because snow is a lot less dense than water. Be generous.

Step 2. Cut the meat into bite-sized chunks and add to the boiling water. Try not to get any of the geographer in it unless you like the taste of human (a bit like pork) and are in a jurisdiction that approves of anthropophagy.

Step 3. Add spuds and carrots, oxo cubes, salt and pepper to taste and cook until tender. There is very little fat in Polar bear meat so it is very healthy (once caught and killed).

I confess that when I was finally rescued I was heartily sick of Polar bear stew and the thought of a bit off the flank of a geographer was beginning to sound attractive, but the question didn't arise until the Commission of Inquiry brought it up after I had cooked it for them. Actually, they were awfully over sensitive about a lot of things that I had endured during that winter but fortunately the fact that when I lit the fire for the stew I had melted the permafrost enough for a nice bubbling spring of tar to boil up seemed to soften their attitude towards me.

'Harpic,' said the Commission Chairman (obviously it was a man, so this appellation is correct), placing a large wad of banknotes on the table before me. 'We think a Confidentiality Agreement is the way forward on this.'

'If I don't say anything, you won't?' I replied.

'That's about the size of it,' he replied.

'It's a deal,' I said, driving a hard bargain.

I even got one of the skins made into a fur coat for Louise, which she flaunts outrageously.

Anyway, the point of this story in regard to my coming encounter with Bill Gon is that, as all Harpics know deep in their hearts, when faced with no choice, one just has to 'Man Up' and eat the bear.

Walking swiftly over to the Nature Reserve, I pass Old Timeon on the other side of the wildflower meadow. He is looking even more Biblical than usual and appears to be preparing to sacrifice something over by the Wicker Man. I give him a cheery wave but all I receive in return is the faint sound of chanting coming down the wind, drowned out mainly by the thumping of a pile-driver in the near vicinity. Coming towards the Nature reserve, I observe a lot of new fencing, several large industrial looking construction vehicles and a number of men in Hi-vis clothing and hard hats. Two of them appear to be holding Denning in a strong arm lock and seem to be frog-marching him out of the immediate surrounds. He is attempting to gesticulate wildly, as he was wont to do when presenting a particularly fine but passionately purchased legal opinion before the highest courts of the land. However, the two blokes who have got hold of him do not seem to be of the legal profession and are not treating his legal brain with the respect he deserves; indeed one of them seems to be clipping poor Denning round the ears. This is surely against *Habeus Corpus*? Denning must surely know.

As I approach closer and more purposefully, a tree – a noble beech! – topples over as the chainsaw bites and the forest screams. The pile-driver piles on as the lash of barbed wire is felt on the mesh fences of imprisoned nature; fence posts linked by the chains of bondage enslave the home of liberty, the land of freedom and the only place left to stick two fingers up to the Nazis before the Yanks got out of bed. Even worse! Behind the toppling forest rears up a lattice of metal and steel, an Eiffel Tower of environmental degradation ready to plunge its biting drill into the ruptured bowels of Olde England. Adorning this monstrous pipe of hydrocarbonical mayhem are stark letters, some feet high, which proclaim the terrible dipper as belonging to G-A-Z, which is a puzzle, but they seem to be still working on it so all may become clearer at a later date.

But a later date can no longer wait for Harpic is on the march! I fly to the aid of my old legal acquaintance who is at this moment being pitched into a ditch by the two goons in Hi-vis jackets worn over the sort of Breton shirts that the old Soviet Spetsnatz special forces used to wear.

'I say!' I cry. 'You can't do that to one of the finest legal minds in the kingdom! It is outrageous.'

There is an echo in the wind that carries with it the distant protests of the soul of Slimstead.

'Shocking,' it says, soughing through the falling elms and crumbling oaks. 'Shouldn't be allowed.'

I come to the side of my defenestrated colleague and stand four square before his granite faced tormentors.

'Pizzorfski,' says the first, a grey, square-jawed chap with all the chiselled blandness of a Kremlin wall gargoyle. 'Orski we chuckski you in bezydes himski.'

Denning is struggling in the undergrowth. There are nettles and brambles that in happier times would present many culinary opportunities for the experienced forager but which are now something of an inconvenience for the dismounted knight errant of the Old Bailey.

'Who the Devil do you think you are?' I demand. 'I take it from your accents that you are not native to the precincts of Slimstead?'

'Healthski and Safetyski,' answers the second, grim enforcer of the despoliation of England. 'Now pizzorfski. Last warningovsky.'

'Never,' I grumble out a defiant warning. 'Never. We shall defend our Nature Reserve whatever the cost may be. We will fight you on the verges, on the puddles, on the ornamental bridge. We shall never surrender. Will we Denning?'

Denning is achieving his feet, but not control of his face, which resembles a burning Stuka spewing oil and smoke and going down in a tailspin. He tries to regain his legal standing by brushing off his coat but has yet to assemble the arguments and precedents necessary for an attempt at the sides of the ditch.

'*Casus belli*!' he storms, brushing a nettle from his fine domed head and screwing up his nose. '*Compos mentis! Fiat Justitia et Pereat Mundus.*'

'Precisely!' I roar at the tank-like jaw of this totalitarian lackey of rampant petrodollar imperialism.

'Wotski fyk youski talkingski aboutov?' says the running dog of unbounded corporate capitalism. Clearly he is confounded by Denning's legal brilliance and my own feisty defiance. 'Fykski ovski or we kickski the shitski out of youski tooski.'

'This is my land not yours, vile invader,' I declare, rolling up my sleeves ready to mete out retribution for the dual outrages committed on the person of Denning and the body of this blessed plot, this realm, this England.

'Pizzorfski lunatikski,' replies Goon #1. 'Or joinski baldy headski prevertski in ditchski.'

I pause and assess the odds before me. Denning, whose legal genius might not be as useful in actual combat as it might be in negotiating the terms of post-combat surrender, is looking doubtful but defiant and is making manful efforts to climb out of the ditch. Will he succeed and come smartly to my aid like Field Marshall Blucher did in bringing the Prussian army to the side of Wellington at Waterloo in the nick of time and so defeating the arrogant machinations and ambitions of Napoleon Bonaparte? Judging by the state of his wind and the slipperiness of the bank, I doubt it. Still, I reason, the odds are no greater than faced Henry V before his great victory at Agincourt.

'England Expects,' says Denning, bolstering my morale no end in the face of these monstrous running dogs of the bourgeoisie. 'I'll be out in a minute.'

'No way,' I declare, spitting defiance in the face of the two environmentally unfriendly hulks. 'As the longest serving Lieutenant in the British Army, I defy you. You Shall Not Pass! Here I stand like a greyhound in the slip, straining upon the start. I think full scorn that any Prince of Europe should dare invade the borders of my realm and cry God for Harry, England and St.George.'

I square up and defy the unacceptable face of capitalism.

There is a flash, a bang, two bangs and the world turns upside down as I tumble arse over tit into the ditch and land squarely on top of Denning. A split second later and two mounds of steaming Hi-vis bouncer beef follow until we are all four combatants entangled in brambles and breathless but not exclusively legal argument.

'Wotski fykski?' cries Kremlin Goon #1. 'Is itski Chechen rebelski againski?'

'Fykski Norovski!' wails Kremlin Goon #2. 'Is worski than Afghanistanski! These Angloskis are madderovski thanski Rasputin.'

'Any ideas, Denning?' I posit, hoping that he might engage his powerful intellect and enlighten us all.

'It's Carruthers,' declares Denning, his trollish features transformed to bright happiness. 'Carruthers to the rescue. *In locus parentis.*'

'*Status Quo,*' I agree, as the welcome face of Carruthers appears above the rim of the ditch. '*Quod erat Demonstrandum.*'

Once out of the ditch, negotiations start in earnest for Bill Gon, attracted by the discharge of Carruthers' elephant gun, has put in an appearance. Gon's Goons are dismissed, leaving him at the mercy of Slimstead's combined legal, armed and dangerous force in the form of Denning, Carruthers and my humble but defiant self. Fair play demands, however, that these advantages in my favour should not be over-played and I ask Denning and Carruthers to retire to a respectful distance so that I may conduct straightforward meaningful negotiations, man to man, as I often did as a Consultant to Large Corporations. They agree; Denning to straighten his attire; Carruthers to re-load.

'I say, Bill,' I demand. 'What is all this nonsense about you fracking? *You* of all people! A decent upstanding member of the community! You! What has happened to your morals? Just because the Cold War is over and the American airbase has gone does not mean that you should have strayed from you honest hobbies of plane spotting and Ham radio and taken up fracking instead.'

'Harpic,' he answers. 'What are you talking about?'

'Fracking,' I reply. 'It's perfectly obvious that you have been led astray by the Communist Ostrakov. Why not give it up and come back into the Slimstead fold? I'm sure all will be forgiven.'

'Harpic,' says Bill Gon, a friendly smile playing about his moustache. 'We're not fracking.'

'You can't expect me to believe that,' I reply, understanding that this is just a cunning opening negotiating ploy. 'Why, even from here I can see the letters G-A-Z on that tower of yours.'

'Look again,' he replies, and turning my eyes to the metal tower I see that a letter P has been added. 'It stands for GAZPACHO, or will do when it's finished.'

'Gazpacho?' I reply.

'We're mining soup, Harpic,' he says, giddily patting me on the back. 'We've hit the motherlode of Gazpacho. There's enough soup down there to feed the hungry of the Third World for the next ten years. All we have to do is pump it out, package it and ship it to the poor, starving millions.'

'Really?' I am stunned, but also relieved. I knew that Bill Gon was not a bad man at bottom.

'Really, Harpic,' he says, peeling off a £50 note and handing it to me. 'And this is a donation from the starving people of Liberia to thank you for all your efforts to relieve them from poverty. This soup will save their bacon.'

I am humbled.

'Bill,' I say, wiping a tear away and shaking his hand. 'Let me apologise for thinking you had been led astray by Communists.'

'No problem, Harpic,' he replies, nobly. 'Anyone can make a mistake. And we'll sort out another Nature Reserve as soon as we've got all the soup out.'

'Please extend my apologies to your friends too,' I reply. 'I fear I may have been rough with them.'

'Ivan and Oleg Kiktabolokov?' he replies. 'They'll be OK, I'm sure.'

I retire and invite Denning and Carruthurs to join me for a *mea culpa* in the Old Queen's Head.

'Rather not, old boy,' says Denning, putting his trousers back in order. 'Rather just forget about the whole thing, eh? Wouldn't want anything to be open to misinterpretation, just in case.'

'I don't understand,' I say.

'Just as well,' he replies, rather anxiously. *'Tacet ire consentire'.*

I ponder this for a while before turning to Carruthers. Being the expert stalker that he is, he has disappeared, blending into the landscape expertly at the merest hint of the police siren atop the Armed Response Unit. Turning back I see Denning making himself scarce too, while from the far side of the Nature Reserve, the raven haired High Priestess Chickadee is emerging from the wood and doing up her dress.

(Wildlife spotted: one fox, two bustards, several large swallows).

Pre-dinner Drinks to Fortify the Soul and reaffirm Your Faith in Human Nature.

I am so delighted to have confirmed that Bill Gon is not a fracker or a Communist but instead an upstanding member of the Slimstead community doing his best to feed the Third World, no doubt at considerable expense to himself in time, money and effort. How could I have thought otherwise? I beat my breast and almost rend my garments. If I could find some sackcloth and ashes or a hair shirt and scourge, I might be tempted to shrive my soul in repentance and beg forgiveness for my transgressions (I'm drawing the line at a cilice though). Instead, I decide to invent a new cocktail to express fully my faith in Human nature and delight Louise when she gets home from leading her little charges towards the kindly light.

Recipe: The *Mea Culpa, Mea Culpa, Mea Maxima Culpa.*

Step 1. Start with a shot of monkish Benedictine to get the whole repentance theme off to a good start. It comes in at 40% abv and as it is officially sanctioned by God, make sure it's a good sized shot. This will give a lovely herby flavour which, given our environmental concerns today, is also appropriate. Add some ice and then top up with Baileys, which is Irish and possibly catholic and so in line with the apostolic.

Step 2. In a separate glass add a shot of Chartreuse. This is also a monkish concoction personally approved by God, so don't stint. The separate glasses are necessary because Benedictine is a reddy-brown colour and Chartreuse is greeny-yellow and if you mix them they end up the colour of a builder's puddle. Add ice, Kahlua and Black Sambuca to remind you of the fires of Hell.

Step 3. In a third glass, put a single shot of Frangelico hazelnut liquor. It is important only to use a single shot as Fra Angelico, the bloke who invented it 1455, was a hermit so he wouldn't want company. Better make sure it's a big shot then.

Step 4. You'll need some rosary beads to help you keep count of how many you've had. This is a good tip. Amen.

'Harpic,' says the fabulous Rainbow of my Dreams, dropping a bag full of marking and looking haggard. 'What enormity are you about to commit on me today?'

'My dear, Louise,' I reply, ecclesiastically. 'You have before you the Father, Son and Holy Ghost of cocktails so may I invite you to imbibe?'

'Harpic,' she replies, gnostically. 'After the day I've had, I will need the full Graeco-Roman Pantheon, Aman-Ra, Anubis, Seth, Thoth, Tutankhamun and more arms than Kali to hold the bloody glasses. Bring more.'

She slurps gratefully and I see the beginnings of Nirvana emerge as from a cloud.

'And you will purchase a Take-Away, Harpic,' she continues, beatifically. 'For I am in no mood to face what you consider to be cuisine.'

'But the car is still unnecessarily in the garage,' I protest.

'Berkstead High Street is only a matter of miles, Harpic,' she pronounces *ex cathedra*. 'It is well within your range.'

I can see there is no point arguing with her when she is in such a pontifical mood.

'Can I stop for a pint in Berkstead?' I punt.

'You may have small half-pint, Harpic,' she concedes. 'But there will be food on this table within an hour and a half or their will be crucifixion shortly afterwards.'

This is cutting it fine, so Harpic doesn't wait until she gets properly theological and is half way down the cul-de-sac before she can ring the Inquisition.

Take-aways: a Culinary Conundrum.

The kebab as Take-away has already been considered, weighed in the balance and found wanting, but if one is hoping to achieve, sustain and maintain as fine a figure as my own then eating Take-aways can be a bit of a challenge. Let us consider the various types of offerings, broadly categorised of course, that are readily available on Britain's High Streets.

Indian: The Nation's favourite. Broadly speaking it consists of several utterly unauthentic dishes unknown outside the Balti houses of Birmingham and regarded with supreme wonder by Indians new to our shores. A typical menu will include Poppodums marked up at loan shark percentages and served with thin yoghurt, apricot jam and an unidentifiable spicy blob that may or may not consist of the corpses of zombies. Main courses include the food colouring intensive Chicken Tikka Masala, something purporting to have been served up to a Mogul (the chef being condemned to be stood on by elephants shortly afterwards) accompanied by a spongy piece of last week's bread, and scraggy mutton disguised in so many ways that it may as well wear a false moustache. Once any of this food has been placed in the foil container and transported for any distance, the copious amounts of oil used in its preparation separates from the other ingredients (a term I use very loosely indeed) to leave a layer several centimetres deep beneath which lurks meat that Gollum might discard. In general, we can describe the typical Indian Take-away as no more than boiled rubber chicken in hot slop. If you want to eat authentic Indian food go to India, or if this isn't possible, the Middle East in general and Abu Dhabi in particular, where the Kwality Restaurant provides the best I've ever tasted.

Pizza. Looking like a teenager's face, this food is often delivered in cardboard boxes by teenagers and is to be avoided, but if you are lucky enough to have a local Italian Take-away, then treasure it. The classic Pizza Margherita was invented to celebrate the red, white and green tricolour of the newly unified (well, most of it) Italy in 1860 and to serve alongside the eponymous Garibaldi biscuit (himself born in Nice) after he had overthrown the Neapolitan Bourbons in a political as well as culinary revolution. The base is made from flour, water, salt, yeast and olive oil. The topping is made from tomatoes, mozzarella cheese and fresh basil. You would think that it would be hard to fuck anything as simple as this up, but depressingly, outside a proper Italian restaurant, it almost always is. The Chicken Tikka Masala pizza is the abomination that springs to mind immediately, followed closely by the BBQ Chicken pizza, but the list is by no means limited to these enormities; I have seen Baked Bean Pizza. Quite recently I came across an alleged restaurant proposing to sell a pizza with a topping of Tuna sashimi, with truffle ponzu, red onions and green chillies which, apparently is an attempt at Japanese-Italian fusion. I might illustrate the flaw in this concept by pointing out that the last Japanese-Italian fusion, when combined with a dash of Nazi, resulted in the Second World War; and just what is 'ponzu', anyway? It does not sound like anything that I would want to put in my mouth, I must say. Mind you, this goes for most of the ingredients found lurking on non-Italian pizza. Take, for example, Mozzarrella cheese; it is rarely to be found on the Take-away pizza; instead a 'cheese fondue' is often used instead, which is a measly bit of dodgy cheese mixed with flour and water to make the price mark-up go skywards. On the whole, therefore, my advice would be to eat the cardboard box; it tastes better and has more nutrients in it. That's if the pimply face of the delivery boy hasn't already put you off.

Chinese. Often described as 'Cantonese' or 'Sechuan' style restaurants, they rarely are, which in some ways is a blessing because anyone who has actually eaten in China will tell you that most Chinese food is bland beyond redemption and that Pot Noodle type products are all the rage there. The only way is up, but not unfortunately, very far up; the Lotus Blossom has as much chance of getting a Michelin Star as the Star of India up the road, turn left. A typical Chinese menu will be numbered to give the impression of variety and choice, but everything will taste of two or three basic flavours; a salty soy sauce bought by the gallon from a warehouse in East London; a sticky jam sauce bought by the gallon from a warehouse in East London; and rice, bought by the gallon from a warehouse in East London, or noodles, which is basically different shaped spaghetti which they fry sometimes. *Chou Mein* actually means *Fried Noodles* and everyone knows that frying spaghetti can only end in *frittata*. The same rule applies to Chinese food transported; by the time you get it home the rice will be grey, flecked only with odd yellowy bits and bearing no relationship to the Special Fried Rice you thought you were getting (and none whatsoever to the Egg Foo Yung you thought you had ordered). A close inspection of the Straw Mushrooms will reveal them to be no different from the closed cup white varieties that you saw Mr.Wong buying in Sainsbury's that morning and that the sauce is basically oxo with a dash of soy. And never eat anything in a dumpling; you really don't know what's in there and Chinese people have a more radical approach to culinary thought than you might be aware of and are willing to experiment with a wider variety of foodstuffs than the conservative English are used to. Fact: we export pig snouts to China. My advice; stick to curry and chips. The curry is thicker and tends to be sweeter than you get at the Indian. Not that they eat this in China either. The ribs aren't bad though. And I'd kill for crispy duck with shredded cucumber, spring onion and plum sauce in those little pancakes. And spring rolls, but on the other hand they do go soggy when transported. Bit of a dilemma for the Confucian philosophers among us there. What time does the Lotus Garden open?

Thai. Same as Chinese, but with more bullshit marketing speak on the menu. True, you might get a bit more coconut milk but the thin watery yellow stuff that the chicken is submerged in will still separate on the way home and the crunchy things will go soggy. The TV chef who described Crab in Thai Green Curry as looking like 'the creature from *Alien* baked in mud' had it about right, I'd say. You don't get crispy duck there either.

Fried Chicken.

Whether from a particular American state or a generic region, the Fried Chicken sold in these Take-aways bears absolutely no resemblance to the real thing. For the record, real fried chicken is marinaded overnight in buttermilk, chilli, garlic and whatever spices take your fancy according to taste and is then coated in a batter of flour and water spiced to your particular recipe. It is then deep fried until brown and then placed in the oven to cook through. It is never to be eaten straight out of the fryer. The fact that many Fried Chicken places skip the oven bit accounts for why it is a dish that, almost uniquely, manages to achieve the virtually impossible trick of being both greasy and dry at the same time. If you then compound this error by transporting it in a cardboard box, you will achieve a triple in that it will be greasy, dry, taste of cardboard and the chips will go soggy. To be honest, Styrofoam isn't much better but it hardly matters – you just can't put lipstick on a pig and expect it to look like a supermodel. Some outlets sell very large 'family size' servings and provide a bucket for convenience in carrying it home; this is to be commended, as at least you have something to throw up into once you have consumed this culinary H-bomb.

Burgers.

Like Fried Chicken, when done properly the humble hamburger is a thing of beauty. Just get some good minced beef, add salt and pepper, then mix it up with ketchup and Dijon mustard to bind it. Some people use eggs or breadcrumbs and some people like to add spices or herbs. This is acceptable. Fried or grilled, then served on a soft white roll, some nice iceberg lettuce, a slice of tomato and perhaps a gherkin, and topped with mayonnaise, it makes a healthy meal or a tasty snack.

What is not acceptable is to scrunch up some 'Head meat' with some 'Mechanically Recovered Meat' and 'Connective Tissue', add artificial sweeteners, some cow's udders to give it enough fat content so it will actually fry, stick it on a pre-sliced tasteless bun with a glop of limp lettuce and disguise it with ketchup. This is because it effectively nukes all flavour, texture, nutrition or aesthetic value, which is fine for Northerners but not for us in the genteel South. In the US, beef is graded into eight categories of which 'Prime' is reserved for the best 3%. After that, 'Choice' and 'Select' are commonly used in restaurants, while 'Commercial' is generally held to be of poor quality but probably OK if you mince it up properly; you could just about make a decent burger out of this if you had to. Below this are the grades of 'Utility', 'Cutter' and 'Canner' and I'd bet a testicle that that's what goes into that dodgy thing you bought for 99p. Feeling queasy? You should be. Remember; burgers are only fine if you like your food pre-chewed.

On the bright side though, we may comfort ourselves that all that BSE stuff was bollocks; if it wasn't we'd all be stark raving bonkers right now, given the number of pies and burgers we got through in the days before Tony Blair invented it to add insult to injury to the farmers in revenge for the miners being shafted by Maggie. He wasn't content with just banning Fox hunting and laughed with maniacal glee when the pyres of the Roast Beef of Olde England flamed like the Apocalypse over the gentle countryside. Bastard. I'd force feed the bastard with Black Puddings and Tripe and Cowheel if I ever got my hands on him.

Looks like it's a Chinese then.

I approach the Lotus Blossom, push open the tinkling door and address Mr.Wong in my best Mandarin, which I picked up when I was an Intelligence Officer before Fatty Pang rusticated me from the Gun Hill Barracks in Hong Kong.

'Ni hau,' I say, bowing low. 'Ching ge wo chau fan, mi fan and some spling lolls?'

'For fuck's sake, Harpic,' he replies. 'I've told you before, I only speak Cantonese and I only have a smattering of that because of my old dad. I was born in Macclesfield.'

'Tse-tse,' I reply, dismissing this as simple inscrutability, for which the Orientals are famed. 'Ying tong, piddle hi ho.'

'Harpic,' says Mr.Wong. 'The next time you come in here with this old pony I'm going to spit in your food and then report you to the Commission for Racial Equality. OK?'

'I say,' I say.

'And any jokes about dirty Chinese windows and Hu Flung Dung will result in smaller portions, heavily laced with bowel-wrenching chillies.'

'I went to a zoo without any animals,' I wittily persist. 'There was only a single dog there. It was a Shitzu!'

'What do you want, Harpic? Please just give me your order and piss off while I cook it,' he says, but I know he's loving it really.

'What do you call a Chinese woman with one leg?'

'Harpic,' he says. 'I'm going to ring your Missus any minute now.'

'Irene!' I triumphantly reveal.

'Harpic, you're having your standard order. The one you always order after you've been through the crap jokes routine, OK?' says Mr.Wong, reaching for the meat cleaver. 'And I'm going to charge you an arm and a leg for not putting strychnine in your Spring Rolls and bleach in your Fried Rice, got it? Not *stwiknine in spling loll* or even *bweach in flied lice*, OK? So piss off to the pub and come back when you're ready to collect it.'

'Will the chicken be rubbery?' I quip, on my way out to enjoy a pint well-earned for my light hearted jests at the *Limp and Splint* around the corner.

'You bet your bleedin' boots it will be,' he inscrutably replies.

Half an hour later and I present myself at the Lotus Blossom where Mr.Wong has my order bagged and ready, keeping warm on the counter. I hand over Bill Gon's £50 note in full and final settlement.

'Haven't you got anything smaller?' says Mr.Wong.

'Put it on my tab,' I reply.

'No,' replies Mr.Wong, a tad testily.

'Well, do you deliver?' I ask.

'We do,' says Mr.Wong.

'Well do so and you can get the money off Louise,' I suggest. 'She's good for it. She even has credit cards.'

'OK,' replies Mr.Wong. 'She is someone with whom it is a pleasure to do business. What she's doing with you is beyond the wisdom of Confucius, the Tau, the I-Ching and Chairman bleedin' Mao.'

'I rescued her in a card game,' I remind him. 'I thought I'd told everyone about that. Now go and get your car out, there's a good Wong.'

'Harpic,' he says, looking tired. 'Do you know what a Triad is?'

'Of course,' I reply, fencing intellectually. 'It's an experimental marketing campaign.'

'I'll get the car out,' he says, a deep furrow appearing across his brow.

Moments later, he has pulled up outside the front of the shop and is coming back inside to collect the take-away.

'No need to trouble yourself,' I say, carrying the carry-out to the car and climbing in.

'Harpic,' says Mr.Wong, somewhat surprised at seeing me riding shotgun. 'What the fuck are you doing?'

'Well you're going to my house anyway, so I thought I'd hitch a lift.'

'Don't ever go back to Hong Kong,' he says with an acquiescent sigh. 'Or I will personally guarantee to introduce you to some experimental marketing executives.'

Day Eleven: Black Thursday.

'Liquid lunches have no calories though they do sometimes have consequences.'

J. Harpic.

The Weigh-in.

Today is a milestone day in that after ten full days on the Beer and Bacon diet you will have lost 10lbs or 5kg, whichever is nearer, minimum. It is important to have milestones as they show you just how far you have come and how far you have left to go, or would do if they hadn't all been removed during the war to confuse the invading Germans. I suppose SatNav has made them rather redundant anyway but I still hanker for them. You know where you are with a milestone and you don't get some mechanical woman banging on at you to turn around at the next roundabout and retrace your steps every time you feel a bit adventurous and want to discover somewhere new. I simply refuse to have one in the car. Mind you, they might come in handy if one is required to travel any distance with Louise because, as Enid Blyton made plain in *The Secret Seven* series of children's books, girls simply cannot carry a map in their heads. This is why all the world's great navigators were men. To illustrate this point, I have compiled a list of rules that seem to sum up the female approach to navigation.

1. Never consult the map until after the junction.
2. Road signs are advisory and do not necessarily represent a more accurate set of directions than the way her dad used to go back in the 1960s before motorways existed.
3. North is directly in front whichever way you are going because that's the way you look at the map.
4. You do not need to know where you have come from to know where you are.
5. Left and Right are not necessarily fixed concepts and you do actually possess 'your other Left'.
6. 'Stop here' does not include the necessity to take into account the requirements for controlled deceleration or consideration for other road users.
7. The fact that she doesn't recognise the location does not necessarily mean you are in the wrong place.

Hope that helps.

So now, having found your way to the bathroom, it is time to triumphantly weigh yourself and to revel in that little flutter of success that is at this moment fellating the inside of your stomach. You have done well, confirmed your inner virtue and built up your character. You are ready for whatever the day can throw at you. You have re-affirmed your status as a living, breathing, fully-fledged member of the human race, validated your ticket to ride and lost quite a lot of ugly adipose tissue in the process. Your BMI is plummeting, you can safely contemplate flying long haul without having to buy two seats, you will feel chipper and fully prepared to entertain supermodel Kate Moss' dictum that 'Nothing tastes as good as skinny feels.' Except bacon, of course. Silly tart; she should stick to being a clothes hanger and not stray onto philosophical grounds.

Cold Breakfasts.

The world is divided in many ways; Arab and Jew, Communist and Capitalist, male and female, the grim north and the supine south, the benighted town and beautiful country, the civilised rich and the undeserving poor, animal and vegetable, intellectual and dullard, the Righteous and the Condemned, football hooligans and sports fans, proper artists and modern artists, Foxhunters and Animal Rights maniacs, responsible drinkers and teetotal Nazis. The list is endless, but perhaps the most profound and strange among these divisions is between those who eat cold, left over curry for breakfast and those who don't. I am one of those who don't because, frankly, it's minging.

Curry is not a breakfast dish. To illustrate this point, I hereby introduce you to that culinary abomination invented in India by Mahatma Gandhi as his prime weapon to undermine British morale and bring down the Raj.

Recipe: Kedgeree.

Step 1. Boil some eggs. You know you are on to a loser right from the start. It gets worse though; you have to have them cold.

Step 2. Boil some unsmoked haddock. Haddock? Are you joking? It smells like sweaty socks and when combined with the hydrogen sulphide from the boiled eggs is likely to bring the UN weapons inspectors in looking for poison gas.

Step 3. Boil some rice up. Rice? For breakfast? And think of the washing up already? Three pans and a whole aerosol of air freshener used and we're not half way through!

Step 4. Allow everything to cool. By now you could have made and consumed the Full Monty twice over.

Step 5. Fry up some spices in ghee. You have ghee in your cupboard. Everyone has ghee in their cupboard. You can't move for the bloody stuff, can you?

Step 6. Put everything together and warm up again. Talk about the size of your gas bill! Then add yoghurt. Honestly; to cool it all down.

Step 7. This is used as one of the tests for those who want to join the SAS as a cook. The successful daredevils who not only cook but also *consume* this horrid mess are awarded a cap badge showing a Winged Spoon underneath which is inscribed the motto: *Who Dares Eat*.

God help us. No wonder the Raj crumbled if this was all they could get hold of for breakfast. If it had been me as Viceroy, I would have been on the boat home in double quick time, I can tell you.

This is not to say that cold curry *never* works. Coronation Chicken, a dish invented to celebrate rather than denigrate the British Raj, is a triumphant *melange* of cold chicken, curry powder, mayonnaise and raisins which when served up around tea time is jolly nice. It is, I think, a development of a similar Indian dish known as Chicken Chaat which is a similar cold curry but which has lots of raw onions mixed in too. It makes a great starter to any meal, Indian or otherwise but to inflict either of these things on a person at breakfast time is a pretty shoddy trick. Breakfast should be served hot except in the case of the Continental cheese and ham fruhstuck, which is good.

To illustrate this point further. People who enjoy eating cold curry for breakfast have been shown to show signs of early onset dementia – the main symptom being eating cold curry for breakfast, of course – and are responsible for several enormities inflicted on the world. A lot of them, like Hitler, are vegetarians and tend to go for Cauliflower bhaji and things with lentils in them, which I'm pretty sure is banned under International Law in some states. Others, like Joseph Stalin, prefer Mutton Madras, mass murder and the violation of the rights of small nations while it is a well-known historical fact that Chairman Mao revelled in Ga Li Sichengzi Re (Trans: Bastard Hot Curry) while millions of his people starved during the Great Famine caused by the usual socialist incompetent fuck up.

And talking about incompetent socialist fuck ups, Bill Clinton was a vegetarian – although clearly Monica Lewinsky wasn't – but it isn't clear if he did or did not have a preference for cold artichoke curry in the morning like fellow vegetarian Ellen DeGeneres. From this side of the pond, our own vegetarian socialist fuck ups include the incomprehensibly thick and whining Morissey who famously declared that 'Meat is Murder' and that 'if your hair is wrong, your whole life is wrong'. Just two points on this: Old Father Timeon has always insisted that he can hear a field of corn scream when it is harvested; put him together with the Maestro of Manchester and welcome to world starvation: and have you seen Morissey's hair? It comes as no surprise therefore that the only three vegan MPs presently in the Mother of all Parliaments are all swivelled eyed socialist loons. That Froggy heejit, Christine Lagarde at the IMF is another vegetarian but possibly one of those half-sane ones who don't extend their definition of sentient animal life to include fish; I know, it stinks of racism to me; it is rumoured that she eats cold bouillabaisse for breakfast. The only place which is now reliably free of vegetarian socialist loons eating cold curry for breakfast is the reliably beef-producing and beef-eating Free State Province, South Africa, which maintains the wholly sensible view that curry should only be eaten hot between the hours of lunchtime until 10pm (they go to bed early down there) and that chicken is a vegetable. It used to be the same in Texas, but its proximity to California means that salad is now offered in many of their legendary steak houses; fortunately, the American commitment to Liberty means you don't have to eat it. They don't have curry there either; it's more on the chilli side.

In my own personal experience and entirely aside from the things I have learned from the unimpeachable sources of the internet, I can say that the cold curry eaters I have known, including non-vegetarians (known colloquially as 'sane people') have been a rum lot. As a Consultant to a Large Corporation I have had to show a deep empathy and understanding for all sorts of people including those on the edges of the diversity spectrum knows as 'complete mad bastards' and I have always tried to be as sympathetic as I could, because they often have money. Remember the Pink Pound! Brighton has been transformed by the Pink Pound from a tawdry, run down Skidrow-on-Sea into a vibrant, go-ahead, Metrosexual paradise and we can nod our heads to the success of the rainbow of diversity that has achieved the regeneration of this run-down yet historic home of the dirty weekend. Unfortunately, this sort of thing attracts swivel-eyed socialist loons in droves so it's best avoided. Where was I? Oh yes; diversity is a wonderful thing especially if it has money in its pocket and although I pride myself on my ability to rub along with all sorts of people (in the figurative sense, of course; I haven't been to an orgy in years) I do have to draw the line at cold curry eaters simply because I suspect Ostrakov to be a cold curry eater too.

Farting

Any discussion of curry and vegetarianism can only really go one way and that is in the direction of farting. This is a serious subject; so stop laughing. It is not necessary to laugh at farts and although this is held to be a universal custom, it is not. As Consultant to a Large Corporation, I was once asked to visit the Celestial Empire to see if the wheels were likely to come off the mandate of heaven any time soon and I naturally began my tour with a visit to a school to assess the state of the education system. Accompanied by several suitably distinguished local dignitaries, I descended upon No.1 High School in Foshan, a town famous for the manufacture of toilets, and whose industry each year needed an appreciable number of well-educated young people to take up the jobs there. I went into the classroom and saw a body of over two hundred diligent little scribes scribbling away diligently at their quadratic equations in absolute complete silence and dedication to their studies. It was amazing. I had never seen anything like it in my life. Not a paper dart or flicked ink blot in sight! Not a mobile phone set to permanent sexting mode, nor a bovine mouth masticating gum; no baseball caps worn backwards; all laces done up and not even a hint of a lit joint. I was almost jumping for joy at the success of the authorities in finding a way to keep teenagers occupied, oppressed and quiet simultaneously without recourse to Ritalin, alcohol or anti-depressants for the teachers. I wish to this day that Louise could have seen it, for then she would, I feel, take a more positive view of the noble profession of pedagogy.

And then, someone farted. I mean, it was an absolute ripper that began like the lowest notes of a tuba, rising steadily through the octaves, rippling through the full audio range until it reached as high as the highest note of a soprano cornet and disappeared into the ether. It was an absolute corker, better than anything that mate of spoilt little brat Holden Caulfield could manage, even if it was in church, and certainly on a par with anything Bludger Casey, the Benbecula Farting Champion three years running, ever produced and far in advance of old 'Breaker' Morant at St,Hilda's who argued that as Latin was the universal language one ought to be able to fart in it (Farto, Fartas , Fartat...). I dare say, La Petomane, the famous French professional flatulist and farteur (1857-1945) would have been moved to tears if he'd heard it.

Was it a male or female? I couldn't tell without smelling, because of course women's farts smell worse than men's because they contain a higher sulphur content, but because the room was so full and so large, it took quite a long time for the smell to reach me and by that time it had diffused to a mere whiff.

What was really eerie though was that *nobody laughed*. No-one! No-one even pointed and sniggered. Not a single peg was produced. Not a single finger was pointed. Not a single nudge indicated the guilty party. In Arabia, a child would instantly have shouted out 'When the desert is silent, the donkey speaks' to tumultuous and raucous applaud. In the remoter parts of the Appalachians, reference would have been made instantly to the presence of the Arkansas Barking Spider while in New Mexico the Call of the Wild Burrito would have been heard; mechanics across the English-speaking world would have been taking their spanners up to fix the Back-end Blow Out on the Mouse Motorcycle; wild life enthusiasts would complain that someone had stood on a duck or disturbed the Trouser Rattler. Farts are regarded as funny the world over but not, it appears, in China. Indeed, the only person laughing out loud was me! Imagine!

So they you are. Not everyone laughs at farts; the practice is idiotic and immature and it is time this subject was given the seriousness it deserves.

Let's start with the smell because really, the noise is neither here nor there be it a Bronx cheer, a raspberry ripple, a blast on the arse trumpet, a quack, a squeak or an innocent, harmless botty pop.

It is a simple truth that you smell of what you eat. If you eat lots of curry, you will smell of curry. If you eat lots of garlic, you will smell of garlic. I know this is contested by the French, who think they smell of perfume, but a quick sniff of a Frog's breathe on a Friday will confirm the truth of my assertion. If you eat lots of sprouts, you will smell of sprouts. It really is that simple. According to some Chinese people, Westerners smell disagreeably of cheese because – guess what? – we eat a lot of cheese. This doesn't stop them going mad for Pizza Hut mind, but this is a multi-cultural globalised world these days, so pretty much anything goes. We English have our own distinctive smell too – cut grass - excepting, of course, that woman who works in the chippy and whose devotion to cheesy chips makes her smell disagreeably of both cheese and vinegar. I once bought her some perfume to mask it but she took it the wrong way. She drank it; she's a bit of an alkie like that.

From this it follows logically that your farts smell of what you eat – but obviously not cut grass; don't be ridiculous. Now while it is perfectly acceptable to fart at night or first thing in the morning – how could it not be? – it really is not acceptable to fart during the day when you are at work or in the lift or on a crowded Tube train. This is because you will cause discomfort to others and although sometimes it is impossible not to fart, you can minimise the disruption by leaving off the cold curry for breakfast, obviously. If you are so misguided as to be a vegetarian and to eat cold curry for breakfast I would implore you not to have the sprout biryani. It really is unpleasant to be near you when you do. On a related note, a mate of mine once did a Post Mortem on a vegetarian and he confirmed everything I have to say on this. Dead vegetarians smell of sprout fart. So eat more meat and don't have curry for breakfast. It's probably what killed the cadaver in the first place.

No, on balance, I think it is time to imitate the Chinese on this issue and have our own Cultural Revolution in our attitude to farting. They should not be laughed at and those who engage in excess and public farting (you know who you are) ought to undergo some sort of re-education, perhaps in a specially established camp staffed by suitably qualified volunteers. Please note that I am not calling for more public expenditure on worthless, heavily pension-entitlemented civil servants or the establishment of Special Farting Counsellors or - God Forbid! – a Fart Police. Rather, this is something that voluntary organisations could take on – the Church, perhaps, or Oxfam. Given the amount of methane that is produced by farting, it might be possible to hand this over to Environmental groups so that they do something useful; we could call them 'Wind Farms' and so meet EU targets for renewable energy without blighting the countryside with all those horrible propeller objects.

I know that Perky Pete shares some of my thinking on this issue, having once banned Carruthers for a period of no less than seven days for letting off a particularly dolorous fart. It was terrible; everyone knew it was Carruthers right away because he attempted to blame it on Ark Slymstead, who though no mean player of the o-ring oboe himself was in this case entirely innocent of the chuff charges against him and simply said 'More tea, Vicar?' upon which he was cleared of cutting the cheese. Carruthers followed up this stratagem by trying to laugh it off with the traditional declaration 'Speak to me, oh Toothless One!' but the brown cloud was too thick to be a laughing matter; Miranda McNulty's hair colouring began to react with it and she actually left her drink in the rush to rescue her coiffure from the worst gas attack England has experienced since the Third Battle of Ypres. After that he attempted to play upon our heart strings by claiming it was no more than the lonely cry of an imprisoned turd; even the dog went outside and refused to come back in to its warm spot by the fire until the place had been fully aired and Carruthers reamed out.

Despite this, Perky Pete retains some reservations on the farting issue. After the hit that the Smoking Ban made on his takings, he is reluctant to further threaten his income by working towards a statutory ban on farting in public places. He thinks this might be difficult to enforce and fears being subjected to inspection by Health and Safety Nazis and charged under EU Laws written in Bulgarian that he never knew existed. He also argues that the Smoker's Shelter cost an arm and a leg to erect and fears that a Farting Shelter might be doubly un-economical because he would have to provide separate ones for male and female. I can see his point but I do feel that it is not beyond the wit and wisdom of our great nation to come up with a solution that takes in full consideration of our traditions of liberty while still getting a handle on rampant arses.

Today's Exercise Regime: A Lovely Walk Spying on Ostrakov the Fracking Communist.

Just before I was rusticated from the Gun Hill Barracks in Hong Kong by Fatty Pang and posted to Benbecula in Ultima Thule, I had been specially selected by the Head of the British Army Intelligence Branch in that former colony to track down a master agent-saboteur in the pay of the Chinese government and whose avowed intent was to hasten the departure of our Sovereign Majesty from the said Colony in as humiliating a fashion as possible.

'There's no doubt about it,' said Major Dunwoody-Tring. 'He's full of nasty plots, he is. Blowing up the Royal Yacht isn't the half of it. Rumour has it that he want to bring down the stand at the Jockey Club in Happy Valley, by Jove!'

'Give me his description and I'll run him to earth,' I enthusiastically declared.

'It's Top Secret, Harpic,' he said. 'No-one must know about this business and it will require you to be away from the Barracks for long periods.'

'I know my duty, Sir,' I replied, cracking off a salute.

'Good man, Harpic,' he said, a smile of sheer pride in finding such a dedicated Soldier of Empire ready to rise to his every challenge spreading across his face. 'The name's Chen; dark hair, brown eyes, average height mainly; known to have a fondness for noodles and last seen in the following locations -....'

I got my trusty pencil out, licked it and prepared to write.

'You'll have to commit this to memory I'm afraid, Harpic,' he said. 'So once you've got it written down, learn it off by heart and eat the paper, OK?'

'No problem, Sir,' I said. 'Go ahead. This is rice paper.'

He gave me a penetrating stare, no doubt wondering if he dare send one so young on such a mission of vital importance to the Empire.

'Harpic,' he said, finally. 'There is no doubt that you are just the man for this job. I congratulate myself on finally finding something that you are perfectly suited to.'

'Tickety-boo,' I said, cracking off another salute. 'You can rely on Harpic to flush out all known saboteurs wherever they are lurking.'

He wiped a tear away from his eye and blew his nose, sobbing a little with joy at the humbling sight of my devotion.

'Right you are then,' he said. 'Here are the locations. Firstly, Fan Lau Fort out at Lantau…'

'Good God, Sir!' I exclaimed. 'Is he spying out the defences of the colony?'

'The Fort was abandoned many years ago, Harpic,' replied Major Dunwoody-Tring, taking a deep breath. 'But it's the sort of remote place from which a Maoist insurgency might be launched. Take your time investigating it, Harpic. It's important.'

'Absolutely, Sir! Next location?'

'Crooked Harbour,' he said, choking with emotion. 'We think he might be doing a bit of cross-border noodle smuggling as a cover for his infiltration and sabotage activities.'

'Noodle smuggling!' I cried. 'Is nothing sacred to these Communist fiends? Noodles indeed!'

'Noodles indeed,' agreed the Major a little giddily. He seemed to be experiencing some kind of hay fever attack. 'Next location; the Stanley-Po Toi Island Ferry. I should try disguising yourself as a Ticket Inspector for this one, Harpic. It'll allow you to blend in more.'

'Ticket Inspector it is, Sir,' I said, writing.

'And then, after that – it shouldn't take more than a week or so of surveillance – check out the bars in Wan Chai,' said the Major, choking a little once more and screwing up his eyes. I thought he may be in danger of apoplexy at this point, but he mastered himself soon enough. 'It may be that he is disguised as a Lady Boy.'

'Suggested disguise, Sir?'

'Something with lots of make-up,' he suggested. 'Excuse me for a moment, I must just nip out.'

I set to with a will to memorise all this vital intelligence while Major Dunwoody-Tring sorted out his hay fever. This was no easy task as there seemed to be a lot of raucous laughter coming from the Officer's Mess where the Major kept his medication, but by the time he returned I had it all pat and had already eaten the rice paper.

'Harpic,' he said, wiping his eyes. 'Make sure you send photographs at regular intervals, won't you? But no telephones, understand? Only contact us by post, understand?'

Well, having sworn to the Official Secrets Act I shall keep the intelligence product (as we say) of those long hot days and freezing cold nights staking out Chen the Chinese Mastermind amid the bleak mountains of Fan Lau Fort, holding my nose through the icy blast of winter storms and the stench of the prawn fisheries at Crooked Bay, gritting my teeth at the sea sickness and dumb insolence I endured on the Stanley ferry and experiencing the louche importuning of Wan Chai as it was meant to be; a secret. But I shall say that my efforts were modestly successful because although I never actually definitively identified him or caught him red-handed in a heinous act of Communist sabotage, he seemed to have been deterred from blowing up any of his targets as a direct result of my dogged pursuit of this oriental fox. Proof of this lies in the fact that both the Royal Yacht and the Jockey Club in Hong Kong are still famous and reasonably priced tourist attractions today, rather than mere smoking ruins. It was in Wan Chai that I met Dim Sum, coincidentally; much good it did me once Fatty Pang decided to put his pallid, pasty face in though. Major Dunwoody-Tring dined out on the story for years, he told me when I Facebooked him briefly; I unfriended him, however, when I found out that he was mysteriously still friends with Fatty Pang, who destroyed the Empire. Still, the experience stood me in good stead when I was asked to perform a similar intelligence role in Bosnia and resulted in me rescuing Louise from a card game and bringing her back to a life of bliss and ease in good old Blighty.

The experience will also stand me in good stead when out hunting for Ostrakov today, for I am determined to undermine his machinations, end his fracking plans and shoot his Communist fox metaphorically if not quite literally. For I *am* convinced that he is fracking *somewhere*. Clearly, Bill Gon's Gazpacho mining is being used by Ostrakov to divert attention away from his own nefarious activities but, unlike Chen the Chinese Saboteur, I have identified him from the crowd already and so all that is left to do is find out what he is actually up to and then confront him with his dastardly plans in a public place. There is a Parish Council meeting tonight. It seems to be the ideal forum for his exposure, but I will need to move fast to assemble the evidence in time. The green fields of England are in danger! To arms!

Tinker, Tailor, Soldier, Rotten Communist Subversive.

Thorough preparation is required for successful sleuthing. Researching your target cannot be skimped and it is a mark of the master counter-intelligence campaign that all existing intelligence is gleaned from all available sources before the stalking of the quarry begins. 'True knowledge is not *what* you know, but knowing where to find out what you *don't* know,' was Major Dunwoody-Tring's maxim and as far as Ostrakov is concerned, the best place to find out all about his subversive activities is through a thorough reading of the village magazine, the trusty and unimpeachable *Slimstead Insinuator*. This is an archive second to none for finding out what Communist machinations are afoot in Slimstead and having built up a good collection – I have never missed an issue and keep them all filed in date order in binders that I have had made specially. They are perfect for the gentleman at stool, although of late I have been reading Rusbridger's Tommy rot (seeing as how I have been buying up Ostrakov's *Guardian* in order to thwart his plans). One day, I intend to read them all and perhaps write a compendious history of the village based on them.

Leafing through the back copies of the *Slimstead Insinuator* now, I find that Ostrakov is a sleeping partner in the village shop, has been behind the raising of capital for the rebirth of the village Post Office, supported a planning application for Mehmet to add some B&B units to the back of The Hanged Man and approved the extension of opening hours at the Old Queen's Head. There is clearly a pattern here; he has been encouraging the expansion of local business so that he can first tax them flat through the Parish Council precept and then expropriate them in a radical programme of mass nationalisation.

I read on and find Ostrakov's fingerprints all over the Sunday School, where he no doubt preaches sermons of revolutionary intent in an attempt to brainwash the young minds of the Cradle Roll into joining a Militant Youth League ready to do his blood thirsty bidding come the day of insurrection. He has been involved in repairing the skateboard facilities to include a graffiti wall upon which he can plaster Communist slogans and propagandise the teenage masses. Not even the cricket team has been spared his attempts to have the tentacles of socialism writhe into a position to strangle all liberty; he has stood in at short notice for players temporarily unavailable on several occasions (middle order batsman, medium pace seam spinner, unusually good for a Communist) and has even made donations to the Afternoon Tea fund in an attempt to pollute that most noble of English games with his Communist blood money.

I note also that the issue of fracking has been kept off the pages of the trusty *Insinuator* in an attempt to stifle debate but having been well trained by Major Dunwoody-Tring, I am not fooled. It is a rule of intelligence gathering that one should always look for what is *not* there as much as for what is right under your nose, so to speak, and act accordingly. So now, it's off to pick up the spoor and having exercised the old grey matter, exercise the rippling muscles of our calves and thighs with such a walk for freedom and liberty as to make Nelson Mandela and the Jarrow Marchers efforts look like a quick stroll down the Pub. Actually, that sounds like a good idea too but duty calls.

Ostrakov's lair is in the modest new housing estate that was built behind The Hanged Man sometime in the 1970s. It is the sort of three bedroomed semi-detached that would provide perfect cover for a Soviet sleeper agent dedicated to the downfall of capitalism and as I approach it from the cover of a convenient wheelie bin, I see that the deception extends to a well-kept lawn and some neat flower beds. I make a mental note to find out if he has infiltrated the Slimstead Horticultural Society, for it is a maxim of the Communist that no area of society can be allowed to exist beyond the control of the dictatorship of the proletariat. I also note that his pot plants are almost exclusively red petunias which gives the game away straight away; no Communist, however deep his cover can resist a love for the colour red. There are a few blue and white petunias mixed in, true, but I suspect they are only awaiting the pruning shears. Pushing the wheelie bin closer, I am able to get closer to his front gate undetected by anyone but Chubble the louche recently privatised Postie.

'He's not in Harpic, you dickhead,' he calls out from the depth of his issue red anorak just as he delivers another wad of unwanted junk mail. 'And put Mrs. Kelly's bin back, for fuck's sake. It's collection day.'

An astute intelligence agent knows when he has been blown so I quickly pretend to innocence.

'Actually I was just testing it for a squeaky wheel,' I say, convincingly off the cuff. 'Do you know where he happens to be today?'

'He's delivering leaflets of some sort,' replies Chubble, louchely. 'But as long as that's all he's delivering, he's welcome to do whatever he wants.'

'Indeed, Chubble,' I say. 'Each to his own, eh?'

'Speak for yourself, mate,' he says, returning to his van. 'I'm more in the free love line myself.'

This is rather disconcerting and I step back onto the pavement smartly as he drives past and away, scattering pebbles in his wake. The news that Chubble the Postie is in favour of free love is a bit of a surprise as he never struck me as the sort to join up with a hippy commune holding their women in common. Perhaps he is a sort of crypto-Communist? And why should he be loitering outside Ostrakov's lair at the very moment that I am about to investigate it? Could it be that he is Ostrakov's stool pigeon? Certainly, his cover as a postman would allow him access to secure channels of communication and an excuse to rove around carrying out all sorts of acts of espionage. I resolve to go through the *Slimstead Insinuator* back issues for any signs that this might be the case as soon as I have completed my dossier on Ostrakov.

Checking that the coast is clear and putting on a hat to change my disguise – an old secret agent's trick – I venture down the garden path and cupping my hand over my eyes, peer in through the window. As expected, there are bookshelves; Communists are always bookish types; it is why they wear glasses. There is a three piece suite, possibly from DFS and a carpet straight out of *Carpets'R'Us* but I spot the real give-away instantly; there is a picture of the Queen over the mantelpiece while below, in faux-silver frames on a small occasional table are portraits of Margaret Thatcher and David Cameron. This for me is the clincher. All Communists like to keep busts or portraits of their enemies to remind them every day of what they are up against and to inspire them to greater efforts to subvert the common man and enslave him in a socialist collective gulag and Ostrakov is clearly no different. It's time to hunt the bastard down.

Carruthers is the expert on tracking having spent an implausible amount of time in Africa and although he is reluctant to give away all trade secrets, I have had occasion to make up a small *aide memoire* of the wisdom that he has imparted to me in carefully controlled parcels over the ~~pints~~ years. I pull it out of the inside pocket of my Norfolk jacket where it is always and without fail to be found.

'*Always shoot early or late,*' is Carruthers' first rule and I have noted beside it that this advice is also followed by photographers who tend to agree that natural light is at its best at these times. It is good advice for the hunter, professional or amateur, too because if you want to slaughter Bambi then you may do so safely just after dawn when the idle unwashed student rabble of the Animal Rights Mob are still in bed, or just before Sunset, when they have trooped off back to their soggy communes to smoke iPads and complain about globalisation to their Friends of the Earth in Canada and Sumatra over the internet. In the present circumstances however, the advice is redundant. In this case the Harpic early bird has missed his worm.

'*Always go for a head shot when possible. Blowing the head apart saves you the problem of running after a wounded animal maddened with fear and pain. Shooting for the heart is second best because to hit the heart you usually have to go through the shoulder blade, which shatters it and sends shards of bone through the carcase and you end up with a disfigured Sunday Roast and bits of bone in your sausages. In the case of Elephant, if you don't hit it in the head and drop it first time you will get stomped on.*'

Carruthers is always interesting but on this particular point, of limited value.

'Always get upwind of the quarry.' This would be a bit more useful if there was a quarry in Slimstead but apart from some gravel extraction back in the 1960s, there hasn't been anything that might be described as a quarry in East Anglia since before the last ice age.

'Rub a bit of animal dung on your clothes to disguise your scent.' No.

'Look out for spoor.' This is more like it. Ostrakov is bound to leave spoor behind if he is delivering leaflets. One leaflet not inserted fully through the letter box and I'm on to him. One leaflet dropped by mistake and whipped away by the prevailing wind and I know he's upwind of me. Good advice that, Carruthers.

'Hunt in the places where the animals are to be found.' Bit obvious that one really. Slimstead springs to mind but it would be good to be a bit more specific. But then again, it could be an idea to look in the Pub because Ostrakov has been seen in there from time to time. Good idea that, Carruthers. And it's nearly lunchtime.

Moving smartly, therefore, in the direction of the Old Queens Head, I keep a weather eye open for stray leaflets but it seems that Ostrakov knows his tradecraft only too well and in his attempts to propagandise the unsuspecting burghers of Slimstead has left no stone unturned in making sure that the leaflets are firmly and decisively posted. It is only when the familiar *crack* of the bolts being thrown back on the doors of the Ancient and Regal Nut reach my ears that I note that Ostrakov has got here first and has left a pile of his noxious publications by the door in the hope that Perky Pete and the Mistress Maureen can be co-opted into his revolutionary plots.

'Hello Harpic,' says Perky Pete, picking up the paper platitudes of the proletarian pariah. 'How's the demo coming along?'

'No need for that now,' I reply. 'Bill Gon has put my mind at rest over the fracking in the Nature Reserve. Gazpacho mining to save the Third World. What a wondrous, generous big-hearted idea. I shall definitely vote for him if he stands for Parish Council Chairman.'

'Really? Gazpacho?' says Perky Pete, throwing wide the welcoming doors of his hostelry. 'I would never have worked that one out. Pint?'

'JCB, please,' I reply, following him in to the familiar fug of stripped wood and treacly beer. 'The game has moved on though. I suspect Ostrakov is up to no good. I believe that *he* is the criminal mastermind bent on devastating the sacred precincts of Slimstead. I believe that it is *he* who is the Moriarty who would tear up our countryside in search of filthy lucre to swell his campaign coffers.'

'What makes you say that?' says Perky Pete pouring a pint.

'I suspect you may have the evidence to hand.'

'The leaflets?' he says. 'Help yourself mate.'

I hand over Bill Gon's £50 note.

'No need,' says Perky Pete, waving away my proffered pelf. 'Ostrakov was in here yesterday saying that he owed you money for your campaign materials. I'll put it on your tab.'

'Good man. Pass me the leaflets,' I say, trousering the loot.

Perky Pete hands over the propaganda and I take up a seat on a settle to pore over it.

> Dear Villagers,

> As you will have noticed, the fracking plant has been set up in the Nature Reserve and drilling operations will begin shortly. We have been assured by Gazpacom that there will be the minimum of disruption and that any damage caused will be made good in the fullness of time. As Chairman of the Parish Council, I would like to take this opportunity to extend a personal 'Thank you' to Bill Gon who has worked so hard to bring about this general benefit to the village.

I am puzzled.

'I say, Pete. I thought that there was no fracking going on in the Nature Reserve. Bill Gon assured me personally that they were pumping Gazpacho out.'

'Gazpacho,' says Perky Pete, polishing a handled mug. 'You do know what Gazpacho is don't you Harpic?'

'Of course, I do. It's soup.'

'Soup. Correct,' he confirms, polishing vigorously. There is an odd flatness to his tone. 'Wait a moment will you? I'm just going to get Maureen through. She deserves to hear this.'

I read on.

> Gazpacom expect to be making the first payment to Parish Council funds within this financial quarter and this will go to repairing the damage to the windows in the Slimstead Social Club caused by the discharge of a shotgun at last week's Parish Council meeting. Bill Gon will continue to be in charge of handling the negotiations around the expected generous payments.

Perky Pete and Maureen appear as I finish the paragraph. They are wreathed in smiles.

'Gazpacho?' says Maureen, through a wide welcoming smile perched above a pleasantly displayed cleavage. 'Gazpacho?'

'Gazpacho,' I confirm. 'Bill Gon is pumping out Gazpacho to feed the Third World but Ostrakov here has written a load of nonsense accusing him of fracking. I have Bill's personal assurance that they have nothing whatsoever to do with hydrocarbon prospecting.'

Maureen and Perky Pete take up a leaflet each and begin to read. After a quick scan, a look of alarm crosses her face.

'Bill Gon is in charge of the money?' she says, seemingly aghast.

'Couldn't choose a more honest man for the job,' I say, supping at the honest froth of a reviving JCB.

'Bill Gon's so crooked he couldn't lie straight in bed,' she says, in a tone of petulance. 'If he swallowed a nail, he'd shit a corkscrew.'

'Nonsense,' I retort. 'He is as honest as the day is long.'

'It must be fucking midwinter in Sweden then,' she replies, reading on.

I am puzzled at her response, but am determined to read the whole leaflet before reaching a balanced judgment against Ostrakov.

We might look forward to a reduction in our gas bills as of next week too as a result of Gazpacom piping natural gas straight into a special village reserve fund, which Bill Gon is also administering at considerable cost to himself in time and effort.

'There you go,' I say. 'What sort of chap would volunteer to do so much work for the village without so much as asking for a shekel in return?'

'Precisely,' says Maureen. 'He's got a new 4x4 hasn't he?'

'His kid has just started at St.Wicca's too,' chimes in Pete. 'That must cost a pretty penny.'

'Dismiss the thought,' I demand. 'This missive is nothing more than a rag designed to deceive us into besmirching Bill's good name and covering up Ostrakov's secret fracking plans.'

'Gazpacho,' says Maureen.

'Bless you,' I reply. 'I knew you wouldn't be fooled by Ostrakov.'

She exchanges a glance with Perky Pete which, under other circumstance, might be construed as a smirk.

> *Predictions of the financial benefits accruing to the village are always difficult to make, but I am assured that we might finally be in a position to repair the roof at St.Moses the Black, upgrade the facilities at the skateboard park, pay off the Cricket Club loan and still have enough left over to allow the Horticultural Society to make a good challenge for the title of Best Kept Village in this year's Britain in Bloom contest. The long held desire for a pedestrian crossing may take a little longer to come to fruition but as long as I am Chairman of the Parish Council, it will remain at the top of the agenda.*
>
> *Yours Sincerely*
>
> *Ivan Ostrakov.*

'Well, there it is in black and white,' I say, laying down the offending pamphlet. 'Ostrakov is fracking and trying to buy the support of the village by bribing them with cheaper gas bills and social spending. It's a typical socialist trick. And at the same time he is actively trying to blacken Bill Gon's good name by pretending that *he* is the one responsible.'

'You need to take this up directly with Ostrakov,' says Perky Pete, tapping Maureen's arm. Though still reading, she is scratching at a stray hair at her temple. 'There is a Parish Council meeting tonight isn't there?'

'Indeed there is,' I declare. 'And I shall confront him with his plots and expose him.'

'This should be good,' says Perky Pete, maintaining a face of stone.

'Oh we'll definitely be there,' agrees Maureen. 'Wouldn't miss it for the world.'

It is always good to know that a righteous cause attracts solid support. Harpic is emboldened.

'Another JCB?' asks Perky Pete.

'Why ever not?' I reply.

'Because you still have a tab the size of the Former Soviet Union,' says Maureen, with an odd sort of smile. 'But if you promise to go to the Parish Council meeting and say what you've just said to us, you can have more than one more on the house.'

Lunch.

Liquid lunches have no calories though they do sometimes have consequences. That said, who can resist the allure of free beer? It is the ordinary tippler's version of a small win on the National Lottery; not life changing but still welcome.

'Mine's a JCB,' I say. 'And keep them coming while I write my speech.'

'You're going to make a speech?' says Perky Pete, with a merry grin. 'Have a chaser to whet the whistle of the wordsmith, eh?'

'Don't mind if I do,' I happily reply.

'Don't drink too much, Harpic,' says Maureen, also merrily grinning. 'Got to be *compos mentis* for the Parish Council, haven't we?'

'I shall regulate my intake according to best practice,' I reply, accepting the hospitality.

Now, I am aware that I have laid down certain strictures about drinking spirits at lunch time and that I have generally come out against their consumption, just as I do not think it wise to drink 5% Knickerdropper lagers in the afternoon. However, these restrictions do not apply to freebies simply because refusing a freebie is just about the most insulting thing you can do to a publican. It is the equivalent of eating with one's left hand at a desert banquet in an Oil Sheik's gorgeous tent. It is akin to farting in church or slurping your soup at the palace. It is to stick chopsticks upright in a bowl of rice in a Chinese restaurant or ask for ketchup in France (or indeed, asking the waiter for *anything* in Paris). It is to take a knife to the potatoes of a Bavarian *Hausfrau*, to trample your muddy boots through a temple in Thailand or burn the flag of the United States of America outside Congress. It is bad manners and only a complete boor would do it. The question before Harpic, therefore, is what is the proper spirit for a lunchtime session, bearing in mind he must write possibly the greatest speech since the Gettysburg Address, deliver it in a style to make Churchill give a standing ovation and be ready with more political wit and repartee than Disraeli, Gladstone, Boris Johnson and Oscar Wilde could muster between them so that he may see off the inevitable cavils of the weasel Ostrakov?

Having shed its Russian connotations, Vodka has recently become associated with a younger, female demographic and is now firmly embraced in the nation's heart as the housewife's favourite and so it should naturally appeal to the hard pressed Househusband. However, I feel that it lacks a certain *je ne sais quoi*, as does Bacardi, the Pirate's Potion although I don't really know why. Gin cannot be recommended. Despite the fruit of the juniper being the very foundation of the Gin and Tonic and therefore the triumph that was the British Empire before Fatty Pang gave it away to the Communists, gin is really best kept for the classic Sundowner. This goes for Brandy too. A fine Cognac or, better still, the infinitely superior Armagnac is too heavy for the middle of the day although I have known it to be used as a *digestif* after a particularly rich lunch of, perhaps, Chateaubriand. On balance though, it is best reserved for after dinner when the table has been cleared, the port taken away and the

Ladies sent off to bed. Whisky is a difficult option because up in Ultima Thule, the crew of the *Tartanic* begin drinking it well before the mid-day strike and so no conscientious worker or Consultant to a Large Corporation can ever drink it without feeling a certain distaste for its North British origins and wishing that the Highland Clearances had not been conducted on a more thorough basis and the dreadful Sporran Munchers relocated to Greenland. Still, it is not unknown for those of a bibulous disposition to drink Loch Ness Monster piss at lunchtime but I declare, it just isn't for me.

A much better alternative may be found in Bourbon or Kentucky Whiskey, which is distilled from corn and 'sour mash' rather than grain and matured for two years in charred oak barrels. 'Sour mash' is a little of the spent corn from the last distillation process added to the new corn to encourage the growth of the same yeast from vat to vat. Tennessee whiskies, the most famous of which is Jack Daniels, are made in the same way. Southern Comfort is a further variation on the theme, having spices and fruit added to give it an agreeable orange or perhaps, peach, flavour. This is probably the best spirit to have at lunchtime as it feels a bit like orange juice and so reminds you of breakfast.

'A Southern Comfort for me,' I call out as I lick my trusty pencil, ready to compose. 'And make it a double.'

When composing a speech, it's always a good idea to have plenty of paper about. Indeed, it is a Harpic Motto to always have plenty of paper to hand and resides on the same level of importance as your Mother's admonitions about never leaving the house without clean underwear in case you get run over by a bus and the ambulance crew getting to see your unsavoury grundies (as if they wouldn't have more important things to do and you wouldn't have more pressing worries, for heaven's sake). This is because you will need to produce draft after draft so that you may hone your message to perfection. We Harpics have always been accomplished wordsmiths and have been involved in writing speeches for the great and good throughout our long and distinguished history (let us not linger on that most misunderstood of sound bites, 'let them eat cake') and have always maintained that keeping plenty of paper close to hand is one of the first rules of speechwriting. Obviously, in Medieval times before paper was invented, this meant 'parchment' or 'stone tablets' or, when my father was doing missionary work in the North, 'slates' but now by 'paper' we mean just that. One thing that we Harpics do continue to share with our Medieval forebears though is an insistence on speeches being produced on scrolls; if it was good enough for the Magna Carta, it is good enough for the Slimstead Parish Council and a speech always sounds better, carries more weight, has more bottom if it is written down on a scroll. Now, admittedly, scrolls are not the first thing one puts ones hand on in the stationary section of WH Smith's but fortunately Izal Medicated Toilet paper is still produced and is widely available. It even comes in a brown colour so it can pass for a medieval scroll at a distance and in bad light.

This may come as a surprise to those not brought up in the State School system during the 1960s when the properties of abrasion and non-absorbancy were still held in such high esteem that school toilet paper was stamped with the logo *Government Property* to ensure that the thief was deterred and the honest citizen reassured that democracy was readily to hand. Now, of course, soft toilet paper, paper impregnated with soothing balms against the raging heat of Gandhi's Revenge – even *moist* varieties are available – all in a variety of colours to match your personal bathroom décor preferences, have all but wiped out any trace of the Klingon's Nemesis. For a while, indeed, it was feared that scratchy old Izal would disappear entirely from the shelves of the nation's supermarkets and the bathrooms of the public sector as people became more sophisticated and demanding in the bathroom. Fortunately, Izal proved as hard to shift as boiled egg sandwiches and survived mainly through teachers using it as a cheaper alternative to tracing paper. For this, Harpic is grateful. For where else would Harpic write a speech than on a trusty scroll of Izal's versatile product? If Izal is good enough for every Labour manifesto since Kier Hardie lost the 1888 election, then it's good enough for Harpic.

I nip to the loo and remove a roll of Montezuma's Messaging Service from its holder, ready to commit pen to paper in a concentrated burst of creative concentration.

Now, as I think I have alluded elsewhere, Thursdays can be a difficult sort of day especially if one is, like me, prone to complete immersion in the task at hand. Once engaged fully, the interruption of the Muse is not something that I would readily attempt when she is in full flow and her wit, charm, sophistication is running down through the pencil and onto the paper. The poet Coleridge was the same, I believe, but not as dedicated; he once answered the door to a caller when in the middle of a poem about Xanadu and when he got back to his parchment and quill, the Muse had got tired of being dissed like this and had gone off and left him swinging so the poem never got finished. This is not something that I would do even if the beer was not free and flowing. The net result is a bit yin yang in that although I now have a fine piece of prose complete with oratorical flourishes, rhetorical devices and lots of ripping inventive, but after looking up at the clock several hours seem to have passed in a flash. It is after 4pm and I am horribly late for my Dear Darling's return from her daily labours.

'You're dead meat,' says Maureen, producing an industrial strength Espresso and smiling. 'Louise will kill you.'

'Heaven's above!' I declare, as the thick black stuff almost straightens my pubes. 'I must be away!'

Dashing off the last line, I then dash out of the Pub and head towards the cul-de-sac as fast as the Harpic pins will carry him in his present state of lubrication. Spying the old homestead ahead and steaming straight towards it, I am surprised to see Patricia Dalrymple's horse-box parked outside and not a little dismayed to see the massively titted Tabitha Greenwood trundling her poonts towards it. I pause to draw breath and see also that Andrea Lloyd's eco-friendly rust bucket is also parked outside *Chez Moi*. It is starting up and heading down the close at a rate of acceleration which will see it hit sixty mph sometime next week, downhill, with a following wind. I give a cheery wave as she goes past and receive a single finger in reply but I do not have time to absorb this cruel jibe as I am forced to duck in order to avoid the wing mirror of Mistress Dalrymple's horse-box as it goes past at a speed which should see it over the jumps at Hickstead for a clear round, no problem. I glimpse a horridly determined frown across her features while the Greenwood moomintrolls quiver like fat whales about to breach. This can only mean one thing; I am late for duty. No cocktails have been prepared, nor a healthy supper prepared. I am in the soup and wonder if I should take a ticket to Switzerland right away or resign myself to shuffling off this mortal coil in a more protracted and inconvenient manner. My feet feel like they are already encased in concrete boots as I plod the last few yards of my life homeward.

'Harpic!' calls my Dearest Louise. 'Have you been drinking in the Pub?'

'Of course,' I reply. 'What else would I be doing in a Pub?'

'Writing speeches for the Parish Council Meeting tonight, by any chance?' she replies.

'How could you possibly guess that?' I am amazed at her perspicacity.

'Because Maureen has been on the phone to the whole village this afternoon,' she says. 'Apparently you are doing some sort of Stand Up Comedy routine this evening.'

'You have been misinformed,' I announce airily.

'No I have not,' she contradicts. '*Gazpacho*, for crying out loud.'

'Bless you,' I reply.

She looks at me carefully for a moment.

'Should I take your temperature, Harpic?'

'As you wish,' I reply. 'As long as it isn't rectally, feel free.'

She looks at me once more, a searching gaze that looks all the way back to the time I rescued her from a card game in Bosnia.

'Harpic,' she says, finally. 'Get me a drink. I think I am going to need it if I am ever to get through this meeting.'

'You are coming to the meeting?' It is difficult to hide my surprise.

'I am, Harpic. Regrettably, I am.'

'That's odd,' I say. 'I didn't think Countesses held much with democratic politics.'

'Harpic,' she says, in *that* tone.

'Dearest?'

'Whatever happens this evening you are not to speak. You are to be seen and not heard, Harpic. Is this clear, Harpic?'

'Crystal, Dearest,' I reply.

'Are your fingers crossed behind your back, Harpic?'

There comes the familiar roar of Rip-Roaring Roopie's throttle heaving to at the end of the driveway and then supplemented with the clarion call of his La Cucaracha horn tooted twice. Having been the longest serving Lieutenant in the British Army, I have already reconnoitred my route out of the regal presence in advance and before Roopie can rip roar a third time, I am beside him in his little red corvette.

'Never in life,' I say, uncrossing my fingers. 'Perish the thought.'

'Fancy a snifter, Harpic?' he says, unleashing the clutch.

'Don't mind if I do, old boy,' I reply. 'For I am feeling rather revolutionary.'

Roopie lets out the clutch and the red speedster roars.

'I say Harpic,' says Roopie. 'Have you eaten today?'

'Serpently,' I reply, taking another tote out of the epns hip flask. 'I had…wait…no….Come to think of it, I didn't. I was put off by the thought of kedgeree.'

'Not surprised, old boy,' says Roopie, taking the bend on two wheels and putting an unexpectedly high spring in the step of two old ladies with La Cucaracha. 'Cold curry; it's an abomination. And you're not much of a lunch man, I recall.'

'Absotively not,' I agree. 'Got to keep the old rig in trim, Roopie. Can't be ballooning up to Zeppelin proportions can we? End up on the *Jeremy Kyle Show*, what?'

'Never a truer word spoken,' says Roopie, cranking up the 1980s Drive Time Classics. 'But I've always thought a good loading of the old stodge before drinking was the way to go.'

'Stodge, ah yes,' I agree. 'Nothing like stodge before a few lighteners, eh? Helps with the old stamina. And I think I shall need stamina tonight.'

'I hear you are top of the bill at the Parish Council tonight,' he says. 'Better get stodged up then, Harpic.'

'Absotively, Roopie,' I say. 'Never a truer word spoken.'

Stodge: The Pre-emptive Strike for Hangovers and other Booze Related Injuries.

There are those who hold to the view that a pint of milk is the best preparation for a night on the moonshine on the grounds that this dairy product is a cheap, effective and readily available method of lining the stomach so as to slow down the rate of alcohol absorption. Those who are not so readily persuaded of this approach argue that slowing down the speed at which the hooch hits the old pleasure centres rather defeats the object. What else are shots for, they complain, than to instantly relieve stress, unchain the shackled inhibition and get the party going? On this issue, I agree with both sides, depending on the circumstances. If you want to have your universe re-ordered as a matter of urgency, avoid anything that will interfere with the magic of the loopy juice. If you are in for a more controlled re-assessment of your chosen approach to reality-numbing, then milk will help. In Spain, *Tapas* was invented to accompany booze - although this is not a fact widely respected in Shagaluf – so that the Mediterranean toper might enjoy his Sherry, Sangria and Cervesas without subsiding into an unscheduled siesta, but though a noble tradition, it is not really part of the English way. Pubs do not normally provide 'small plates' as a matter of course and crisps and peanuts do not really come up to scratch over the longer term. If you're in for a session, only proper stodge will do if you don't want to get completely plastered from the outset and thereafter spend the evening calling for the Deity on the Great White Telephone.

Thoughts naturally turn to mashed potato when this issue is discussed for it is solid, cheap, easily made and does the job, no question. The only difficulty with mashed potato is that it bears more than a passing resemblance to baby food, especially when combined with any sort of sauce or gravy, and so what goes down easily has a tendency to display the same properties when moving in the opposite direction. This goes for any sort of mashed vegetable, including the famous carrot but also the less well known but increasingly popular sweet potato. Spicy foods should also be avoided as they tend to be imbibed later on in the evening and so a double helping can cause a certain amount of stress the following morning.

Bread is an obvious contender in the stodge stakes and there are those who swear by the cheese sandwich as combining the absorption properties of the humble crumb with the lining properties ascribed to related dairy products. It is a highly regarded approach but does have the disadvantage of slowing down the intestinal transit in the same way that egg and cress sandwiches do. Improvements may be sought in toast, of course, as this acts in the same way as Fullers Earth or Charcoal tablets to ameliorate the effects of accidental poisoning or the excess acidity sometimes experienced during a good spew but cheese on toast should be avoided because of its soporific effects. If you are going to fall asleep in the pub, you may as well have your behaviour ascribed to the booze rather than (pathetically) to the cheese. No one will believe it isn't the booze anyway.

The ideal stodge for a night out is actually that perfect synthesis of bread and potato known as the chip butty. It is just about the only thing of value that the North has ever given to the south and even the seeker of the svelte may enjoy it as an occasional indulgence because although it does contain calories, these are more than cancelled out by the absence of calories in the hooch. Enjoy it with lashings of salt and vinegar – perhaps even with some HP Sauce - and be confident that your preparations for a night on the firewater have been completed to the highest culinary standard. Do not, however, be tempted any further towards Northern culinary 'culture'; the 'Pie Barm' – a meat and potato pie on a large bread roll – is an abomination on the same scale as the deep fried Mars bar.

'Good chips, Harpic?' says Roopie, demolishing a battered sausage and a large cod thoughtfully provided by the Barkingham Fryer.

'Just the ticket,' I reply, cleaning up with a wet wipe. 'Jolly crunchy.'

'A cheeky one before the meeting then?' he says.

'It would be undemocratic not to,' I agree.

'As you are aware, Harpic, there are two suitable hostelries in Barkingham,' says Roopie, starting up the corvette and sounding the Cucaracha call to arms. 'There is the *Forlorn Hope*, an ancient and respectable establishment purveying the finest ales and porters locally brewed by master craftsmen. Alternatively, there is the *Last Chance*, a testimony to the evolutionary nature of the Licensed Trade, a modern, hip, up-to-date, swinging gastropub. Which shall it be?'

'Both,' I reply.

'Indubitably,' says Roopie. 'I admire your indecision.'

It is, of course, always a mistake to rush a quick beer so Roopie and I decide not to. Instead we savour our JCBs as they were intended to be savoured, enjoying the hoppy aromas, the light zesty citrus notes and the long, smooth finish at our leisure and then, comforted by the horse brasses, red velvet furniture and reassuringly Victorian prints, have another. Impressed by the cellar keeping abilities of the landlord of the *Forlorn Hope* we decide that the proud vintners of the *Last Chance* should not be deprived of our appreciation and so enjoy a couple more among the bright stripped wood of the floorboards and the impressively chalked boards promising the most marvellous of gastronomies.

'I say Roopie,' I say perusing the starters. 'Bill Gon is already doing his sterling work here. They have Gazpacho on the menu.'

'Sure you want to attend the parish Council meeting, Harpic?' says Roopie, running a hand through his salt and pepper hair and peering directly at a spot on the ceiling. 'After all, the beer here is jolly good.'

'Get behind me, Satan,' I declare. 'Harpic has his duty to do.'

'As you wish, Harpic,' he says, picking up his car keys and swaying only slightly. 'But I hear it might be a bit bloody.'

'It will be more than bloody,' I reply, getting up my dander. 'For tonight Ostrakov is finally going to get his comeuppance!'

'And Louise knows about all this, I take it?' There is an unmistakeable note of caution in his voice.

'After a fashion,' I reply, warily. Can he perhaps doubt my resolve?

'Well, if you're sure Harpic,' he replies, raising his eyebrows. 'To the Batmobile.'

It is but a short, exciting ride down to the Slimstead Social Club and Roopie completes it at warp speed, bagging two pigeons and a scuttling squirrel in the process. Upon arrival though, I am amazed at the level of activity that news of the meeting has generated. In one corner of the club's front lawn, Old Timeon has established a tepee underneath a large banner reading 'The Earth Groans' and is handing out 'Frack Off' placards to an assortment of very smelly hippies and general undesirables with dreadlocks and badly knitted sweaters. They look like the aftermath of an Oxfam bomb in a paisley factory and are badly in need of a pressure washer. I note the presence of several cadaverous vegans too and make a mental note to persuade them away from their folly at a convenient moment by offering them a bacon sandwich as soon as they have finished warming up their didgeridoos. Close by, Chickadee has assembled what can only be called the Sisters of the Moon, a circle of decidedly gothic ladies, each face paler than the next as it emerges from the close fitting collars of their matching, full length dark blue velvet dresses, each nail painted a shade of purple or scarlet according to rank. The senior witches have pointy hats, mysterious runic tattoos and more than a hint of bared breast about them. Their eyelids also seem to be flickering at a rate that must require a lot of practice and as Roopie tames the skidding corvette beast and anchors her on the pea shingle, the acrid smell of skunk marijuana strikes like a lit fag stuck up a nostril.

'There are wild-eyed fanatics here, Harpic and they are chanting,' says Roopie, darkly as a minor descant fills the void under the night. 'It may be a spell.'

'Mere superstition,' I reply, stepping out of the vehicle and stubbing my toe painfully on the kerb.

'Even so,' replies Roopie, handing over the epns medicine cabinet. 'Better take precautions, what?'

'Indeed,' I say, regaining my composure. 'Just to be on the safe side.'

Fascinated though I am by this gathering of the heathen, the presence of Carruthers rummaging around in the back of a small pick-up truck quickly draws my attention. Roopie and I go over and see that he is busily engaged in wrapping tar-soaked rags around sturdy sticks. There is a crate of empty milk bottles there too and a large, green Jerry can of petrol standing by another pile of rags.

'Ah Carruthers,' I say, eyeing up a collection of agricultural implements – principally pitchforks - only partially concealed by a tarpaulin. 'Preparing for a bit of midnight farming, are we?'

'Just in case,' he replies, without looking up. 'Just in case. I've put the Neighbourhood Watch on full stand by in case a State of Emergency is called.'

There is an admirable sense of urgency about his action but I confess to feeling a little unsettled at the sight of two blunderbusses and several rather worn airguns.

'Do you think a State of Emergency is likely, Carruthers?' I ask.

'Can't hurt to be prepared,' he mutters. 'You don't get much warning when the natives rise and the country is up. Better to be ready for them. And don't fire until you see the whites of their eyes.'

'There'll be a state of emergency declared if I don't get another drink soon,' says Roopie distractedly eyeing the welcoming windows of the Old Queens Head just a short hop across the road. 'And look at all the Yummy Mummies in there! Like shooting fish in a barrel! Come on, Harpic!'

Roopie is quivering like an altar boy in the Convent showers, a look of ardent fire glittering in his eyes. My eyes follow his through the latticed windows and into the purdah of the lounge bar where I discern not just an array of orange tans, designer leatherwear, diamond talons and Gucci handbags swilling Prosecco like a hen party convention, but also half the staffroom of St.Wicca's, including the blue stockings and Roman nose of Miss Ward. I recognise the Miss Pound screech immediately and wince nervously.

'Vipers, mate,' I warn him. 'Those are sharks swimming in oceans of white wine, Roopie, old boy. Believe me, you do not want to dip so much as a toe in those waters. I've seen them at the gym and they can be very ascerbic in response to a gentlemanly overture.'

'Really, Harpic?' says Roopie, a note of disappointed disbelief creeping into his tone. 'That bad?'

'Rape alarms and pepper spray aren't the half of it,' I say. 'They send their kids to St. Wicca's.'

A thrill of horror passes across Roopie's features and he shudders a little before mastering himself.

'They hatched those little blighters?' He puts a hand out to steady himself and finds Harpic's sturdy shoulder. 'I never thought….And is that Labiaplasty Nolan in there too?'

I confirm his worst fears. The blood drains from his face.

'Thanks, old man,' he says, after a moment's pause. 'I appreciate it. But where did they all come from? From which woodwork did they crawl?'

It appears to me that Perky Pete has assembled his thirsty, high spending middle class protest group independently of my aid.

The sound of mechanical grumbling temporarily drowns out the sound of occult chanting and the drone of the didgeridoo and I look up to see the *convoi exceptionnel* horsebox of Patricia Dalrymple, Mistress of Five Chimneys farm and Queen of All She Surveys, pull up. She is accompanied by fierce dogs lightly leashed and has a determined furrow across her brow as if she has arrived to finish things one way or the other for good. I think of William the Conqueror or Queen Elizabeth I but can't decide which she more resembles. More worryingly, I have a flash of a mental picture of Custer at his Last Stand.

As the engine dies, and the chanting begins to build to a didgeridoo accompanied crescendo, the massively-titted Medea of Slimstead alights from the vehicle like a cumulonimbus in bottle green taffeta to gasps of amazement. The shimmer under the street light is like gold lightning on the smooth scales of the original satanic serpent while the deep red and copper hues of her *a l'imperatrice* hair flame up like the fires of hell. Her smile is like a freshly slit throat and there is an air of undeniable triumphant victory about her, which I find worrying because on past experience alone, a victory for Tabitha Greenwood is unlikely to be without unpleasant complications for Harpic. She moves towards the doors of the Slimstead ~~Mens~~ Social Club like an over-botoxed Marylin Monroe, sashaying as though she were on a catwalk and provoking awe from the smelly hippies, one of whom at least is choking on his didgeridoo and getting slapped by his girlfriend. Even the Sisters of the Moon fall momentarily silent.

'The Goddess is among us!' shrieks a purple-nailed citizen of Loonyville.

'The Horned God shall surely be among us soon!' answers Old Timeon, standing and staring wildly at this unexpected vision of the Earth Mother. 'The Earth Groans! The Horned God Comes!'

'The Horned God in my trousers is certainly in danger of coming very shortly,' says Roopie. 'By Jove! Those titties are magnificent! Where can I purchase a pound or two?'

'Bulk orders only, I'm afraid,' I reply. 'I had my head between them this time last week.'

He looks at me with renewed admiration.

'Harpic,' he says. 'I am in the presence of an intrepid explorer indeed.'

'You are in the presence of an idiot, Rupert' says Patricia Dalyrmple, marching past, tugging her ferocious dogs out of his crotch. 'And an idiot who is about to be put into proper restraint when his wife arrives.'

'Don't speak about Old Timeon like that,' I protest. 'He may be a little eccentric but he is still a valued member of the community and jibes about his wife are inappropriate since she is unlikely to return from a luxury yacht in the Mediterranean bought with the proceeds of successful speculation during the Dotcom boom. I dare say he is still devastated by her departure and you should have more sympathy.'

'Harpic,' she replies, in a tone to wither crops. 'Come up to Five Chimneys soon won't you? My dogs are in need of training.'

She leaves amidst a trail of red-eyed canine growl and slaver and I ponder on the thought that one might need more than a doggy choc and a rolled up newspaper to train those hounds.

Before I have fully formulated an approach to effective obedience training however, the wheeze and back-firing of Andrea Lloyd's *convoy manqué* jalopy brings me back to more immediate concerns.

'Dear Lord, Harpic,' says Roopie, taking in the methane gas bag and bumper stickers. 'Is that thing still afloat? I seem to remember running that into a lake at least twenty years ago.'

'Andrea Lloyd has taken the eco-recycling method to heart,' I reply, marvelling at the artistic tension generated by the juxtaposition of her elegant coiffure and the wreck of her rust bucket car. 'She can certainly be relied upon to back me in my fight to scupper Ostrakov's fracking schemes. Indeed, she adds a welcome rational counterpoint to the wailings of the lunatic fringe so well represented here tonight.'

She emerges from the classical antiquity of mechanical heap carrying an impressive number of files, each marked with an array of post-it notes, treasury tags, bookmarks and colour-coded pegs.

'Seems jolly well prepared,' says Roopie. 'You are certain that she is one your side in all this?'

'No question,' I reply, batting away his rumbling scepticism. 'She is a skilled political operator, big in the Brownies and *au fait* with the nooks and crannies of local governance procedures. I rely on her implicitly.'

Closely behind the Andrea Lloyd string-welded speedster, I spy my very own Third Party, Fire and Theft motor vehicle and a thrill of alarm courses through my veins.

'Cripes, Roopie,' I declare. 'It's the Memsahib. I need to get under cover.'

'I thought she was aware of your intentions tonight, Harpic?' he replies, raising a quizzical eyebrow. 'Not a person to cross, your Louise, if memory serves me right, Harpic. Not if you value an attachment to the old family jewels, Harpic.'

'She is aware *after a fashion*,' I reiterate. 'But in some respects she can be a little like the Jehovah's Witnesses; not someone you want to get into a discussion with when the Pubs are about to open.'

'Ah,' says Roopie, understandingly. 'Bushes or a disguise, then?'

'Disguise might be best,' I say. 'Especially as I shall have to insinuate myself into the meeting, Roopie. If I go dressed as a bush, I'm likely to draw attention to myself. Indeed, given the unfolding revelations of Timeon and Chickadee's theology, I might end up being worshipped.'

'Not a bad thing to have the old Horned God worshipped by mysterious women, Harpic,' says Roopie. 'Not a bad thing at all.'

'Perhaps,' I concede. 'But tonight the big head must do the thinking for the little head.'

'Disguise it is,' says Roopie. 'Let's try the smelly hippies, eh?'

'Must we?' My heart quails a little.

'Afraid so, Harpic,' replies Roopie, steering me towards Timeon's tepee by way of a handy screening of hedges. I see my own Dearest Louise exit the vehicle in a smart fashion and march straight through the milling crowd of protestors, her pale skin and dark hair crackling and flashing like a summer storm, her face tigerish in contained fury. She resembles something so magnificently imperious that neither the massively-titted Tabitha Greenwood nor the distressed aristocrat Patricia Dalrymple can match her for sheer presence. She sweeps down the path, not bothering to stoop to conquer but hands out clipped ears liberally and with gusto to anyone in her path. The White Witch of Narnia couldn't hold a candle to her; I make a mental note to advise her to employ Turkish Delight as a classroom management strategy. And dungeons. And serve the little beasts right.

'Here, Harpic, try this on,' says Roopie, who has made rapid acquaintance with the anti-materialistic hippies by means of a proffered £20. 'And this. And this. And, definitely, this.'

He hands me a selection of woollen items, mostly of apparently Peruvian origin, which smell of yurt, cannabis and have bobbles.

'I say, Roopie, can't we just slap on a false beard and moustache?' I protest, holding the items between thumb and forefinger and giving them a sniff. 'This is damned disheartening for a man who is about to make the speech of his life, expose a Communist conspiracy and bring down the government of Slimstead.'

'Needs must, Harpic,' replies Roopie, handing me an alarmingly multi-coloured poncho made from alpaca and guinea pig hair. 'Think of England's green and pleasant land, Harpic. Think on Rupert Brooke and Rudyard Kipling, Harpic. *Vitae Lampadae*, Harpic, and Rule Britannia. Perhaps a shot of Dutch courage might help?'

He hands over the epns morale booster and I take a long, pube-straightening pull.

'Good Lord, Roopie,' I gasp. 'Just what is that stuff?'

'Latvian Brandy,' he replies. 'I swear by it for motorway driving. Does more than pass the time of day, I can tell you.'

I go into the tepee and change. Timeon has been burning incense to deodorise the armpits of the Old Gods, no doubt, and I now smell like patchouli, skunk marijuana and acrid strawberries. Luckily, I still have my taupe chinos to remind me of my usual sartorial elegance, having declined the low crutched pyjamas fervently offered for the out lay of a mere extra tenner by a woad painted young man who assures me that he has rejected the world and all its works.

'You can, like, have a tote on my, like...er.. you know...like, joint, man.'

It is dark and close in the tepee and the lighted tip of his marijuana cigarette glows diabolically as he draws on it. His face looks stony, like a fall of boulders on a mountain after an underground nuclear test.

'And be under the influence of drugs at a time like this?' I am horrified.

'You seem...like...like...you know, man...like you've had a drink, like...er...man,' he replies through bloodshot eyes. 'Alcohol is...er..like a drug too...er...like...er...man. And it's only...er...a tenner, dude.'

'Alcohol a drug?' I reply, choking slightly and inhaling deeply. 'Do not be ridiculous young man. Alcohol is a perfectly harmless, calorie free chemical element. Do you work for some dreadful preachy branch of the NHS? The Health and Safety Executive? The National Obesity Forum?'

'I'm like…er…on benefits…man….It's like a protest…er…against the system. Peace, man…er…you sure? It's only like a tenner….'

I sweep him and his light-headed alternative culture aside. I do not have time for this sort of burbling insanity and need to concentrate on building support for my anti-fracking campaign. Commending my trusty blazer and regimental tie to Roopie's care, I emerge as if re-born from the tepee clad in poncho and Peruvian beanie, complete with ear flaps and woollen strings dangling.

'How do I look, Roopie?'

'Unrecognisable,' he replies, brushing off my blazer and folding the regimental tie into its pocket.

'Well, that's not strictly true is it?' I say, a little dismayed. 'Otherwise you wouldn't have known it was me, would you?'

'You could add the pyjamis,' he offers.

'This will do,' I declare. 'The disguise does not have to hold for long.'

From the Old Queens Head comes the sound of revelry approaching. It has the high pitch common to ladies out on the town without their husbands to restrain them. It has the timbre of vodka at the Chippendales. It has the quality of crocodile tears in alimony hearings. It has the squeal of the wheels of vengeance grinding the metal of male gears and a look of alarm explodes across Roopie's face.

'Quick! Back in the tepee,' he cries and bundles me back inside, following closely behind. 'I know that sound. I heard it just before a troop of Amazons just like that wiped out a whole SAS Sabre Squadron in four minutes flat in bar room brawl in Amsterdam. No holds barred it was and not a sight I'd like to see ever again.'

There are now three of us nose to nose in this confined, marijuana fumigated space and there is not a lot of room to move.

'So…like…you want the pyjamis then, man?' comes the plaintive punt from the drug-addled benefit scrounger and smelly hippy. 'Only…like…man…it's gonna cost you…like… twenty now, man.'

'I thought you had renounced the world,' I say, rather exasperatedly and trying not to be unmanned by the sounds of merriment coming from without. Once again, I have a vision of Custer surrounded by shrieking hordes of ~~blood thirsty Red Indian savages~~ brave, entirely justified Native American fighters employing a forceful but proportionate response to totally unjustified colonialist aggression.

'I have…like…well….Step by step, dude,' he replies, exhaling acrid smoke mixed with breath like a donkey's fart. His eyes are flickering like a black and white movie. 'It's…like…the free market, man, like…bread, dude.'

'Shhh!' says Roopie. 'The Yummy Mummies approach.'

'Cool,' says the blowsy tyke. 'Do you think I can...like...score some...like, coke from them?'

'Very probably,' hisses Roopie. 'And you'll get Ritalin at good rates from the Staff too. But right now, you stick your head into that den of dragons and the only thing you're likely to score is taloned fingernails down your cheeks. They've been at the Prosecco, for crying out loud.'

'Yeah, man...like,' says the horrible hippy wild child. 'But like...coke is coke, man....'

'Here,' says Roopie, handing him the epns bomb. 'Have a slug of this. Sort you out good and proper, it will.'

The woolly vegan troll takes the flask, imbibes deeply and appreciatively, then begins to sway.

'Dude...wow....'

'Catch him, Harpic,' says Roopie, grabbing the flask. 'He's done for, the dashed lightweight.'

There is a slow cascade of bad knitwear, a slight whump of patchouli and the expressing of a sickly sweet fart as the expiring eco-warrior slumps on the floor of the tepee. Outside, the sounds of vicious revelry change tone as the Doppler effect combines with high heels and Prosecco to produce a sound like an overwound clockwork frilly train driven by Barbara Windsor in *Carry On Camping*.

'I think we made it,' says Roopie, after an agonising moment when Labiaplasty Nolan seemed to stop and sniff the air, as though recognising an after shave. 'No! Lay doggo. It's the Wednesday Night Volcanoes!'

The sound of Barney the Builder, Higgins the Trucker and Ark Slymstead comes barrelling across the road from the Old Queens Head where they have been observing from the Tap room and waiting for the coast to clear. Behind them comes the yapping of Bark the dog from which I deduct that the Venerable Gentlemen are also in motion.

'These are my natural allies, Roopie,' I declare. 'But I shall try out my disguise on them anyway.'

'As you wish,' says Roopie. 'It stinks in here, Harpic, and I'll be glad of the fresh air.'

Stepping outside, the chanting is muted but extant and the didgeridoo seems to have tailed off a little. Certainly the player bears all the hallmarks of a casual hand-bagging and I am moved to wonder whether he was foolish enough to venture a louche comment in the presence of Labiaplasty Nolan or Miss Walsh. Either would be beyond his capacity to resist, in my humble opinion.

'Jesus, Harpic, you gave me a scare there,' says Ark, head down, bullishly heading for the ~~Mens~~ Club gate.

'Is this part of the act?' asks Barney, not waiting for an answer but following on up the path to the waiting doors.

'You smell like a doped up alpaca,' says Higgins, steaming by. 'Reminds me of my first girlfriend back in Lima.'

The Venerable Gentlemen are reassuring in their neutrality regarding my disguise.

'Shocking.'

'Outrageous.'

'Shouldn't be allowed.'

'Bark.'

This helps.

'The Earth groans, strange brother,' says Old Timeon, appearing at my elbow like the ancestral ghost. 'The Horned God must be appeased.'

'There you go, Roopie,' I say triumphantly. 'The disguise is, on balance, effective.'

'Whatever you say, Harpic,' he replies, sniffing at his Hound tooth jacket and wrinkling his nose. 'Shall we go in to the meeting?'

'Indeed. Lead on, MacDuff.'

Leaving behind the Eco-warriors of Loonyville, we slide in to the rear of the meeting where the good burghers of Slimstead are sitting in boisterous anticipation of a hectic meeting, on chairs, in two blocks divided by an aisle. At the front, entrenched behind the blanket covered official Parish Council trestle table is the Communist Ostrakov, fiddling with his agenda papers as though he is about to sign a warrant for the mass deportation of a subject minority. His light bulb head is bent forward a little and he is twiddling his moustache, fondling his goatee beard and snuffling like a badger with TB. Next to him is the much put-upon and maligned hero of Third World Aid, Bill Gon, flicking through his wallet to count the money that he has already earmarked for his noble Gazpacho famine relief schemes and smiling like genial Uncle Joe under his yard brush moustache and jolly brows. I note that the Kiktabolokov brothers are also in attendance providing a reassuring Health and Safety presence in what is a jolly packed ~~Mens~~ Social Club although it is odd that they have had to borrow their Hi-vis jackets from Ostrakov's arch-frackers, Gazpacom.

Andrea Lloyd is going over her papers and rearranging some of her bookmarks, while Patricia Dalrymple is eyeing up Bill Gon in what might be deemed to be a threatening manner, all the while patting her fearsome dogs and feeding them tasty meaty morsels. The Right Reverend Richardson is there too and as he raises his head from its encircling dog collar like a tortoise from its shell, his eyes land on me and bulge rather comically. He is probably having an attack of guilt at not making the acquaintance of this new parishioner; the disguise is working well indeed although I confess the price of my effective deception is that the poncho seems to have become impregnated with marijuana fumes and I am experiencing a certain light-headedness.

I spy Denning standing behind a rickety chair to the right rear of Patricia Dalrymple, keeping a close watch upon the Dobermanns. He has graced the occasion with wig and robes, and his stern, stiff, legal demeanour will add weighty legal weight to the dignity of the proceedings, if only he can keep his face under control. I keep my eyes down, but continue to survey the situation through hooded lids, just as I had learned to do all those years ago in the Intelligence Branch before Fatty pang rusticated me from the Gun Hill Barracks in Hong Kong. Sitting in the middle of the audience is Tabitha Greenwood looking like a steep pine clad hillside in Norway while beside her is Professor Birch from the Barkingham Red Bus Transport Café who has donned a new striped apron for the occasion but has not gone so far as to tame the struggle of wispy hair that surrounds his IQ intensive pate. He is also looking rather nervous, being dangerously close to the Yummy Mummies of St.Wicca's and attracting the attention of one of the Dobermanns who has detected his meat-smelling odour. Nearby is my own Dearest Louise, sitting stock still, thrumming with puissance yet maintaining the haughty, detached demeanour of the defenestrated Countess she is. The noise is growing, handbags are being rooted in, arms being folded and nobbly elbows settling on comfortable, well-earned paunches, while outside I see Carruthers lighting his flaming brands and handing them out to his Neighbourhood watch lynch mob in anticipation of a good tarring and feathering. There is a palpable air of expectation as the Communist Ostrakov looks from one to the other of his Parish Council Commissars and calls the meeting to order.

'Oh, er, hello everyone,' he smarms. 'It's so jolly nice of so many of you to turn out for a second Parish Council meeting in as many weeks....'

'Get Harpic on!' shouts a voice from the crowd, to general approval. My heart swells with pride that so many people have turned out to support my cause.

'Well, I'm sure we will be calling on Mr.Harpic shortly,' says Ostrakov, shiftily evading the righteous demands of the people. 'But we must just run through a few things to do with the Gazpacom contract. So I shall ask Bill Gon if he would like to give us an update.'

'Bollocks to that!' cries a voice that might well have come from Ark Slymstead. 'We want Harpic!'

'Yeay!' cries a bevy a St.Wicca's beauties amidst a burst of hysterical but essentially good humoured shrieking. 'Harpic! Harpic! We want Harpic!'

'I'm afraid I really must insist...' says Ostrakov, attempting to deny the demands of the masses.

'Harpic! Harpic! Harpic!' chants the crowd; so loudly indeed that the faint rhythmic rumbling of the Sisters of the Moon is completely drowned out. Only the didgeridoo maintains its presence of droning undertone. 'Harpic! Harpic! Harpic!'

'... on going through the contract....'

'Harpic! Harpic! Harpic!' chants my public.

I see Louise is looking around trying to locate me, all the while ignoring the calls for me to make an entrance. She is a little flushed, as though surprised by my evident popularity and embarrassed by her good fortune in having a spouse who not only rescued her from a card game in Bosnia but is also held in such high esteem by the *Vox Populi Slimsteadorum*. I duck down a little behind Roopie to ensure the integrity of my masquerade.

'Harpic! Harpic! Harpic!'

'Looks like this is your moment, Harpic,' says Roopie, out of the side of his mouth. '*Carpe diem*, what? Onward Christian Soldiers into the Valley of Death and all that?'

'Harpic! Harpic!'

'You may be right, I say,' pushing the Peruvian beanie back on my head and wafting the acrid smell of skunk marijuana away. 'It is time for me to reveal myself and reveal my revelations.'

'Best foot forward then.'

'Hold hard, citizens of Slimstead!' I cry above the fray. 'Friends, Slimstead, Countrymen! Lend me your ears!'

The crowd cheers. Louise covers her brow with her hand in humility before her heroic husband.

'Harpic! Harpic! Three cheers for Harpic!'

Ostrakov is looking tight-faced, frustrated in his designs and bitterly preparing himself for the exile to come. Bill Gon is smiling in anticipation of fine oratory, as indeed are most of the audience, while Patricia Dalrymple and Andrea Lloyd exchange puzzled glances. The Dobermanns sit up. As the noise subsides, Denning sits down. I spot Miranda MacNulty twinkling at me from the stalls. She has a new turban which is jumping up and down on her head in a very unusual fashion.

'Very well then,' says Ostrakov, a note of irritation in his voice. 'Mr. Harpic, you have the floor.'

I step out bravely, best foot forward and stride through the aisle to the front, drawing gasps of admiration at my wondrous garb. I see Louise sit up but, in the best tradition of oratorical technique decide not to meet her eye as this might put me off. I have got past the point of overcoming any possible nervousness or stage fright by imagining my audience naked - it really is too horrible an image to dwell on – but I do fix my eyes on a point three feet above the furthest person at the back of the hall before proceeding. It is Maureen, our Northern refugee and wife to Perky Pete. She gives me an encouraging grin and accompanying thumbs up. Her form is strangely indistinct though and she appears to have grown an extra head.

I reach into my pocket and pull out my scroll of Izal bathroom parchment and begin to read. Needless to say, my flights of rhetoric soar up to the rafters, plumb the depths of the soul of Slimstead and tie knots of logic of such complexity as to make the Gordian knot look like a simple sheepshank. My poignards of invective make Ostrakov wince in intellectual agony as my razor wit rips shreds in his inflated ego and self-esteem. He tries to interrupt but I brush him aside. My audience is rapt, stunned by the brilliance of my argument, the clarity of my diction and the conviction of my delivery. Before long, Ostrakov is holding his head in his hands and I move in for the kill.

'There, citizens of Slimstead, sits the criminal Ostrakov! The *Communist* Ostrakov! He who would despoil our native heath with his plans to frack the life out of our green and pleasant land. He who would enslave us to a foreign power and subvert the natural order of our civilised democracy with a miserable socialist collective! He who would send our children to the gulag and who would commit mass murder on the way home from the club once he has drawn the reins of power fully into his dictatorial hands. Stand up, Slimstead!' I cry, throwing out an accusatory arm and identifying finger in his direction. 'Throw out the Red Tsar Ostrakov and be fracking free!'

I wait for the cheers.

There is a silence, so I wait a bit more. There is still silence. Funny, but I thought Slimstead folk were a bit quicker on the uptake than this and wonder if I might have laid the rhetorical flourishes on a bit thick and stunned them. I see Louise, exhausted by the brilliance of my presentation, has slumped down in her seat and holds her head in her hands as though struggling to comprehend the brilliance of my theory. Strangely though, there seem to be several people whose heads seem to bear more resemblance to the common Mallard than to their normal human visages. This is oddness of a whole new order.

There is a cough from Ostrakov.

'Mr.Harpic,' he says.

I turn to the Parish Commune. Bill Gon has a broad, supportive grin plastered across his features. The Reverend is praying silently. Andrea Lloyd appears not to have paid any attention at all and is still busily making notes on her files. Patricia Dalrymple is restraining her hounds.

'Mr.Harpic,' he repeats. 'I was under the impression that you knew I was a member of the Conservative Party. Indeed, since my family fled Soviet Russia during the 1970s and sought asylum and subsequent naturalisation as British citizens, we have devoted ourselves to the cause of Queen and Country. I can assure you quite categorically that I am not, nor have I ever been, a Communist.'

'Lies and evasion!' I cry.

'No they aren't, Harpic, you idiot,' says Andrea Lloyd, without looking up from her files.

'Shall I set the dogs on him?' adds Patricia Dalrymple.

I confess that I am nonplussed. Especially as the Dobermanns seem to be riding bicycles across the ceiling.

'But you have been spreading unfounded rumours about Bill Gon's Third World Gazpacho Relief plans, haven't you?' I counter.

'Gazpacho?' says Ostrakov.

'G-A-Z-P-A-C-H-O,' I say, spelling it out for him. 'Gazpacho.'

There is a splutter from the crowd. Then a titter. Then a snigger. Then a giggle. Then a guffaw and then a riotous explosion of chortling which rapidly builds into a howling of convulsive hysterics. Barney the Builder falls backwards off his chair. Tabitha Greenwood's titanic tits are wobbling like politicians before a free vote. Miss Walsh looks like she is about to have an accident in the lady department while one of the Yummy Mummies has bitten through the string on her bead necklace and red balls are bouncing and rolling around under the chairs; attempts to retrieve them are adding to the general hilarity. Not only that, but the number of people whose heads resemble zebras and giraffes has increased beyond the point that one might think reasonable for a small English village. I ignore them as an unwanted distraction.

I confess that this is not the reaction that I was expecting at all. Can Harpic have miscalculated in his analysis of the competing political factors? Is it possible? I look for succour but only Roopie offers it in the form of a waved hip flask of Latvian Brandy. I decide to take it, if only to gain time to reassess the situation in the light of information received. I take a tentative stride towards the gleam of the epns but am arrested by a further outbreak of exuberance led by two elephants and an alarmingly green rhinoceros.

'Harpic!' cries the crowd. 'Encore! Encore!'

Whatever can they mean? I am doubly non-plussed. The bobbles on my Peruvian beanie are beginning to spin as I turn from one hooting collection of faces before me to the next while the smell of wacky baccy about my person continues to be quite pronounced.

'Sit down, Harpic, you idiot,' says Patricia Dalrymple. 'And do something about that revolting poncho, will you? The dogs want to mate with it.'

'Here, mate,' says Bill Gon, handing me a £50 and wiping tears of mirth from his eyes. 'Priceless mate, priceless. You should take it up to the Edinburgh Fringe.'

Something seems to have gone dreadfully wrong but I am at a loss as to what it actually is. Roopie waves the flask once more like a vision of the Holy Grail. Mesmerised and slightly light-headed, I take one more faltering step towards it, then spread my wings and am assumed into heaven.

*

Some little time later, after having failed the Pearly Gate Entrance Exam, I return to Earth swimming up into consciousness in the grateful company of Roopie's Latvian Brandy.

'There, there old chap,' he says, pouring another arse-shrivelling dose down my cake hole. 'It's all over now. Andrea Lloyd is just demolishing Bill Gon's credibility with an impressive array of documentation drawn from diverse sources.'

'The rotter!' I mumble.

'Not really, old boy,' says Roopie, sympathetically. 'Seems that Bill Gon was a KGB sleeper agent during the Cold War and is back working for his old boss President Putin. He's been trousering more than his fair and due share of the loot from the fracking operation in return for letting Gazpacom loose in the nature reserve.'

'What?' The foundations of my world totter. 'What about the Gazpacho?'

'I'm afraid he has pulled the wool over your eyes there, Harpic.'

I am crestfallen.

'Don't worry, Harpic,' he says, comforting me with another reviving shot of Latvian Liberty. 'Anyone could have made the same mistake. Jolly glib chap, Gon is.'

At that moment Denning hoves over the meniscus of my limited horizon and, though dribbling a little, smiles as though he has just delivered bad news to the Birthday Boy.

'Gon's gone,' he says. 'Pursuant to Clause three, paragraph 2.1 Local Government Exigent Circumstance regulations, he has been replaced by Andrea Lloyd in respect of any and all dealings with Gazpacom and the fracking operation.'

'Well,' I say weakly. 'I suppose all's well that ends well. There will be no more fracking.'

'Oh I wouldn't go so far as that Harpic,' says Denning warily. 'Given the possibility of cheap, clean gas and the opportunity to reduce our dependence on Russian Oligarchs and Middle Eastern medieval tyrants, the village has rather taken the view that, *ceterus paribus*, they rather like the idea of fracking.'

I lay back in despair.

'I have failed,' I declare, placing a wan hand across my pale brow. 'My own dear Slimstead will be despoiled and turned into a Northern slag heap.'

'Not really,' says Denning. 'In fact, Patricia Dalrymple is proposing that the proceeds be used to enhance several areas of potentially natural beauty around the village. Looks like she's going to succeed too.'

'And what of Ostrakov the Communist?' I ask.

'Best forget about that for the time being,' says Roopie, manfully. 'In fact, he's just announced his resignation.'

'On what grounds? Treason? Subversion? What?'

'On the grounds that he feels responsible for not keeping a tighter rein on Bill Gon,' says Roopie. 'Damned decent of him really. That woman with the massive tits is taking over from him.'

'Tabitha Greenwood? A Feminist woman in charge of the Parish Council? This is too shocking.'

'Outrageous,' agrees Denning.

'Shouldn't be allowed,' chimes Roopie.

'It is a *coup d'etat*,' I declare, struggling to my feet. 'We must resist it! Root it out before it grows branches! We must to arms! Where is Carruthers and his stout Neighbourhood Watch lynch mob? We must strike while the iron is hot! You can't get to Corfu from Switzerland in a boat, you know!'

'Yes, well,' says Denning, looking at me as if I was an oddity. 'I'm afraid Carruthers is busy with some extra-judicial justice involving Bill Gon, the Kiktabolokovs and a Wicker Man – all of which I am completely and legally unaware of, you understand.'

'Then call the eco-warriors to my banner!' I appeal.

'That might be difficult too,' continues Denning, who appears to have grown another nose and at least one extra ear. 'Half of them have followed in Carruthers' footsteps hoping that the sacrifice of Bill Gon may hasten the appearance of the Horned God – an individual who has no status in Law as I'm sure you are aware and thus may be required to check his immigration status before proceeding - and the other half are strewn about the village in various deep degrees of intoxication.'

'And it's probably better to consult with your Missus before starting a counter-revolution,' says Roopie, producing a rough bandage and beginning to wind it around my head.

'Popacatpetl wasn't built in a day, Roopie,' I remind him. 'So what has Louise got to do with Tabitha Titwood taking over as titular tyrant?'

'Apparently it was her idea,' he says, binding the bandage a little tighter around the old bonce. 'Cooked it up at a dinner party while you were doing your alpaca racing stunt apparently.'

I take another glug from the epns and swoon once more.

Harpic is betrayed.

Harpic is defeated.

Harpic. All Washed Up.

One Year Later: Just Desserts

'The Secret to a Happy Life is to Always Do what She Wants. That - and Pots of Money. And Plenty of Bacon, of Course.'

J.Harpic.

'Morning, Harpic,' says Louise, bustling through from the kitchen. 'Now, I have Newmarket, Lincolnshire or Cumberland ring on the go and there is a choice of smoked streaky, green middle and unsmoked back. Which is it to be?'

'I think I'll go for the Newmarket and some smoked streaky, if that's OK,' I reply.

'Certainly, Harpic,' says Louise. 'Shall I make a fresh pot?'

I survey the snowy linen, the finest silver and the delicate bone china awaiting the Earl Grey. The mustard spoon curves gracefully out of its trim cruet while the lime marmalade shimmers in its crystal serving dish. There is my freshly ironed copy of the *Telegraph* waiting on its stand while there are four freshly toasted triangles of wholemeal cobber lined up in the rack as smart as Pythagoras.

'A fresh pot would be lovely,' I reply, glancing at the headlines and reaching for the curled butter in its dish. 'Anything in the post to day?'

'Oh nothing much,' says Louise laying a starched napkin across my lap. 'But I hear Chubble has actually proposed to Mrs Johnson and she has accepted.'

'How lovely,' I chime. 'My best wishes to the happy couple.'

'The rest of the post is on the platter,' she says. 'You may as well have a flick through while I bring your breakfast.'

Of course, this is a task natural and fitting for the man of the house and I take the bone handled letter opener to the first missive.

'It's just the gas bill,' I call out. 'Hardly worth opening these days.'

There is a comforting sizzle of sausage from the six ring gas cooker in the newly fitted kitchen. A whiff of frying bacon sails into the breakfast parlour like a welcome zephyr causing me to pause for a moment.

'Is the bacon from Barkingham?' I call out.

'Of course,' comes the reply. 'From your own acorn fed Gloucester Old Spots, Harpic.'

'Ah,' I say, a swell of proprietorial pride welling up inside me. 'And here is a letter from St.Wicca's addressed to you, my dear.'

'Oh do open it for me,' replies Louise, popping her head around the door. 'It can't be anything important.'

I run the knife through the seal and glance through the contents.

'It's another letter begging you to come back,' I say. 'The third one this month isn't it? Are you sure you don't want to return to work?'

'Not likely,' she says in mock indignation. 'Why on earth would I want to do that?'

I move on to the next item.

'Dividend statement from the Slimstead Community Shale Gas PLC,' I call out. 'Looks like you'll be able to book that spa break in Monte Carlo this afternoon.'

'Oh jolly good,' she replies, bustling in with sausages and bacon. 'I'll call Andrea Lloyd and Tabitha to see if they would like to come too.'

'Good idea,' I say. 'Why not invite Miranda and Patricia too? A private charter is so much more fun - and cheaper too if there are a few of you.'

'Really, Harpic? Do you think things will stretch that far?' She takes a seat, rearranges her Gucci dressing gown and gives a little polish to the Cartier wrist watch that I gave her for our anniversary yesterday.

'Of course, Dearest,' I reply, spotting a little HP by the streaky. 'Will you go for one week or two?'

'Just a week, I think. Patricia still has the farm to run.'

'I thought Old Timeon has that in hand?' I say, munching a sausage.

'Well he does – and Chickadee is doing some amazing things with the GM soya trials – but he does tend to get a little distracted these days.' She pours a steaming cup of Arabica for me and tops up my glass with freshly squeezed Florida orange.

'How so?' I ask, opening up my stockbroker's statement.

'Too many Wicker Men, I'm afraid,' she replies. 'And he spends too much time instructing Bill Gon in the finer points of charcoal burning.'

'Well, everyone needs hobbies,' I reply. 'Shame about Bill Gon's 4x4 going back to the dealers. I know he was fond of it. Still, hiring Denning isn't cheap.'

'Serves him right,' says Louise, a flash of the old Countess blazing in her eyes. 'Being in the pay of the KGB all those years and not declaring it. We all have to pay our taxes. It is the responsible thing to do.'

'Quite right, Dearest,' I reply, looking at the statement from the broker. 'But I still wish that there was not so much Capital Gains Tax to pay on share dealing.'

'Hush,' she says, waving a finger in playful admonition. 'Your decision to invest in all those shale gas companies when there was all that blether from Greenpeace was a stroke of genius. I confess, Harpic, I had my doubts about your theories on stock selection back then. Darts and runes hardly seemed very scientific to me.'

'Ah, my Dear. That's because you have never been a Consultant to a Large Corporation.'

'Too true, Harpic. Too true,' she says buttering me a piece of toast. 'But beating the stock market by 2000% still seems an amazing stroke of fortune.'

'Oh, it was nothing,' I say, modesty being my middle name. 'Just native genius really.'

We pause in our intercourse to enjoy the coffee and sausages.

'Will you be meeting Roopie and the Volcanoes for lunch?' enquires Louise. 'I only ask because I thought I might take the Jaguar today. You'll be OK with the Beamer, I take it?'

'I'll probably go by cab,' I reply. 'There isn't much parking by the Heliport.'

'Well and good,' she says, delicately handling a croissant. 'Do have a good lunch and don't feel that you need to rush back. Tabitha and I will be sharing a bottle of fizz and discussing the refurbishment of the Social Club. I say, Harpic, what do you think? A heated indoor pool or a new chef?'

'Why not both?' I reply. 'Now that the church roof is fixed and the new school opened, there should be a few spare bob hanging around.'

'Oh and there's the matter of Ostrakov coming up too,' she says. 'Tabitha thinks it's time he was let back on the Council, given all the good work he did in unpicking the Gazpacom contract and reallocating it to the Slimstead Community Shale Gas PLC.'

'Whatever you say, Dearest,' I reply. 'I admit I have been a little off with Ostrakov from time to time but I'm only too willing to let bygones be bygones.'

'His view exactly,' she says. 'Where are you off to for your lunch?'

'Oh just the usual,' I reply. 'We are giving Carruthers a bit of a send-off before he goes Big Game Hunting in Africa again. Would you like me to pick up a couple of cases of something special in Le Touquet? Perfume? Champagne?'

'I think we're alright for fizz, Harpic,' she replies. 'But I'll check the cellar. Perfume would be nice though.'

I sit back and take a sigh of pure happiness, fulfilment and wellbeing.

'Whatever you say, darling,' I say, finishing off the streaky and reaching for another chipolata. 'Whatever you say.'